THE MINDSPAN DIET

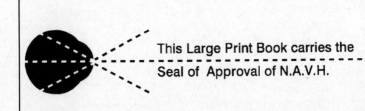

This Large Print Book carries the
Seal of Approval of N.A.V.H.

THE MINDSPAN DIET

REDUCE ALZHEIMER'S RISK, MINIMIZE MEMORY LOSS, AND KEEP YOUR BRAIN YOUNG

PRESTON ESTEP III, PH.D.

THORNDIKE PRESS
A part of Gale, Cengage Learning

GALE
CENGAGE Learning·

Farmington Hills, Mich • San Francisco • New York • Waterville, Maine
Meriden, Conn • Mason, Ohio • Chicago

GALE
CENGAGE Learning®

LIBRARY OF CONGRESS CATALOGING-IN-PUBLICATION DATA

Names: Estep, Preston, author.
Title: The mindspan diet : reduce alzheimer's risk, minimize memory loss, and keep your brain young / by Preston Estep III, Ph.D.
Description: Large print edition. | Waterville, Maine : Thorndike Press, a part of Gale, Cengage Learning, [2016] | Includes bibliographical references and index.
Identifiers: LCCN 2016024669| ISBN 9781410493972 (hardcover) | ISBN 1410493970 (hardcover)
Subjects: LCSH: Alzheimer's disease--Diet therapy. | Large type books.
Classification: LCC RC523 .E88 2016a | DDC 616.8/310654--dc23
LC record available at https://lccn.loc.gov/2016024669

Published in 2016 by arrangement with Ballantine Books, an imprint of Random House, a division of Penguin Random House LLC

Printed in Mexico
4 5 6 7 8 9 20 19 18 17 16

*To my wonderful extended family,
all of whom have seen the effects
of dementia firsthand, and to all of
my colleagues in determined
pursuit of maximum mindspan*

CONTENTS

PART 3. IN CONTROL WITH THE MINDSPAN DIET

INTRODUCTION

I was motivated to write this book for a few interrelated reasons. First and foremost, I believe people's minds and memories — the basis for all their thoughts and wisdom, feelings and relationships — are humanity's most valuable treasures, and dementia is their greatest threat.

I have seen dementias and neurodegeneration firsthand. I have lived through the progressive mental decline of grandparents on both sides of my family. I know personally the slow-motion tragedy of a loved one's mind fading, one uncertain recollection at a time, into oblivion. I have been asked the same question repeatedly — one that I answered only moments before. A middle-aged woman told me of an unsettling interaction she had with her father, a man in his late seventies. He asked her, in a way that seemed to beg for both guidance and forgiveness, "Are you my wife?" The man was what remained of my grandfather, and that woman was my mother. His plaintive question — posed over twenty years ago — overshadows my memories of a young, robust man with a deeply resonant voice and confident bearing.

As director of gerontology at the Harvard Personal Genome Project (PGP), the research study I help run at Harvard Medical School, I have interacted with adults of all ages, including many older ones. I occasionally meet very old people who remain mentally sharp, but unfortunately, mental decline and memory loss are the norm. From these experiences I have learned that life is — more than anything else — life of the mind. There is nothing more important than staying physically and mentally fit and healthy as long as possible; there is nothing more precious than the mind.

This book is about the life of the mind — about living and thinking as well and as long as possible. To write it, I have pulled together many disparate sources of information to identify and control the primary risk factors for Alzheimer's disease and other dementias. I want to show you how to use this information in your everyday life to help you and your loved ones to substantially reduce the risk of dementia — without prescription drugs or expensive medical treatments.

Lifespan measures how long we live, but how fulfilling that life is depends on how well your mind works during that time.* I use the term "mindspan" to capture this essential idea. Lifespan refers only to longevity, while mindspan refers to the mind's length of life *plus* its breadth and height of performance. The pinnacle of living isn't just a long lifespan, it is *maximum mindspan*. This book is the definitive guide on how to achieve this enormously important goal.

Everyone — from young to old, lean to overweight, and layperson to expert — will benefit greatly from this book. I think no one will be surprised to find some of the usual suspects on my list of unhealthful foods, but you will be surprised to discover the risks associated with foods commonly regarded as healthful, such as iron-fortified foods.

People are living longer than ever. While this trend is good, there is a serious downside: record numbers of people are experiencing greater levels and degrees of cognitive

---

* The brain is the physical organ in your head; the mind is slightly more abstract. It isn't a thing but a dynamic process: the brain interacting with the inputs and outputs of the body and the environment. It consists of thoughts, memories, responses, behaviors, and the like.

decline and other brain disorders in later life. They aren't the only ones affected; their communities, neighbors, friends, and families also must deal with these challenges. But some people seem mostly immune to such problems.

I call these people the Mindspan Elite. They live very long lives and remain as alert, active, and autonomous as people decades younger. Important discoveries from many sources have shed substantial light on the keys to their success, and now show the rest of us the way. They have achieved their extraordinary success because they've enjoyed some extremely important advantages the rest of us haven't had. But this book shows you what these advantages are and how you can get them — plus, you now have in your possession the key to some advantages for achieving longevity and mindspan that they've never had.

The biggest advantage possessed by the Mindspan Elite can be summarized in a single short and simple word: diet. That's why I happily use the word "diet" in the title — even though the main purpose of this book isn't to get you whittled down to a size 4 or chiseled like an Olympic athlete. When I looked into the origins of the word, I learned it derives from the Latin and Greek words meaning a way of life or a regular mode of living, which is, after all, what this book is about.

However simple the word might be, the real-world practice can be quite different. My first attempt at emulating Mindspan Elite eating habits was a series of misadventures. I started with Mediterranean and did most things according to my superficial understanding at the time. I began to use more olive oil. I upped my dark chocolate and red wine. I also consumed more milk and yogurt, pasta and bread. The results? I got more headaches. I experienced more pain during and after exercise, and increased symptoms of inflammation. I didn't feel any better and looked tired. My cholesterol went up. I was only in my forties and I was supposed to be feeling better, not worse. I knew something wasn't right.

Only when I dug deeper did I discover that many of my newly adopted foods were only superficially Mediterranean. Critical differences made them extremely poor additions to my diet; some are even dangerous. My genes are also different enough to have made some of my otherwise good food choices bad ones. This book shows you these critical differences so that you won't make the mistakes that I did. *The Mindspan Diet* also features

15

discoveries at the frontiers of laboratory science — especially in genetics and longevity research. It pulls together essential bits from these vast repositories of still-disconnected information and combines them into knowledge — knowledge to achieve a long, healthy, smart, and autonomous life. All health, lifestyle, diet, nutrition, and fitness websites, articles, and books give advice, but nearly all of them fail at the most fundamental level: they don't know or they don't understand how and why we live as long as we do, and how and why we age. Many provide information that is good for a thirty-year-old to build lean muscle or for a forty-year-old to lose a few pounds, but many of them provide information that is likely to age you — and your brain — faster. I am very alarmed by this prospect, and you should be too.

Recent studies have identified genetic factors that have an impact on cognitive function in the latest years of life. These and other developments have provided a new perspective on the nature of aging and the prevention of disease and cognitive decline. As a result, we can now remain fit and healthy for longer and even control aging to some degree, and we are on our way to controlling it much more precisely and extensively in the future.

Other important scientific research has underscored the principle that genes are not fate; instead, GENES + ENVIRONMENT = TRAIT. In other words, environmental factors interact with genes, and can even control or override their effects, to shape a trait. This is critically important, because you currently cannot change your genes, but you can change how they are controlled. Among the most important environmental factors are those in the diet. *The Mindspan Diet* shows how diet can accelerate or slow aging, and how today's most healthful cuisines and modes of living contribute to longevity. It also reveals the dangerous interaction between genes and modern foods and lifestyles.

View *The Mindspan Diet* as your guide to the essentials of Mount Evidence, and reading it is like taking an elevator to the top. From this summit, you'll see more and farther than ever before. One of the ways we have been able to ascend it is through powerful yet simple tools such as surveys and counts. Through these methods, we have gained fantastic insight into human health by learning what people eat and how they live, then following their health outcomes over decades.

We've also added more complex tools,

such as DNA sequencing machines and powerful computers and software to analyze the resulting enormous quantities of DNA data. The first draft of the human genome,* published in 2001, has fundamentally altered all of human biology and medicine. Its effects are just now being felt in routine research and medical practice, as individuals begin to have their entire genomes decoded. As these huge amounts of data accumulate, Mount Evidence rises precipitously, changing the landscape rapidly — and sometimes radically.

While interpreting biomedical research remains difficult, detailed analyses of risk factors and genetic variants that protect against diseases such as Alzheimer's allow us to quantify people's genes, environments, and traits to a depth that was previously impossible. At the Harvard Personal Genome Project, we've already made important differences in people's lives by what we've discovered in their genomes.

One public example is the story of Bloomberg News reporter John Lauerman, who came to us while he was writing a series of articles on personalized medicine and the

---

* The genome is the entire collection of an individual's DNA found within each single cell.

emergence of genomics. He decided there was no better way to become immersed in the process than to enroll in the PGP. We drew John's blood and began the process of sequencing his DNA. When his genome sequence was done, we analyzed it with our automated computer interpretation system, and top, front, and center of his report was a huge red flag. John has a rare DNA variant that causes a potentially serious blood clotting disorder. Neither of his parents had the variant, so it must have been a mutation that occurred in one of John's cells at some point in his life. Similar to a cancer, this cell had proliferated excessively.

It turned out that John had been experiencing medical complications from this mutation for maybe a decade, but he hadn't known why. The information in his genome allowed John and his doctors to know the precise cause of his illness, and he began a fairly simple treatment regimen that put him on a healthier course into the future. John began his series of articles — and a completely new and unexpected chapter in his life. He concluded his last article in the series saying he had no regrets, and that he was glad he had discovered and addressed a serious and previously unidentified threat to his health.

We've had other similar cases in the PGP, where discovery of gene variants has led to simple yet potentially lifesaving knowledge and treatments. One notable example: a sixty-something male participant who came to us a few years ago experiencing early symptoms of Parkinson's disease. It turns out he'd been taking a daily iron supplement for years to feel more energetic. Recent research suggests that Parkinson's can be caused by iron accumulation and the resultant increased oxidative damage in key brain regions. When we sequenced and analyzed his genome, we found he had a genetic variant for the iron overload disorder called hemochromatosis, which is fairly common and has been found in some recent studies to be a risk factor for a range of neurodegenerative diseases, including Parkinson's and Alzheimer's. The genetic finding was confirmed by a blood test showing extremely high blood iron. He eliminated the iron supplements and began conventional treatment for his Parkinson's. Now it seems progression of the disease has been slowed greatly, and maybe even stopped.

These and similar examples show that genomics is ushering us into a new era of confidence about our discoveries. But change often comes slowly, and much of the advice dispensed by even well-meaning and credentialed biomedical experts will not produce desired results. The reason is simple but virtually always overlooked: few understand the primary force that stands in opposition to long-term health goals. That force is senescence, which begins in the second half of life. As we gradually make this midlife transition, some of the things that were good for us when we were young can actually harm us. Conversely, other practices thought to be less than ideal or possibly harmful become beneficial, extending life and preserving mindspan. The life of the bodies and minds of you and all of those you hold dear depends on knowing — rather than guessing — which is which.

HOW TO USE THIS BOOK
The Mindspan Diet is grouped into three sections.

Part 1 will give you the backdrop to the science to come in the book. It explains the concept of mindspan and offers a primer on how your body works and why it needs various nutritional building blocks found in food. This part also introduces genes and important genetic determinants of the mindspan. Here too I introduce the commonalities of traditional cuisines of the Mindspan

Elite, select populations and special individuals who enjoy the greatest validated lifespans and mindspans in human history. Part 1 also contains information from the cutting edge of various biological and nutritional sciences that reveals how your body and food interact and how your needs change with age. It shows you the dangers lurking in everyday foods and how these dangers grow in magnitude as you get older.

Part 2 reveals the critical importance of diet in longevity and mindspan. It shows you the most healthful sources of carbs, fat, and protein, and which foods to avoid, making it easier to get and stay fit and active in both body and mind.

In Part 3 you'll find a summary of dietary keys of the mindspan leaders of the world. This part also has lists of ingredients you should stock up on, practical advice on healthful Mindspan Diet eating and cooking, and seventy-two recipes to get you on the path to maximum mindspan!

■ ■ ■ ■

PART 1
MINDSPAN
BASICS

■ ■ ■ ■

It's important to have a good understanding of the building blocks of life and how they make and maintain your body; you're more likely to stick to the program if you understand why it's working. This section will give you that basic information, reveal the true nature and scope of Alzheimer's disease and other dementias, and show you the commonalities of cuisines of select people and populations that live the longest cognitively healthy lives.

1.
MINDSPANS ON THE MOVE

It ain't so much the things we don't know
that get us into trouble. It's the things we
know that just ain't so.
— Probably said first by
Henry Wheeler Shaw (pen name
Josh Billings), but also attributed to
Artemus Ward and to Mark Twain

Our highest aspiration should be to make
our mindspans soar — to maximize both
longevity and mental performance. With our
best possible minds we can confidently tackle
the most challenging problems; we can better forecast and plan for the future; and we
can live the fullest and happiest lives. In other
words, we can experience and do *everything*
better. Now, however, we face our days with
less certainty and confidence.

According to recent polls, Alzheimer's disease is the most feared diagnosis. Some of

our uncertainty and fear about the future comes from the lack of scientific consensus on the most healthful path forward. There are all manner of claims, from hopelessly bleak to hopeful and inspiring. Some say nothing can prevent or substantially slow the decline. Others say cognitive decline can be stopped and even reversed by some implausible miracle cure. Both are wrong. I selected the Josh Billings quote to head this chapter because, of all the health-related information that inundates us these days, critical parts just ain't so. They just ain't. And, as Mr. Billings said, that gets us into trouble.

CHOOSING A DIET

I have seen and heard about countless diets over the decades. Most focus on weight loss, others on physical fitness or athletic performance, some on health. These are all laudable goals, but neglect what is most important: the long-term performance and health of your mind — and the minds of your loved ones. Think about being a caretaker for many years for someone you love as he or she slowly descends into the abyss of mental darkness we call dementia. Now reverse the roles and picture your loved ones caring for you as all of your memories and relationships fade one by one, leaving them to care for your progressively debilitated body and your ravaged mind. We want to remember the best of our loved ones, but it is difficult to disregard the repeated questions, odd behaviors, incontinence, and the like. The only reasonable goal in choosing a diet is maximum mindspan.

In recent years, both fatty foods and carbs have been vilified. Common assertions are that we're being poisoned by our foods, we're suffering from our bounty, and our diets and health are worse than ever. I agree generally with the first two of these claims, but not with the specifics. As for the state of our diets, in some important ways, they are better than ever. But that doesn't stop the grim downpour of gripes and the rising tide of misguided solutions.

Some health gurus harken back to bygone days. They say if we could go back many millennia we'd see people living in pristine health. As we'd chat around the campfire with our cave kin, they'd be amazed by our descriptions of computers, cellphones, and routine airplane travel while being equally puzzled by our relatively recent ailments such as heart attacks, cancer, and dementia. These gurus are fascinated by our Paleolithic ancestors' health, speculating as to why, for example, starches made up such a tiny fraction of their daily diet.

While our kin of millennia ago were leaner and far more active and diabetes was much less common, the juiciest parts of these stories — especially those used to justify currently popular Paleo diets — come from imaginations gone wild. Genetic evidence shows that over time humans have been evolving an increasing ability to digest starches and sugars. (Today, for example, we produce more than five times the amount of digestive enzymes needed to break down starches as chimps, our closest ape relatives.) The changes with the largest effect date to at least 50,000 years ago, which contradicts the belief that starch consumption is recent and therefore evolutionarily unimportant.

Scientists agree that diseases of older age such as heart disease, cancer, and dementia were less common many thousands of years ago — but primarily because old age as we know it was less common. In fact, mummies from around the world are found with cancer, atherosclerosis, arthritis, and other diseases, which appear to have been at least as common then as they are now when age is taken into account.

If we flash back to the turn of the twentieth century, we'll see that the current ailments of old age were common. In fact, the age-adjusted rates of cardiovascular diseases —

which remain leading killers today—occurred more frequently, as did age-adjusted rates of other deadly diseases, such as pathogenic infections.

Still, more than a hundred years later, it is clear we have some big problems, one of which is that many people have an unnecessarily high risk of cognitive impairment. It is very disturbing that as people and countries become wealthier, cognitive problems in later life become more common.* But to see the best direction forward in dealing with such risks, we must get our facts straight.

MAXIMUM MINDSPAN MEANS OPTIMAL HEALTH

Mindspan translates to longevity and performance of the mind, and it is the ultimate measure of overall long-term health. If the cardiovascular system is in poor shape, blood flow to the brain is impaired. Similarly, poorly functioning kidneys, lungs, or liver also impact mental performance. It is therefore unsurprising that a host of leading health problems, including diabetes and high cholesterol, are risk factors for mental

* People of the same age get dementia more frequently (age-adjusted dementia rates are higher).

decline. Optimal health and longevity of the body come baked into the overall recipe for achieving maximum mindspan. If you are eating a conventional diet — even one typically considered healthful — my dietary program will reduce your risk of all killer diseases.

MINDSPAN RISING, MINDSPAN FALLING

First, the good news: We've made impressive headway in just the last few generations, both in overall longevity and in performance of the mind. Over the last 150 years, industrialized countries have achieved the greatest longevity increases in history. Improved prenatal care and reduced infant mortality have driven huge gains not just in overall life expectancy,[*] but in adult years too. My great-grandparents were born just before the turn of last century. When they were children in the year 1900, a seventy-year-old woman living in the United States could expect to live about nine more years, a statistic that has increased to fifteen years today. And

---

[*] Overall life expectancy at birth is the age to which 50 percent of people born in a given year are projected to live.

recent trends in record long life show accelerating growth. Between 2000 and 2010, the percentage of centenarians (age one hundred and up) of many populations increased dramatically — even more than doubling in some, including in Japan, which leads the world in longevity.

The realm of the mind has experienced similar gains. Modern mental testing didn't become common until after the turn of the twentieth century; but once started and applied widely, testing showed gradual increases similar to those observed for longevity. The mental realm is highly complex and important changes are less easily measured than those in longevity, but measured gains in memory, IQ, and other cognitive functions are impressive: reportedly as high as 25 percent over the twentieth century. As with life expectancy, previous increases of this magnitude likely took many times longer.

While these gains are most often measured in children and adolescents, tests on adults show gains across the board, including in older adults (which is one of the important developments opposing the trend toward increased dementia as people live longer). In other words, it appears people are living longer than ever at about the highest-ever cognitive level. According to these mental test data, adults today are more intelligent than those of generations ago. The fact that these gains are both substantial and persist into later years shows they are at least as impressive as gains in overall longevity. Sensationalist headlines like "Aging Reversal Process Discovered!" aside, these two important types of gains are synergistic and together constitute increasing mindspan.

When we look deeper into the historical and global trends of rising mindspan, there is reason for hope . . . but also for serious worry. And unfortunately the bad news seems pretty grim. Mindspans of some developing nations are still on the rise, but there are alarming signs that mindspan growth has plateaued in developed nations. Most concerning, recent reports suggest that dementias and other neurodegenerative diseases such as Parkinson's are already much higher in developed nations (comparing people of the same age), and might still be on the rise in the United States, Europe, and most other affluent nations of the world. Some of these reports suggest that many in higher-risk countries begin to develop memory problems as early as their forties.

According to a recent study, "deaths from Alzheimer's disease and other dementias rose more than three-fold, and deaths from

Parkinson's disease doubled" globally between 1990 and 2010. It's not just longevity driving this trend. These diseases appear to be increasing in frequency at every age, and in fact the age-standardized death rate from Alzheimer's and other dementias doubled over just two decades.

However, even this alarming trend might seriously underestimate the magnitude of both current and future problems. Alzheimer's disease is responsible for over 500,000 deaths annually in the United States, which is six times higher than the official estimate of the Centers for Disease Control and Prevention. This level of mortality makes Alzheimer's disease the number three killer (maybe even number two) and suggests that it could become the number one killer in the near future. You may have been hearing for years of the coming wave of dementia as the baby boom generation ages, but this study — and others — shows that the worrisome wave is likely to become a devastating tsunami if this trend isn't reversed very soon.

GETTING A GRIP

Our genes haven't changed in the past two or three decades, but our foods, diets, and lifestyles have — radically. But I believe we can reduce risk to far below what it was even before then. Why? Because many independent strands of solid scientific evidence tell us that *we have substantial control over mindspan.* Dietary and lifestyle factors in developed countries have contributed negatively to dementia rates, yet certain stealth factors have produced the opposite effect. The Rolling Stones famously lamented that "you can't always get what you want," but I say sometimes you get more of a good thing when trying to get something else. Some of the gains in longevity and cognition have come from a focus on comfort and quality of life. As discussed at length in later chapters, coffee, tea, and red wine are flavorful ways to improve energy and mood, and certain modern pain relievers like ibuprofen reduce inflammation, but they also reduce dementia and produce other benefits. People seeking immediate mood or energy tweaks or relief from the pain of a bad back or balky knee have achieved long-term cognitive side benefits without intending to.

Other factors that have produced increased mindspan as side benefits include improved sanitation, water and food abundance and quality, and a range of other public health measures. But while these gains may have come easily, we've probably reaped most of the benefits we can from them. If we want to make more headway, we need to look for new sources. Even greater future mindspan gains are possible, but going forward, we need to apply key scientific knowledge and technologies more thoughtfully and precisely.

EATING BETTER AS YOU AGE

The second half of life is regarded somewhat differently across cultures, but one universal among them is that older means wiser, and thus we tend to entrust older people with more responsibility. Here in the United States, where we have a law that restricts the office of the presidency to people thirty-five and older, the average age at the start of all presidential terms is fifty-five, and our youngest president — John F. Kennedy — was just shy of his forty-fourth birthday when he took office. Even in countries without such laws, ultimate responsibility is almost always given to someone well into the second half of life; in the United Kingdom between 1800 and today, for example, the average age a prime minister first took office is about fifty-six.

People begin to slow down physically before this peak in wisdom and leadership (some have even theorized that this physical slowdown is an essential part of the rise to emotional and mental maturity). The tech-

35

nical term for this slowdown is senescence. But we don't just get slower, our needs actually change. We respond differently to food, drink, exercise, and sleep, among other things. Over the decades of the second half of life, these changes add up, as do the benefits or costs of our choices. The importance of this change is underscored by focusing on the leading risk factors for Alzheimer's disease.

Mainstream science has identified the most important genetic contributors to Alzheimer's disease (which we'll discuss in detail in chapter 5). The medical community has pursued treatments to correct the problem caused by one of these genes. Yet most experts don't realize that the interaction of this gene with a ubiquitous environmental trigger negatively impacts cognitive functioning in virtually all older people.

Alzheimer's disease is diagnosed in less than 10 percent of Western populations, but according to the Alzheimer's Association, less than half of Alzheimer's sufferers or their caregivers are told of their diagnosis (possibly because so many believe nothing can be done anyway). It's also widely believed that an additional 10 to 20 percent of people suffer from other lesser or unrelated forms of dementia. Some estimates using relaxed criteria say more than 40 percent have some impairment. But even this figure underestimates the extent of age-dependent cognitive compromise. As chapter 5 explains in detail, most cases of Alzheimer's disease and dementia have the same primary genetic cause, and it is not an uncommon genetic variant. In fact, this root genetic cause is so common it is nearly universal.

All forms of dementia also have common environmental causes, such as the ingredients in our foods. The public remains unaware of these dangers despite being assaulted by them every day. At the moment it is impossible to prove which influence cognition more, genetic or dietary factors, but my belief is that diet has a substantial and possibly greater capacity to either increase or decrease mindspan. Many dietary factors act as volume controls to turn the level of genes up or down or as switches to turn them on or off. In fact, iron is a primary dietary risk for neurodegeneration and dementia because it turns up the volume on this key gene that increases the risk of Alzheimer's disease.

Currently we cannot change our genes, but we can change how they behave with a few potent factors: exercise and physical activity, sleep, drugs, and even our state of mind. But diet exerts the most profound and lasting effect. The critical role of diet isn't very surprising, given that a typical person will eat about forty tons of food in a lifetime.

An outstanding dietary and lifestyle pattern reduces risk of heart attack, stroke, and other cardiovascular complications by 90 percent or more. The Lyon, France, heart study produced a 76 percent reduction in all-cause mortality by boosting the Mediterranean components in the diets of people already eating typical French diets — which are better and result in fewer cardiovascular events than other standard Western diets.

Compare this to the benefits of the best cardiovascular drug therapies. If you are at high risk for a heart attack, statin therapy cuts your risk by up to a third, while an experimental, potentially blockbuster drug for treating heart disease appears to reduce mortality in initial trials by up to 20 percent. As you can see clearly from these numbers, the best blockbuster drug doesn't even come close to the benefits of a good diet.

Very soon you'll find that dangers such as excessive iron are probably abundant in your diet and the diets of people you care about. However, you will also discover that you'll be able to get on a much healthier trajectory with relative ease because while *the main genetic cause of dementia is nearly universal, so is the ability to control it.* Let's turn now to the interaction of these important factors.

2.
GENES AND ENVIRONMENT, FUEL AND FIRE

The unique complexity that is each of us can be represented simply and compactly: we are our environment plus our biology. Factors such as food, drink, air, and temperature together make up the environment. Innate biology is vastly complex and dynamic, but is often represented by its single most important component: DNA, the physical stuff of genes and genomes (collectively all the genes found within each single cell). Here again is the basic formula: GENES + ENVIRONMENT = TRAIT, and all traits are shaped this way. But of a trait's building blocks, which is more important, genes or environment?

Many people have long thought that nothing is more important than heritable, innate biology. After all, family resemblances are more than superficial. We know that certain diseases and disorders run in families, right? Some do, but in truth, a more common answer is "It depends." Genes determine some traits irrespective of environmental influences, and these cases have gotten loads of press and popular attention. But the past few decades of scientific searching have turned up lots of data on what influences health and longevity, enough to upend prior beliefs about genes and environment. Currently, most experts agree that genes are responsible for between 20 and 35 percent of extreme longevity, and the rest is due to environmental factors, such as diet, sleep, mental stimulation, mood, and exercise.

We now know that health and longevity are very complex, but this is good news, showing that our genes are not our fate and that we have substantial control over our future health. Plus, these complexities can be reduced to a few universals for essentially everyone, with a nod to some key information that applies to people with certain genetic variants.

Some genes provide an edge in achieving exceptional longevity and the combination of certain gene variants and good environments can produce very impressive results. Consider one extraordinary example: the extreme longevity of the Frenchwoman Jeanne Calment, who gave up her long habit of smoking one cigarette a day and eating two pounds of chocolate a week — but only when she was nearly a hundred twenty years old! While Madame Calment came from a family of long-lived people, it's important to point out that, except for that one daily cigarette and perhaps a little too much chocolate, she lived a nearly textbook healthful life of good food and drink, plus regular exercise. So she had both exceptional lifestyle factors and exceptional genes, and the two meshed perfectly together.

VARIABLE AND CONTROLLABLE AGING

It is typically thought that all people age at about the same rate, and that a person who lives to ninety or a hundred years simply spends more years in a state of decrepitude and senility. When many think of longevity record holders, like Jeanne Calment, they envision decades of dependency in a nursing home or hospital bed. But this view is wrong. Madame Calment was very active, even riding her bicycle at over one hundred years old! And she remained happy and cognitively aware her whole life. At over age one hundred she appeared decades younger, and her vitality matched her appearance.

Most leading researchers agree that rate

of aging varies greatly from person to person, and even in an individual over time. The rate can even be regulated by various factors, like exercise, diet, and certain drug therapies. So the idea that we are powerless to slow aging is simply wrong. The reason this flawed perception is so harmful is that it can manifest as resignation and be used to rationalize unhealthy behaviors.

To create a more optimistic vision of future possibilities for yourself, imagine a healthy life of average length — say, eighty years — and now stretch it out to a minimum of a hundred twenty years. Envision yourself active and healthy at ages over a hundred, doing all the activities you want — even taking your bicycle out for a relaxing scenic ride! If you are an optimist, think beyond a hundred twenty; stretch it out indefinitely, with no end in sight.

THE THREAD OF LIFE

Everyone has an ideal environment to complement their genes, including you. Yours might be different from Madame Calment's, but there's a substantial core of similarity, thanks to nearly identical genes. The occasional genetic variants each of us has are responsible for any differences. But what are these genes, exactly? They're made of DNA, the molecule that is at the root of all life.

DNA is a vanishingly thin threadlike molecule that has information encoded along its entire length. It's so thin that winding up six feet of it into molecular spools results in a particle so tiny that tens of thousands of them bundled together are the size of a period, like the one at the end of this sentence. When we zoom in tight on the DNA thread, we find it is actually a chain. You can visualize this DNA chain as a long, punctuated message or book written in four letters or chemical units — referred to as bases and named A, C, G, and T — that are linked together one after another to make the long slender molecules we call chromosomes.

Each of your approximately 40 trillion cells contains a total of about six feet of these DNA chains in twenty-three pairs of individual chromosomes. This entire collection of over 6 billion letters of DNA is your genome. One member of each chromosome pair came from your father and one from your mother. Your genes, the individual units that shape your life, are spaced along these DNA chains. There is no physical change along a DNA chain that obviously defines one gene from the next, but the genes and the spaces between them are coded for by the order of the bases along the DNA chain — like punctuation and capitalization to mark the end of a sentence and the beginning of a new one. From the outside of the book all the pages look the same, but the start and stop of a chapter are clear when you know language and the layout of books.

Genes are units of many different functions that do many different things to assemble the body and make it work. To use an analogy, if your body is a car, then genes are the thousands of parts working together dynamically to convert energy (gasoline or electricity) into motion. A few genes encode seats, others encode wheels and tires, and some of these genes might be used in slightly different combinations with other genes to produce a similar but slightly different function, such as making the steering wheel and so on.

The word "encode" is key to understanding what genes actually do. They do not move from where they reside in the center of each cell in your body; they are more like a master plan, blueprint, and mold for physically casting the working parts of the body. Your body is made primarily of trillions of these tiny individual cells, each of which is like a balloon full of highly organized material. A cell is a miniature factory that imports materials, processes them on a production line, and exports a variety of finished goods and waste products.

In your body, many of the different pieces that function as the seats, steering wheel, etc., are proteins, which are essentially chains made from hundreds to thousands of small links. A primary job of the production factory of the cell is to take apart and create links between many different biochemical structures. In general, each human gene encodes one protein, and proteins are used to build bones, skin, hair, and other tissues that make us what we are.

Of the tens of thousands of genes in a human genome, most have some similarity to those of a chicken or a fish, and many are even similar to those in plants. Indeed, all life-forms are evolutionarily related, and the molecules they produce to function are the raw materials of our diets. We require these raw materials from our diets to develop and grow, and to maintain, repair, and replace cells and tissues. We also require food energy as fuel to get around, think, breathe, pump blood and nutrients through the circulatory system, and perform many other normal functions.

Your genes make the cellular factories that take the raw materials provided by the food you eat and convert it into energy and the appropriate parts your body needs to work properly. When we consume food, we are basically "rearranging" the materials in a way to better suit us, but it is essentially the same stuff, the basic building blocks and energy sources of life. So there is truth to the old aphorism "You are what you eat."

This is also true for the things you eat: they are what they eat. Salmon and other cold-water fish are widely known for their high levels of healthful omega fatty acids. These fats are not made by the fish themselves, but by microscopic plankton, which are eaten by larger plankton and so on up the fish food chain to the large fish we eat. So you aren't just what *you* eat but are to some degree what was eaten by whatever you ate, and so on and so on, all the way down to the plants and other organisms that harvest energy from the sun. And since your foods can vary greatly in composition, they can have greatly different effects on your health. Mindspan Elite people of the world have rich food traditions and believe that diet is a primary determinant of health. Older Okinawans say that good food is *nuchi gusui,* or medicine for life.

Examples like Madame Calment show that genes make a minor but important contribution to longevity, and that other factors are even more crucial determinants of our health and well-being. But how important are controllable factors like diet and lifestyle, really? Look no further than Japan, Greece, or Italy. Their traditional diets have fueled their rise to membership in the Mindspan Elite, but are being replaced with more modern, processed foods. There are growing rates of obesity, diabetes, heart disease, and dementia in many areas of these countries. But older people in more rural locations haven't been exposed to as many changes and are as healthy as ever.

Not long ago it was conventional wisdom — and just plain common sense — that genes were primary determinants of health, disease risk, and longevity, but only moderately important in determining personality and cognition. But these beliefs had the facts exactly backward. Identical twins (who have identical genes) score nearly identically on tests of personality and cognition, but their health histories over their lives typically are quite divergent — so much so in fact that their perceived ages can differ substantially in later life.

We sometimes hear the old saying "You can't choose your parents," which is essentially shorthand for you can't choose your genes. While this is true, even though you can't change your genes — at least not yet — you can change how they behave, and our power to control our genes is growing. We are learning how environmental factors, such as nutrients in our diets, can turn certain genes on or off, or up or down. Through the application of key information about lifestyle, diet, drugs and supplements, and other therapies, we can achieve a large degree of specific control over the activities of key genes.

Switches Upon Switches

Genes are regulated at many levels and in many ways, including by other genes. When a gene is turned on, a messenger is created and transported to other machinery that processes it and translates it into a protein before sending it to its proper location.

ENVIRONMENTS CONTROL GENES

Traits — including health, disease, and overall mindspan — are the outcome of a combination of genetic and environmental factors. Environmental factors are multi-

---

layered. The environment of a given gene can be influenced or controlled by many factors, including diet, dietary supplements, and drugs, and even by the products of other genes. Key genes involved in regulating mindspan are controllable by dietary factors. So remember that genes are not fate, and keep in mind this critical formula:

GENES + ENVIRONMENT = TRAIT

Until the day when we can safely upgrade our genes, let's focus on the powerful environmental controls available to us — which have been proven to allow mindspans of well over a hundred ten years.

But even after a gene is turned on, the process can be modified by switches or volume controls at every stage. The messengers can be intercepted or destroyed, for example, or the translation machinery can be slowed or halted.

A TABLE FOR ONE . . . HUNDRED TRILLION

Another way in which diet regulates gene activity and overall health is by establishing conditions for the 100 trillion microbes in the gut (called the gut microbiome). This community is made of hundreds of species of microscopic single-celled organisms that depend completely upon us for their existence. They provide benefits to us, like synthesizing vitamins we can't, such as vitamin B12. Nevertheless, what is best for them isn't always best for us. Some thrive on certain foods, and they have ways to up-regulate our appetites to this end. This important community in your gut influences your body and your mind. The bag of tricks employed by these tiny critters is well developed and powerful, and we have only just begun to plumb their depths. But we already know that they play very important roles in our health and longevity, as you'll see in the chapters to come.

FOOD AS FUEL: KEY MACRONUTRIENTS

To begin to understand the critical role of diet in the regulation of genes — and ultimately of lifespan — let's meet the most abundant constituents of the diet: macronutrients.

Food macronutrients provide the fuel for you to do all you do. They are the energy that powers the symphony of life. We routinely hear about fat, carbs, and protein, but there are others that provide a stable foundation for our overall health. These include ethanol, organic acids, and short-chain fatty acids (SCFAs). Some of these are components of the foods we eat, and others are produced by fermentation of carbohydrates by our gut microbiome. Fermentable carbohydrates are typically fiber, resistant starches, and other carbs that escape digestion. Since so much of the Mindspan Diet is about what you eat and how the macronutrients in your diet interact with your genes, it's important to look at each of these categories a little more closely.

Carbohydrates

Carbohydrates (carbs) are either individual sugars or chains in which the links are sugars. A single sugar unit is referred to as a monosaccharide. One common monosaccharide is glucose, which is found in many foods, including grains, fruits, and vegetables. Another one is fructose, a sugar commonly found in fruits and berries. These single rings can be linked together to form chains of varying lengths. No matter how long these chains are, they are *very* small. Remember how long and thin chains of DNA are? Well, chains of carbs are much shorter and even thinner. A human hair is about half a million times thicker.

Short polysaccharide chains of two or three links have a sweet flavor and are considered sugars. One very common two-link chain, or disaccharide, is sucrose, which is also known as table sugar or just plain sugar. Another disaccharide is lactose, the primary sugar in milk. All starches, including corn, potato, wheat, and rice starches, are just chains of many sugars linked together. These linkages make these starches "complex carbs," and are readily digested by enzymes that specifically recognize them. Breaking the links of the polysaccharide converts it into monosaccharides, and only monosaccharides can be absorbed into the bloodstream through the intestinal wall.

It takes some time for enzymes in the gut to break all of the links in long chains, so longer-chain carbs generally have a lower impact on blood sugar than do shorter-chain carbs. Monosaccharides are the most rapidly absorbed carbs because they don't need to meet up with and be cleaved by an enzyme in the gut. They're also considered the most dangerous to sedentary people, which is one reason why scientists have come up with the glycemic index method of rating foods.

Carbs contain about 4 calories per gram. One teaspoon of sugar contains about 3 to 3.5 grams and about 12 to 14 calories. A heaping teaspoon of sugar can contain more like 5 grams, so be careful in estimating how many calories you are ingesting by such crude measures!

Fat

Like most carbohydrates and proteins, fats are chains of smaller molecules. Fats come in many different varieties that have different effects on health and fitness. Single fat chains are found in foods and in the bloodstream and are referred to as free fatty acids (FFA). The vast majority of dietary fat comes in one basic type of molecular structure: a triglyceride (also called a triacylglycerol), which is three fatty acid chains connected to a molecule of glycerol. The different fat types are grouped into different classes based on what types of fat chains are connected to the glycerol molecule.

Extending our car analogy, your body can use dietary fat for fuel, but did you know that cars can also run on dietary oil or fat, which are very similar to gasoline? Gasoline is derived from crude oil that is made from living things from millions of years ago; it has been converted into a form that can power combustion engines. The engine in your car and the cells in your body derive energy from gasoline and fat in much the same way, although in your cells the process is much more orderly.

There are four broad classes of common dietary fat: saturated, monounsaturated, polyunsaturated, and trans. These classes can be further subdivided depending on the length of the fat chain and the type of bonds in the chain. Both are important features of fat that give it certain biological properties. Saturation refers to whether or not the fat chain has a kink (resulting from a carbon-carbon double bond) in it. Saturated fatty acids have no kinks. Monounsaturated fatty acids (MUFAs) have one kink, and polyunsaturated fatty acids (PUFAs) have more than one kink. Omega-3 and omega-6 refer to different kink positions in the chains of polyunsaturated fatty acids.

Trans fats have kinks that cause their chains to zigzag. These fats occur in small quantities in natural foods, such as dairy products. Artificial trans fats are made by heating unsaturated fats in the presence of metal catalysts in a process called hydrogenation. These fats are referred to as hydrogenated and partially hydrogenated. Evidence suggests that naturally occurring trans fats are not harmful to health; it's the differently structured artificial trans fats that cause disease.

Ketone bodies are strictly speaking not a

fat; they are a class of small compounds produced by the liver and metabolized as fuel by various tissues. Ketone bodies represent only a tiny percentage of the typical dietary calories we consume, generally from meat and dairy products. But much larger numbers of ketone bodies can be produced within our own bodies when carbohydrates are very limited. Under such conditions, ketone bodies are used as primary metabolic fuels. This is why very high-fat eating is sometimes called a ketogenic diet.

Protein
Proteins are similar to carbohydrates in calories and in their chainlike structure. But protein chains are made of about twenty different types of chemical structures called amino acids linked together in different combinations. While amino acids are somewhat different from one another, they have one universal property: each has two chemical groups and is able to link to any two other amino acids, to make linear chains of any length. These chains can fold into countless complex three-dimensional shapes, and these shapes are critical features of proteins.

Our bodies are able to synthesize only eight of the twenty basic amino acids. We have to get the remaining twelve from dietary sources

— the plants and animals we eat for food. Since they all have different biology and needs and live in different environments, they're made up of differing amounts of each amino acid. This is the rationale for why some people become hyperfocused on combining certain foods together, such as beans and rice, to get a "complete" protein.

Organic Compounds and X Factor Fuels

Though the vast majority of our calories come from fats, carbohydrates, and proteins, we do use other compounds as fuel calories. These fuels typically don't appear on food pyramids or nutritional labels. There are two general classes of these underaccounted fuels: organic compounds and what I call X factors. X factors are the end products of microbial metabolism, a.k.a. fermentation, which means these factors are essentially the waste products of these microscopic critters. Not only do we use these factors as fuel, they are crucial for optimal body function and mindspan.

• **Organic acids/organic compounds:** You've probably heard of common organic compounds in our diets, some of which are weak organic acids. One is citric acid, which gives citrus fruits their tart flavor. Another is malic acid, which gives apples a distinctive flavor and aroma.

- **Short-chain fatty acids (SCFAs), X factor fuels:** Some fuels are very short fat chains, and as a group they are aptly named short-chain fatty acids. Although they are fats, they have important properties different from other fats. One difference is that they are produced by microbial metabolism, or fermentation. Important SCFAs in our diets are lactic, acetic, butyric, and propionic acid.* Lactic acid is responsible for the tartness of yogurt, sour cream, sourdough bread, buttermilk, and many cheeses. Butyric acid gives old butter a distinctive aroma. Dilute acetic acid can be found in most homes by its common name: vinegar.

- **Alcohol, an X factor fuel:** For many people, a source of these other calories is alcohol, also known as ethanol, which is the product of yeast fermentation. Ethanol packs a pretty good caloric punch at about 7 calories per gram. Wine has about 9 to 14 percent ethanol, beer be-

---

* These compounds are also known by the names of their nonacidic forms: lactate, acetate, butyrate, and propionate.

tween 3.5 and 6 percent. People of many nations regularly consume 8 to 10 percent of their daily calories in the form of ethanol. Most ethanol is produced by yeast fermentation of starches or sugars.

The amounts of citric, malic, and lactic acid in our foods are small but significant. Citric acid has 3.5 calories per gram. The amount of citric acid in a 6-ounce (170 grams) orange is about 2 to 2.5 grams, which is about 8 calories, or a little less than 10 percent of the total calories in the orange. One 8-ounce (230 grams) cup of low-fat plain yogurt contains about 2.3 to 2.7 grams of lactic acid, for a total of about 10 calories, or about 7 percent of the total calories in the yogurt. Vinegar also provides a small number of calories in a typical diet, but as you will soon discover, the effects vinegar and other X factor fuels have on your body are akin to their potent flavors: a small amount packs a major punch.

The Unbreakable Chain: Fiber
Some carbohydrate chains have special links that can't be broken down by enzymes in your GI tract. These indigestible links are called fiber.

Fiber can be found all around us, and not

just in our food. The wood in trees is composed mostly of sugar — mostly in the forms of cellulose and hemicellulose — as is paper, cotton clothing, etc. As strange as it may sound, if you live in a wooden house, your house is made of sugar in the form of fiber. So those of you in cotton clothing and wooden houses are literally clothed and sheltered by sugars!

Fiber is usually categorized as soluble fiber or insoluble fiber, but that misses what is really important about fiber, which is whether or not it can be digested, or "fermented," by intestinal flora. Even though fermentable fiber is eventually broken down into monosaccharides by gut enzymes, these sugars have very different effects on a person's physiology than dietary sugar or starches do. The degree of difference is so dramatic that it's hard to believe they're made of the same basic building blocks.

Some scientists and authors of popular diet books say that fiber provides no calories in the diet. This is simply not true. In fact, even the average low-fiber Western diet provides on the order of 6 to 10 percent of calories through fiber fermentation, which is quite a lot. When fiber makes its way into the lower part of the large intestine, it is fermented by your bacterial flora. These bacteria break down the fiber into monosaccharide sugars and metabolize most of it, with the remainder metabolized by the cells lining your large intestine.

These by-products of floral fermentation — mainly alcohol and short-chain fatty acids — aren't normally used by other bacteria for fuel, but they can be used by colonocytes, cells that line the colon, the lower portion of the large intestine. Some of these fermentation products also make it into the bloodstream, eventually ending up in muscles, fat, and even your GI tract and liver. Propionate, for example, alters liver metabolism, which is a primary regulator of cholesterol and explains how dietary fiber alters your good (HDL) and bad (LDL) cholesterol.

Another important characteristic of fiber is viscosity, which measures how thick fiber makes a solution and its ability to "trap" foods in a weblike matrix. Barley and oatmeal are gummy and gelatinous, for example, because of fermentable beta-glucan fiber. The cholesterol-lowering effect of these grains is due to fiber's ability to trap cholesterol and prevent its reabsorption into your body.

Some fibers are so nonviscous they are not even thought of as fibers. Take lactose, the sugar in milk. Many people are lactose intolerant (also known as hypolactasia), which simply means they can't digest lactose.* Well, if they can't digest it, where does it go? If you guessed it goes into the lower part of the GI tract and gets fermented by intestinal flora, you're catching on to how the body works. Naturally, we all can digest lactose when we're babies, but many people lose this ability beyond the age of about four years.

One characteristic of the Mindspan Elite, which we'll discuss in later chapters, is the large quantities of fermentable carbs in their diets. While we're still unsure of how much food is digested by a person — as opposed to their flora — we've made great leaps forward in understanding why fiber and fermentation are so important to overall health. In the next chapter, we'll look at some other similarities of Mindspan Elite diets.

* The percentage of adults who cannot digest lactose ranges greatly by ethnicity, from less than 5 percent of northern Europeans and Scandinavians to over 95 percent of Asians.

3.
KEY SIMILARITIES OF MINDSPAN ELITE CUISINES

If a coded message from extremely long-lived beings within our galaxy provided a compelling description of an ideal way of eating to boost mindspan, what might it say? Would it recommend low carbs and loads of omega-3 fats? A caveman diet? Or maybe something incomprehensibly complex involving lots of supplement powders and capsules?

This is a trick question, because we have received such a message — in fact, many of them. They originate from far-flung and exotic intragalactic locales such as Naha, Nicoya, PACA, and Liguria. Ace geographers will notice a deeper level of trickery to this question: these aren't faraway planets, they are places right here on earth. But by typical earth standards they might seem to belong to another galaxy: Naha is the capital city of Okinawa, the southernmost prefecture in Japan; Nicoya is a southern region of Costa Rica; and PACA (Provence–Alpes–

Côte d'Azur) and Liguria are neighboring French and Italian regions on the Mediterranean coast, commonly known as the Rivieras.

These areas are widely separated geographically and culturally but are members of what I call the Mindspan Elite — places and people blessed with longevity of both body and mind. While each has its own unique foods and ways of life, they do share clear commonalities critical to health and cognitive longevity. And most important, their commonalities are *not* shared by peoples and cultures at the other end of the mindspan spectrum (those with poor health and shorter cognitive longevity). I call that other end of the spectrum the Mindspan Risk countries and populations.

We've all seen dramatic weight loss before and after photos in magazines, in television infomercials for dietary supplements, and in popular diet books. Or perhaps you've read claims of the newest fad diet that is based on selected blood biomarkers like homocysteine or cholesterol as ultimate measures of success. But all of these claims are usually devoid of statistically solid examples of long-term successes. This is why the Mindspan Elite are so valuable: they represent real-world outcomes of billions of very long-term human experiments.

LONGEVITY AND MINDSPAN

Longevity can be measured in several ways. The most common is current life expectancy, or average life expectancy at birth (LEB), but early life mortality rates can skew this number. Life expectancy can also be estimated for people at certain ages — for example, average life expectancy of a sixty-year-old or an eighty-year-old. I generally prefer these measures since they show how long an older person in a given country or area is likely to live if he or she has already lived to that base age.

Regardless of method, however, the list of global longevity leaders includes France, Italy, Iceland, Finland, Denmark, Norway, the Netherlands, Sweden, Japan, Thailand, Singapore, and Costa Rica. Most of these populations are also historically leaner than those in the United States, which makes sense when you consider we have only moderate longevity and the highest rate of obesity in the world. Other recognized longevity hot spots in southern Europe are certain areas in Spain and the three tiny countries San Marino, Andorra, and Monaco.

But even among these longevity leaders, there are some stark differences. A key study finding in some of these countries is that long life is usually accompanied by an increasing risk of mental impairment such as Alzheimer's disease and other forms of dementia. Finland, Iceland, the United States, Sweden, and the Netherlands, for example, all have good healthcare and longevity, but they suffer the highest rates of Alzheimer's disease incidence and mortality in the world.*

Other countries, however, experience even greater longevity and much better late-life cognitive functioning. The best of the best is Japan, followed closely by a few others such as France and Italy. But even within countries there are pockets of longevity that best their long-lived compatriots. Here is a look at the Mindspan spectrum — from the true Elite to Mindspan Risk populations.

The Mindspan Elite

Japan
Japan leads the world in virtually all longevity categories and has low levels of dementia.

* "Age-specific incidence" is the proportion of people of a given age diagnosed with Alzheimer's disease. This is the key measure for comparing two groups. Other measures, especially prevalence, are misleading.

It has consistently suffered lower rates of dementia than other developed countries, including the United States and all of Europe. One reason for Japan's extreme longevity is its very low rate of obesity. In 2008 the Japanese government enacted legislation to combat this disease, but even before then, their overall obesity rate was the lowest in the developed world: less than 5 percent, compared to almost 40 percent in the United States! Japanese women are the real stars of longevity and mindspan, living six to seven years longer than Japanese men.

Mediterranean France and Italy

Regions of France and Italy near the Mediterranean Sea and spanning their shared border have the highest longevity in Europe and are close behind leader Japan. The proportion of centenarians and supercentenarians (age one hundred ten and up) is second only to Japan. Southern Europe has overall lower dementia incidence than northern Europe, and Liguria and the Provence–Alpes–Côte d'Azur region (PACA) appear to have even lower rates. I refer to these Mindspan Elite areas collectively as the Mediterranean Rivieras. Sardinia is an Italian island across the Ligurian Sea (part of the Mediterranean) from the Rivieras. An interior hilly region of

Sardinia is one of five *National Geographic* longevity hot spots (so-called Blue Zones).

Spain

Certain areas of Spain have proportions of centenarians and supercentenarians nearly as high as the Mediterranean Rivieras, and rates of dementia that are low for Europe. The highest longevity concentration occurs in a geographical band that begins just northeast of Madrid and stretches north and westward to the north and western coasts above Portugal.

Health-Conscious Vegetarians and Pescatarians

Seventh-day Adventists (SDA) typically eat little red meat and enjoy exceptional longevity. In the United States, vegetarian and pescatarian (eat fish but not red meat or poultry) Adventists suffer less dementia than their meat-eating peers. SDA are the best studied of these health-conscious groups, but it's likely that these findings can be applied to all health-conscious vegetarians and pescatarians, which I'll discuss in later chapters.

The Mindspan Prospective

Cambodia, Costa Rica (Nicoya), Colombia,

Greece (Ikaria and Crete), Panama, Singapore, and Thailand

These places are reported to have outstanding longevity and to have hot spots of truly exceptional longevity, but dementia hasn't been studied sufficiently well to grant them Mindspan Elite status. However, developing countries typically have lower dementia risk than developed countries, especially Mindspan Risk countries, and initial studies in East Asia and Latin America show low dementia rates.

The Mindspan Risk

Finland, Iceland, the United States, Sweden, Netherlands, and Certain Areas of Northern Europe and the United Kingdom

These countries and regions have the unfortunate distinction of leading the world in Alzheimer's disease incidence and mortality.

THE LONGEST-LIVED PEOPLE IN THE WORLD

- The town of Arles in the Provence–Alpes–Côte d'Azur (PACA) region was the birthplace and residence of Jeanne Calment, the longest-lived person ever at over a hundred twenty-two years!

- Liguria, the physically smallest of Italy's regions, boasts the highest concentration of centenarians and supercentenarians in all of Europe.
- The Italian region of Piedmont has two of seven living Italian supercentenarians, including one-hundred-sixteen-year-old Emma Morano, the oldest living person in Europe, and the second oldest in the world! Emma lives independently and prepares her own meals. On her every-day menu: pasta for lunch, eggs, and a daily dose of her homemade brandy.
- Japan leads the world in life expectancy in all ages, and has the highest proportions of centenarians and super-centenarians.
- Except for Sardinia, women in all developed regions of the world outlive men, and they make up the majority of cente-narians and an even greater proportion of supercentenarians. Sardinia has a very high proportion of centenarian men, and local provinces Nuoro and Ogliastra feature both the highest longevity among Sardinians and an equal proportion of men and women centenarians.

DIVERSE CUISINES, SIMILAR DIETS

There's no doubt that diet plays a key role in driving longevity *and* mindspan. Over the past twenty to thirty years, supermarkets in many nations have become filled with a wide variety of foods from around the world, but for most of the twentieth century, people ate locally and traditionally. Older people stick with their traditional diets, so they resisted the changing food landscapes. Traditional cuisines such as those in Japan, France, and Italy not only are well known and loved but also have been tracked and analyzed in great detail for decades. We know the favored foods and routine diets of people of average longevity, and of the longest-lived of Mindspan Elite and Mindspan Risk. The cuisines of the Mindspan Elite of Mediterranean Europe and Asia differ greatly and feature vastly different flavors, aromas, and ingredients. No two countries exemplify this contrast better than France and Japan.

Among European nations, France consumes the most fat and far-above-average quantities of alcohol, cheese, and butter. Contrary to popular belief, Mediterranean French traditionally haven't eaten a lot of fish — mainly because the Mediterranean is not a rich source of fish and seafood — whereas the Japanese eat it (in the form of sushi and sashimi) in quantity. (We'll discuss this more at length in part 2.) The French eat lots of vegetables and a fair amount of fruit. The Japanese? Not so much. The Japanese eat low to moderate amounts of fat, only small amounts of meats and dairy, and moderate amounts of fruits and vegetables — including few fresh ones. The Japanese drink a lot of green tea (the French do not) — and they drink substantially less alcohol than the French.

And yet even with such diverse cuisines, they have two crucial things in common: both have very low levels of obesity and disease. France is last and Japan second to last in risk of heart disease, the number one killer in developed countries. So what is responsible for their typical leanness, good health, *and* mindspan?

Once we look beyond the many differences, we can readily identify a common core of features between the cuisines of France and Japan, and among all of the Mindspan Elite. And in some ways the key dietary components of PACA and Liguria are even more similar to Japan and the other longevity leaders of Asia than they are to the rest of Europe.

SOME CORE COMMONALITIES OF THE MINDSPAN ELITE

- Less red meat and added sugar.
- Less liquid milk (moderate amounts of cheese, butter, sour cream).
- Moderate to fairly high amounts of fish and seafood, typically not deep-fried.
- More beans and other legumes.
- Fat consumption varies, but if it is high, then it is mostly monounsaturated.
- Alcohol consumption varies but is routine, usually with meals, and is not extreme among the longest-lived.
- Abundant dietary phytochemicals, such as polyphenols and tannins, consumed with meals and present in fruits, vegetables, red wine, coffee, and tea (including herbal teas, like mint, pennyroyal, chamomile).
- Fermented, pickled, and preserved foods, such as vinegar and dried fish (mostly bonito in Japan and cod in the Mediterranean Rivieras).
- Greens. Key Mediterranean cuisines feature an abundance of greens and herbs, including Swiss chard, borage, escarole, purslane, basil, thyme, marjoram (oregano), and many more. In Japan, sea vegetables (seaweed, kelp, etc.) are found in many meals.

You can begin right now to shift your diet in a more healthful direction by incorporating common factors among Mindspan Elite cuisines.

1. Consume less meat. Relative to Mindspan Risk countries over the past half century, the Japanese have averaged only about a third to a half as much meat. If you eat a substantial amount of meat most days, gradually shift toward better health by replacing it in some and then most meals with half the amount of fish or legumes.

2. Cut out excess sugar. The Mindspan Elite aren't sugar-free, but they consume 35 to 40 percent less sugar than the Mindspan Risk average. Regular and substantial doses of added sugar, soft drinks, sugary juices, candies, pastries, muffins, doughnuts, and the like contribute to obesity and mental decline. The message is clear and simple: too much sugar will accelerate aging of your body and mind.

3. Drink more tea, coffee, or small

amounts of red wine *with meals.* The reasons for drinking these beverages with meals are detailed in chapter 10, but the essential and immediate take-home message is that they must accompany meals to have maximum effect. Most Mindspan Elite cuisines include one or all of these beverages at various meals. In Japan, for example, green tea is commonly drunk at every meal. Okinawans drink green tea and jasmine tea. In Italy, they drink more coffee and red wine, and in France, they drink all three. In the Italian Riviera regions, they drink two to three times as much tea as those in other parts of Italy. Green, oolong, jasmine, and black teas all are excellent choices. I drink mostly green tea because it is the top choice in Japan, but I drink plenty of other kinds of tea. Decaf tea doesn't have equivalent benefits, although certain herbal teas, like chamomile, possess some. Decaf coffee appears to have nearly equivalent benefits to caffeinated coffee.

NEWS FLASH: SOME REFINED GRAINS ARE GOOD

Although "refined" is a good thing in other contexts — e.g., it connotes high class — when it comes to food, the typical connotation is unhealthful. Refined is most often associated with "prepared" or packaged, and thus assumed to be nutrient deficient, since the process of refining anything takes it further from its natural state. When it comes to grains, however, the reverse is true! At least it can be. But as with good fats and bad fats, you have to know which refined grains are good and which are bad.

A whole grain hasn't had its outer bran and germ removed. Sounds good, right? Refined grains, in contrast, are milled or "polished," which means they've been stripped of both bran and germ. The advantage is a finer texture and a longer shelf life (because of the reduction of fats that can be oxidized, which causes the grain to smell and taste rancid), but the downside is that fiber and many nutrients are reduced.* Sounds bad.

Knowing that, it makes sense to assume whole grains are better for your health. Not necessarily. Many commercial whole grain

---

* A notable exception is barley, which retains most of its fiber when stripped of bran and germ.

crackers, muffins, and breads are made of flour ground so finely that most potential health benefits are lost. Even worse, this fine grinding exposes the natural grain oils to more rapid oxidation, which, as you'll see in later chapters, is detrimental to your health.

This may help explain a puzzling fact about the Mindspan Elite: not only do they eat large amounts of grain, but they, to the horror of many nutritionists and epidemiologists, *eat substantial amounts of refined carbs.* In Japan and other longevity leaders of Asia, they traditionally have eaten and continue to eat mostly refined white rice, and very little brown rice. In PACA, Liguria, Sardinia, and the rest of the Mediterranean Mindspan Elite, they eat many kinds of breads and pastas with almost every meal — and most are made with refined wheat flour. These aren't just side dishes; they are the very foundation of these cuisines. In fact, Italy leads Europe in present and historical starch consumption *and* in centenarians and supercentenarians. A traditional serving size of pasta in the Mediterranean Riviera is 7 ounces (200 grams).

Proof that these grains are the bedrock foods of these cuisines is further found in the words for meals. Rice is so central to Japanese cuisine that two words for it, *gohan* and *meshi,* also mean "meal." If you ate a meal, you ate rice. Similarly, in Italian, *pasto* and *pasti* are the singular and plural of "meal."

Copious consumption of refined carbs among the Mindspan Elite isn't usually overtly denied — almost certainly because denial would be so obviously untrue and easily exposed. Instead, it is simply swept under the rug like any inconvenient truth in disagreement with accepted dogma. For example, two widely promoted diet pyramids for Mediterranean and Asian cuisines show grains at the base of these pyramids, but only whole grains are explicitly mentioned. Despite the known preference for white rice in Asia, the pyramid shows "Rice, noodles, breads, corn, and other whole grains."

See the magic trick, the sleight of hand performed here? We are given a list of grains plus "other whole grains," implying that all grains in the pyramid are whole. These misdirections are routine practice. Search for authoritative descriptions of Asian and Mediterranean cuisines, and you'll find them everywhere. We are told that healthy Mediterranean and Asian people eat cuisines based on whole grains, and that they avoid refined grains. We are expected to join this conspiracy of convention. We are instructed to look the other way, to avert our eyes from this starch-filled Pandora's box. But facts impel us onward toward understanding.

In Liguria and Sardinia, two mindspan leaders of the Mediterranean, the diets are similar to those in PACA, but they eat more pasta — much more — and their wheat is also refined, probably very similar to the regular pasta at your local grocer (except it isn't enriched with iron). Pasta and couscous are made from durum wheat semolina. Typical semolina consists of coarse bits of the starch granule of the durum wheat kernel, although it is usually ground more finely for breads. Rivierans do have some mixed pastas, which include some chestnut flour or whole wheat flour, but the vast majority of pasta is made from 100 percent semolina.

Both Ligurians and Sardinians eat a wide variety of breads, most of which are made of refined flours. All Italians eat focaccia, made from refined flour, but Ligurians are known for their particular fondness for it. In his classic book *Flavors of the Riviera: Discovering Real Mediterranean Cooking,* Colman Andrews says focaccia of many kinds "is Ligurian fast food."

In addition to white flour, Ligurians and Sardinians also use semolina in a wide variety of pastas and to make soups, cakes, pastries, crackers, puddings, and breads, including the Sardinian favorite flatbread known as carta di musica (that is, "sheet music," because of its resemblance to a piece of paper, and because of the noisy crunch produced when eating it). A similar semolina flatbread, pane carasau, is favored by Sardinian shepherds for their long journeys from home. Longevity-leading Greeks in Crete and Ikaria eat white and semolina breads and phyllo at most traditional meals (they also eat lots of potatoes, contributing to their high carb intake). Some claims about Mediterranean bread and pasta being typically whole grain seem to be based on the incorrect notion that semolina is unrefined wheat. It is not; it's refined.

Semolina is also used to make Sardinian sourdough bread, which has been a staple for generations. Barley and barley bread were also traditional staples in the Sardinian mountainous interior, which is the true longevity hot spot of the island. Combined intake of barley and wheat provided the majority of dietary energy in the traditional diet in the middle of the twentieth century, and carbs were 60 percent of the diet. As civilization gradually encroached, this level dropped slightly but remains over 50 percent — although semolina has almost completely replaced barley.

As is true in regard to semolina, most people are confused by barley. The most common type of barley is called pearled barley. Like white rice, it lacks the bran and germ. In other words, it isn't a whole grain; it is just as refined as white rice.

As in other Mindspan Elite regions like Piedmont, Italy, longevity and grain go together. The longevity belt in the north of Spain largely overlaps the region called Castile and León (Castilla y León), which has been called Spain's grain belt, because most of the country's grain is grown there. Just as with their Mediterranean neighbors, and again in contrast to common assertions, agricultural and commercial records reveal that less than 10 percent of bread eaten in Spain is whole grain.

Exactly what quantities of refined carbs do the Mindspan Elite eat? In 1961, about 45 percent of food energy in Italy came from grains, 90 percent of which was refined wheat in the form of breads and pasta. This level has declined steadily to about 32 percent today, although Ligurians reportedly eat more pasta and other grains than most other Italians (Liguria is one of the famed pasta regions of Italy, and there pasta remains *the* staple food). In addition to relatively high consumption of refined carbs, Mediterraneans consume copious amounts of olive oil, which contributes phenolic compounds and other so-called phytochemicals to the diet, but otherwise has little established nutritional value relative to its energy content.

In Japan, about half of calories consumed come from grains, about 40 percent from refined sources. Okinawans still get about 60 percent of their calories from carbs, which is down from 85 percent in the middle of the twentieth century. I often see claims that the Okinawan diet is based on the purple sweet potato, and that is a main reason they are so healthy and long-lived. But Okinawans haven't consumed more than 3 percent of their calories as sweet potatoes since the 1950s, and less than 1 percent since the early 1960s. During the 1950s Okinawans transitioned to eating more white rice and bread, just like the rest of Japan.

What nerve of these mindspan champs — willfully ignoring the sage advice of the world's nutritional brain trusts! Their grain is not brown, it is not whole, and it is not a pure and natural gift from Mother Earth — unless by pure, we mean nearly pure starch. Overall, Mindspan Elite still get over 50 percent of their daily food energy from refined starches and oils, sources that are widely considered to be nearly "empty" calories — that is, calories with comparatively low levels of vitamins, minerals, and fiber. If you add alcohol and sugar (also commonly considered to be empty calories), the level increases to over 60 percent. In decades past this level was even higher, approaching 70 percent of food energy in most Mindspan Elite locations. This is a diet clearly contrary to the healthful diet that is commonly promoted — even without considering the minimal fruits and vegetables in the Japanese diet, most of which are not fresh but pickled.

How about other mindspan leaders? Take a look at Central and South America, where Costa Ricans, Panamanians, and Colombians follow the same formula: less meat, more seafood, routine and moderate alcohol intake, abundant phytochemicals, including coffee with meals, and lots of white rice. Like the Japanese, these people use white rice as the base for every meal, including breakfast, and they get more of their daily calories from it than from any other food. They pair it with their other carb-rich staples, including beans and fried plantains. Gallo pinto, a mixture of rice and beans (usually black), is ubiquitous in Costa Rican cuisine. The ratio of rice to beans varies but is always largely rice.

You were warned at the beginning of this chapter that this message would seem like an alien transmission. Given widespread warnings about "empty calories," promotions of fresh fruits and vegetables, and the current status of refined carbs as the whipping boy of virtually every dietary philosophy, I consider this a reasonable warning. By the way, I happen to love fruits, vegetables, and whole grain foods and have no agenda other than to report and interpret the facts as they are, not as I would like them to be. These facts might come as a shock to you, but only because you've been hearing and reading highly sanitized accounts of these traditional cuisines.

The Mindspan Elite who continue to eat their way are living longer than ever, defying conventional wisdom. Those deviating far from traditional foods and dietary patterns — especially adopters of Western-style fast foods — aren't faring as well. The lifespan and mindspan successes of the Mindspan Elite provide the best reason of all for why they — and we — should be skeptical of the prevailing orthodoxy about refined carbs, and the guidance to abandon what has been proven beyond doubt to work.

While dietary influences are clear and substantial, a somewhat surprising primary risk factor has emerged: national affluence. In other words, at the same age, people in poorer and developing countries have lower levels of Alzheimer's disease and other dementias than people in wealthy countries. Many explanations have been offered for this problem, but only one is completely consistent with all the evidence: diet is responsible for most of the difference.

As we look deeper into this puzzle and you are introduced to various elements of the Mindspan Diet solution, you'll likely be surprised to discover that the underlying drivers of dementias of affluence aren't just fast and junk foods, but even many foods that are portrayed as healthful. In the next chapter you'll begin to see why these foods might be okay or even healthful for some people, especially the young, but in the long term they gradually but surely undermine the health of your body and mind.

4.
CHANGING BODIES, CHANGING NEEDS

Life's tragedy is that we get old too soon
and wise too late.
— Benjamin Franklin

From early childhood we see a few key differences among people. We know there are
boys and girls and men and women. We see
there are little people, big ones, and everything in between. We see clear differences of
many kinds between infants, children, adults,
and the elderly. When young, we are smooth-
skinned, flexible, speedy, seemingly indefati-
gable, and resilient, with full heads of hair in
all colors but gray. We bump, bruise, and
break, scratch, scuff, and bleed, but we heal
quickly. Adults, on the other hand, are very
different, both physically and mentally. They
are large, but while they don't get taller,
some continue to grow — sideways. Some
have gray hair and some men lack hair on

86

their heads. Healing doesn't happen as quickly as it once did.

ESSENCE AND SENESCENCE

We age all through our lives, but as we all reach middle age, we also begin to *senesce*. Senescence is the array of physical changes that accompany the decline of our most important evolutionary objective: our reproductive ability. In other words, around the time we lose our ability to reproduce, we begin to senesce. Modern healthcare is helping us control this process. With many advances in our living conditions and healthcare, we are slowing the age of onset and rate of senescence.

Of course, many adults transition into the second half of life showing only subtle signs of senescence; we all know people who look half their age. Even when they do start to show some signs of advancing age, like decreasing muscle and bone mass, gray hair and skin wrinkles, most remain very active. Women transition more abruptly than men do. They stop menstruating regularly and then completely as they go through menopause. Men undergo a similar but much more gradual transition called andropause, marked by the decline of testosterone and the sex hormone dehydroepiandrosterone

(DHEA).

During the last sixty years, the study of senescence has helped us understand just how primary reproductive ability is to setting the tempo of this process. From an evolutionary perspective, the very essence of life is reproduction, and this shapes how our genes shape us. Any gene variant that tends to favor reproduction early in life enjoys a selective advantage. And there is little or no selective pressure against gene variants that exert negative effects if they occur past the age of reproduction. Thus a given gene variant that has a positive effect early in life will be favored by natural selection even if it has serious negative effects later in life. This double-edged-sword effect is dubbed antagonistic pleiotropy (let's call it the AP rule).

The AP rule is a very tricky concept, and if you understand it, you have passed your AP exam and are way ahead of many recognized biomedical experts with advanced degrees. Now that you know this rule, you'll see and hear assertions that natural selection weeds out harmful genes, so only rare genes cause disease. But this is true only of diseases that occur up to the end of reproductive age. Genes that contribute to the diseases and degenerative processes of older age are not necessarily rare. In fact, many are extremely common or even predominant. This misunderstanding is widespread in the biomedical sciences outside of gerontology and is a primary reason incorrect and even dangerous medical and dietary advice is so common.

Together with the AP rule, another rule gives us a complete framework for optimizing our health and maximizing mindspan. I call this one *synchrony of senescence.* A very large number of studies have been done to understand the biology of aging and senescence. There have been studies on cells in dishes, on experimental organisms such as worms and mice, and on people. Countless bodily and cellular functions and variables have been measured as they change with age: circulatory function, heart and other organ functions and stress responses, brain anatomy and function, and accumulations of damage to DNA and other cellular components, just to name a few. From these studies, one thing is clear: all attributes and processes peak and decline, and they do so in approximate synchrony — i.e., on about the same schedule set by reproduction. Of course, some lives are longer and the shapes of life history curves can differ greatly, but the overall trend is the same. This general synchrony results from natural selection acting on all of our genes to provide a peak of reproductive fitness at about the same time.

At this peak, your body is like a new high-performance car. After this peak, performance declines at an imperceptible rate. An aged car can malfunction in any one of multiple ways that will end its life. The engine (heart) can quit; the electrical system (the brain and nerves) can go; or the transmission can grind to a halt. Nothing in a twenty-year-old car with 200,000 miles on it looks or functions like new, which is why it isn't worth it to install a new engine or transmission. The car doesn't expire all at once, but all of it declines on about the same gradual schedule. Likewise, very old people in declining health typically have multiple maladies.

Still, like a car, the body can be tuned and maintained. The vast majority of cars from sixty or seventy years ago have completely rusted away and disappeared, but those meticulously maintained by collectors look better than newer cars on the road today. Similarly, supercentenarians have good biology, but their genes work well with their environments and they take care of themselves. The latter makes an enormous difference in how well you look and perform over the years. The key is, you have to know exactly how to perform the necessary maintenance.

Human lives have changed substantially over millennia. We have progressively freed ourselves from many stresses of bygone days. Most of us don't spend most of our days exposed to the sun and elements, and modern food safety laws, sanitation, and medicine have spared us from routine exposures to many harmful toxins and pathogens. But at older ages, the synchronous schedule of senescence begins to break down. If you look at the skin of people who have experienced excessive sun exposure, you can see clearly that the aging of one part or organ system can be accelerated. A similar thing happens to other organ systems under chronic assault — including the brain.

It is essential to understand that, similar to a car with a bad engine or transmission or electrical system, any one unhealthy factor or body component trumps all else. Very high cholesterol is harmful, and in the long term it is a killer. Although much more rare, very low cholesterol is also a health risk. The same is true with very low or high blood sugar, or extremely short or overly long telomeres (the protective coat at the end of your chromosomes). People who are models of extreme longevity of body and mind are free from any serious pathology at a time when others are beginning to experience declining health. In other words, they enjoy very late onset and slow progression of senescence. Those on their way to living over a hundred years don't even start to look or feel old until most other people in their age group around the world have died.

WHICH IS MORE IMPORTANT, GENES OR ENVIRONMENT?

It is commonly believed that centenarians and supercentenarians have special genes that allow them to age slowly. Most experts agree that the contribution of genes explains between 20 and 35 percent of their extreme longevity. That means environment is responsible for the remaining 65 to 80 percent of the longevity equation, and diet is a major component of the environment.

When Japanese move to other countries, their health typically goes downhill. Japanese in the U.S. with the highest rates of disease, including Alzheimer's disease and other dementias, have a more Western eating pattern. Their rates of dementia are similar to those of Americans of European ancestry. So bad diet produces bad results — but luckily, this works both ways. Many

---

studies have shown that people who adopt healthy Asian and Mediterranean-style diets have lower levels of disease.

DIFFERENT NEEDS, DIFFERENT DIETS

The AP rule describes why we have the genes that we do, and reveals the risks they pose as we get older. It also helps us to identify the dietary and other environmental factors that regulate these genes and can exacerbate their good or bad long-term effects. The AP rule has far-reaching consequences for diet, nutrition, and overall longevity and mindspan, and we can apply it to understand the long-term costs of nutritional deficiency or excess.

First consider deficiency. Some people insist that nature has optimized our bodies to get all the nutrients we need out of good natural foods, which is all we need to fix nutritional problems. This general view is known as the naturalistic fallacy. While I agree that most of us can eat better, the AP rule explains why certain nutritional deficiencies happen more frequently as we get older. Take vitamin B12, for example. Many complex steps are required for B12 to be absorbed sufficiently. Natural selection has ensured that all these steps occur efficiently in youth, but it has not ensured that they continue to be equally efficient as the years go by. The same is true for other nutrients. A diet that once provided enough of all nutrients might fail to provide sufficient amounts of at least some of them in later life.

Now let's turn to nutritional excess. Lucretius wrote over 2,000 years ago, "What is food to one, is to others bitter poison." What wasn't understood until the twentieth century (and what Lucretius probably didn't know) is that the one and the other — these two seemingly different people — can be the same person at a different time of life.

We all know that young people are more robust and can tolerate stresses that harm older people, but what is not widely understood or appreciated is that some things that are good for us when we are young can harm us as we age. A given amount of a certain nutrient that might be highly beneficial for an eighteen-year-old woman can become excessive, harming her as she gets older — either because of the cumulative insults of chronic stress over time or because of dramatic changes in her body's requirements for good health, or both. The same is true for men. The cumulative negative effects of uninformed decisions add up over time, so it is critical to identify as early as possible the current dangers to your long-term health. Our best strategy for doing this is to follow the example of the Mindspan Elite, and we can be aided in setting our mindspan course by using detailed information about them.

BIOMARKERS: BAROMETERS OF YOUR HEALTH

A biomarker is simply something that can be measured and might provide useful information about the state of your health. When you put a thermometer in your mouth, you are measuring a biomarker: body temperature. Common blood biomarkers include insulin, glucose, cholesterol, triglycerides, testosterone, estrogen, and electrolytes such as sodium and potassium. Non-blood biomarkers include percent body fat, height, weight, body mass index (BMI), lung volume and function, and the like. Biomarkers can be subfractions of other biomarkers, such as LDL (a.k.a. LDL-C, or "bad" cholesterol) and HDL ("good" cholesterol).

Continuing our car analogy, we can call a biomarker the equivalent of, say, a fuel gauge, oil dipstick, or odometer, as well as other trickier measurements, such as the condition of the brake pads or tire-wear depth and pattern. Just as these measurements enable a car mechanic to diagnose and correct or prevent a problem with your car, biomarkers allow you and a healthcare provider to give your health a tune-up to correct or prevent more serious problems (see appendix B for a list of biomarkers I recommend you get tested for).

As you weigh the importance of any biomarker relevant to longevity and mindspan, keep in mind the following key points:

The Mindspan Elite are the proven pinnacle of mindspan, and Japanese women live longest of all. Any biomarker data should be compared to their biomarkers — primarily of the past, if they are available. Mindspan Elite biomarkers of the present are relevant only if we are sure critical factors, such as diet and physical activity, haven't changed substantially since they got on the path to maximum mindspan.

So biomarkers are useful, but we must be careful in attempting to interpret them. For example, be wary of treatments claimed to reverse aging or make you younger by establishing a more youthful hormonal or other biomarker profile, since some of these are more likely to shorten rather than lengthen your life! These sorts of simplistic strategies to recapture youth are the hormonal equivalent of excessive tanning. When you are young, suntanned skin looks attractive and healthy, but too much tanning over time results in unhealthy and old-looking skin.

CHRONOLOGICAL VERSUS BIOLOGICAL AGE

We all know people who look much older or younger than their ages. Chronological age (how old you actually are, measured with a calendar) and biological age (how old you seem, measured by appearance and advanced biomarker testing) can differ by nearly twofold. These apparent age differences are more than skin-deep. People who look younger typically live longer than those who look older. This is true even for twin siblings. And the difference can be measured in their biomarkers, like telomere length.

Some biomarkers are simply symptoms of a certain state or underlying process. Take gray hair, for example. It is a marker of older age but doesn't make you old. And dyeing your hair another color makes you feel better when you look in the mirror but doesn't make you younger. But other biomarkers, such as telomere length (which we'll investigate shortly), are more than just markers; they play critical roles in setting the pace of aging and senescence.

Cardiovascular Biomarkers

Two of the most important and commonly measured cardiovascular biomarkers are cholesterol and triglyceride levels. If these are moderately elevated on their own, it's not necessarily reason for alarm. Longevity and mindspan are at much greater risk if these high biomarker levels are accompanied by high blood iron levels, which accelerate the oxidation of LDL cholesterol. Blood and body iron stores are complicated to measure, but two relatively common measurements are hemoglobin and serum ferritin (a storage depot for iron).

There is always some minimal level of oxidation occurring in the body since we need it to live. Therefore, elevated LDL is always somewhat worrisome because it is inevitably accompanied by some elevation of oxidized LDL. However, when oxidative potential is high, even moderate LDL becomes more oxidized, and high oxidation *plus* high LDL is deadly for both your heart and your brain.

There are many independent lines of evidence implicating LDL in heart disease, but it is the genetic evidence that has raised the level of believability to a virtual certainty. Some variants of the gene PCSK9 reduce LDL cholesterol and provide extremely strong protection (one variant reduces risk by over 80 percent) against heart disease. Other genes have less pronounced effects, but these effects can be additive or synergistic.

I still occasionally run across the claim that cholesterol can't be bad for you because it is a natural component of all cells, produced by the body in a regulated manner. This is another naturalistic fallacy, and we can use the AP rule to correct this misunderstanding. Even if our ancestors did eat diets that promoted high levels of oxidized LDL cholesterol, and even if this promoted youthful health and reproduction in those bygone days, the costs in later life of such a diet today are well established and must be avoided. The data implicating LDL cholesterol in heart disease are complex but rock solid.

We can't yet say the same for HDL. For decades, countless studies have shown that higher HDL cholesterol is associated with lower heart disease risk. But clinical trials of HDL-boosting drugs don't show any benefit, unlike increasing HDL through diet or exercise. Similarly, increases in HDL by gene variants involved in cholesterol metabolism fail to reduce risk of heart attack. And while HDL level has been shown in a landmark study of Ashkenazi Jewish centenarians and their children to be a key marker of longevity, attempts to replicate the association in other populations have met with mixed success. These independent strands of evidence suggest that HDL is simply a marker and not a critical frontline player in the development of heart disease. While HDL might play some role in cardiovascular health, it is not as important as LDL or certain other blood biomarkers.

Longevity Biomarkers

Research shows that three biomarkers predict longevity in men: core body temperature (lower is better), blood levels of insulin (lower is better), and DHEA-S, the sulfated form of the sex hormone dehydroepiandrosterone (slower decline of blood levels in old age is better). The authors of this study note that these biomarkers are also associated with a calorie restriction diet in lab animals, which extends longevity relative to animals given unlimited food.

This discovery about DHEA-S has created a market for DHEA-S supplements in the form of a pill. It's easy to assume that artificially altering hormone levels — by, say, taking a DHEA supplement — will improve longevity, but that's probably not the case. Such treatments may temporarily improve your body's blood levels, but they won't get to the real root of the problem. A low DHEA level, for example, is more likely an indicator of another, more fundamental problem with your adrenal gland.

Similarly, lowering body temperature artificially has not proven to be a recipe for longevity. In fact, it seems that the opposite is true: artificially raising body temperature is associated with increased longevity. Therefore, tinkering with biomarkers — even those proven to be associated with longevity — can prove fruitless or counterproductive. Nevertheless, as I mentioned before, there are some biomarkers that aren't just symptoms, but frontline players in advancing age.

Insulin might be one of those players. Multiple approaches and drugs exist for reducing high insulin. Exercise and better diet are effective and tend to cure many who suffer from metabolic syndrome (prediabetes). Metformin is a first-line drug in type 2 diabetes and is even given to some type 1 (insulin dependent) diabetics. It is one of the few drugs shown to reproducibly extend longevity in lab animals. Metformin has complex effects on the body, but a primary function is to reduce the amount of glucose produced by the liver.

Metformin also boosts insulin sensitivity and stimulates the uptake of glucose by muscle and other tissues. As a result of these beneficial effects, metformin substantially reduces fasting insulin levels. Even though insulin is an important hormone and an essential player in the regulation of glucose metabolism, it is also an indicator of other, more primary benefits occurring in the body. Absent these other positive changes, substantially reducing insulin would be harmful and would be similar to early stages of type 1 diabetes. A group of gerontologists in the United States is proposing to conduct the first clinical trial of any drug to slow aging, and the drug they chose to test is metformin.

Telomeres

Imagine that human chromosomes are shoelaces. Like the little plastic sheath (called an aglet) covering the end of a shoelace, the tip of each chromosome is protected by a telomere, a specialized stretch of DNA. Each time a cell divides to either add body mass during development or replace damaged cells, the telomere shortens. Over many years of life, the telomeres in some cells get so short that chromosomes can become damaged, leading to a number of diseases, including cancer, heart disease, and dementias.

Long, stable telomeres are robust predictors of good health and longevity.* As we age, telomeres get broken down and become shorter. Eventually they get to a point where they're so short, the cells in which they reside stop functioning and the telomeres destabilize your chromosomes, greatly increasing cancer risk as well as other health issues. In general, the shorter your telomeres are, the shorter your lifespan. Most long-lived people in their eighties and nineties have telomeres as long as or longer than most people in their seventies!†

Just as with other regulators of the pace of aging (like insulin), the shortening of telomeres can be accelerated by certain environmental variables — including diet. But here is the positive flip side: good diet and lifestyle factors can counteract this erosion. Higher intake of omega-3 fats, good sleep, low stress,

---

* Excessively long telomeres are also a problem and are associated with an increased risk of some cancers.

† This is probably due to the survivor effect: people with short telomeres die and those who are still alive have longer telomeres.

and routine exercise are all associated with longer telomere length.

Through Thick or Thin:
Body Weight and Mindspan

You have probably heard about BMI and getting to an ideal level — both in the news and probably from your doctor. And it is an important biomarker. It makes sense that carrying around too much body fat — even if you exercise regularly — is a risk for a number of health issues. Some small studies show that obesity increases the risk of Alzheimer's disease. But the largest and most impressive study shows otherwise: A 2015 study of over 2 million people in the United Kingdom (published in *The Lancet Diabetes & Endocrinology*) found decreasing risk of dementia with increasing body weight, even for people who are obese.

But before you get too comfortable and smug about those extra pounds you're carrying around, let's look at some other relevant research. One 2009 *Lancet* review that looked at around 900,000 Europeans ages thirty-five to eighty-nine found that overall mortality from all causes is actually lowest when you have a BMI of about 24.

So what's the take-home message? *There's a substantially higher mortality risk associated with being either too lean or too heavy.* The protective effect against Alzheimer's that might accompany increasing obesity is greatly outweighed by the higher risk of death from other causes, such as heart disease. These findings are consistent with observations that centenarians are never obese, but many are slightly plump. Most are lean when they are younger and slowly increase their BMI as they get older. In later years, a moderate level of body fat is not only tolerable but likely beneficial, providing a metabolic buffer and energy reserve when challenges occur (like incapacitation or illness).

These data are also consistent with average BMI measures of Mindspan Elite countries during their rise to the pinnacle of mindspan. For example, the average BMI of Japanese and Okinawan adults over the second half of the twentieth century was a bit over 23.* The

* Through the 1950s, Okinawan adult average BMI was about 21; it increased to about 24 by the year 2000. In the 1980s and 1990s, Okinawa led the world in longevity and mindspan; centenarians at that time would have been in their sixties or seventies during the leaner 1950s. This pattern of leanness in youth and gradual and slight weight gain (up to a BMI of about 23) into one's older years is typical of the long-lived.

BMI of Mediterranean Riverans over this time was about 24, and Italians were the only Europeans to have about the same BMI in the year 2000 as they had in 1980. All others showed a substantial increase. Currently, French and Italians still have among the lowest BMI values in Europe, while the U.K. has the highest — though, at about 27.5, it is far short of the U.S. value, at 29+.

For middle-aged and older women, the sweet spot for BMI is about 23 or 24, or about 140 to 145 pounds for a 5-foot 5-inch woman (and less if she is younger). If you have a leaner or more robust build, your BMI can be somewhat lower or higher than this number, respectively. Taking this into account, a BMI range between about 21 and 27 is fine. For middle-aged and older men, the ideal BMI is about the same (about 24), but the best range starts a bit higher and spans from about 22 to 27.

Even though there are many negatives associated with obesity, if we can identify the underlying mechanisms that protect against dementia, we can potentially use them as part of an overall preventive strategy. One, paradoxically, is that being heavy increases exercise, by increasing the load on your muscles. Obesity also causes iron deficiency. How? It increases chronic inflammation in your body, which in turn increases binding of iron by ferritin and thus reduces available iron. This helps explain why so many obese people are diagnosed with anemia, despite having sufficient body iron stores.

People of Mindspan Elite regions have low iron, low dementia, and relatively low obesity (case in point is Japan, which boasts both low dementia and the lowest level of obesity in the developed world). Therefore, one needn't suffer the associated negative health risks of obesity to achieve maximum mindspan. Still, these apparent protective effects of obesity against dementia provide additional perspective on common claims that restricted food intake prolongs life.

Should You Starve Your Body (and Brain)?
Calorie restriction (CR) came into vogue as early as the fifteenth century, when the Venetian nobleman Luigi Cornaro wrote about improving his ill health by eating less. But it wasn't until the mid-1930s that a more scientific approach was used to study the practice. Dr. Clive McCay, a scientist at Cornell University, was the first to show that limiting food intake extends lifespan in rats. Dr. McCay's discovery continues to surprise many people. Eating less might be expected to shorten the lifespan of a lean individual, but

the results of many decades of laboratory experiments suggest the opposite is true.

However, some recent and careful studies show little or no life extension benefit in animal experiments. So what is happening here? I think the quality of the diet is one key to this puzzle. What is the closest human food counterpart to the food fed to rats and mice in the experiments that produced longer life with CR? A sugar cookie (although a typical sugar cookie has less sugar than the food these animals eat). So it is unsurprising that animals allowed to eat as much as they want generally become fat and sick, and that those that eat less don't become as sick or die as early. I sometimes jokingly refer to this kind of CR as "cookie restriction."

Nevertheless, CR is associated with some benefits in people: it seems to lower body temperature and blood insulin, and it slows late life decline of DHEA-S and telomere length. Whether this translates into longer life is an unanswered question. Research shows that the longest-lived people don't practice a CR diet — at least, not in their older years. Again, most are lean in youth, and many lived through difficult privations when little food was available, but in their last few decades of life, they were well nourished. But Mindspan Elite do have minimal consumption of animal foods. This limits dietary iron, and as we'll see in a later chapter, it also provides many of the benefits of CR without one having to be bone-thin or go hungry.

HOW TO USE BIOMARKERS

All of the key biomarkers we've reviewed are greatly influenced by diet and lifestyle factors, and we can use them to best effect by comparing our own values (today and over time) with data from Mindspan Elite people and countries. We can begin with the Seven Countries Study, which was started back in the late 1950s. One publication from this study showed that telomeres in white blood cells are longer in men from Crete than in men from Zutphen in the Netherlands. As a result, men in Crete have a biological age about five years younger. They also have ferritin levels about half the average level in Zutphen, which is consistent with their significantly lower risk of stroke, cancer, diabetes, and heart attack.

According to Japan's 2006 National Health and Nutrition Survey, people in Japan and Okinawa also have low ferritin, and a large proportion are iron deficient (50 percent of women of childbearing age have ferritin below 20 ng/mL). Japanese also have low hemoglobin.

The World Health Organization defines anemia as hemoglobin levels below 12 g/dL for women and 13 g/dL for men. This difference in minimum acceptable value for men and women is arbitrary, simply because women tend to have lower levels — not because a value between 12 and 13 g/dL is unhealthy for men. The *average* hemoglobin levels for older Japanese (including centenarians) are often even lower than this minimum. In a publication from 1996, average hemoglobin levels in healthy Japanese centenarians were reported to be 11.5 g/dL for women and 11.8 g/dL for men. We can't be certain that their hemoglobin has always been so low, but we can be sure that their diets and lifestyles haven't changed much, and these values are lower than those measured in elderly people in Mindspan Risk countries.

Below is a table that compares Mindspan Elite and Mindspan Risk biomarkers.

KEY BIOMARKER SUMMARY: MINDSPAN ELITE VERSUS RISK

Biomarker	Mindspan Elite
Cholesterol, total*	Lower (0 to −15%)

— LDL	Lower (0 to –23%)
— HDL	Higher (0 to +18%)
Triglycerides	Lower (0 to –19%)
C-reactive protein	Lower
Fasting glucose	Lower (0 to –15%)
Fasting insulin	Lower (–5 to –23%)
Iron, serum ferritin	Lower (–10 to –60%)
Iron, hemoglobin	Lower (–10 to –25%)
Telomere length	About 5 years longer
Blood pressure	Better, see graph opposite
BMI	Better, obesity below 10%

* The formula for total cholesterol is HDL + LDL + (triglycerides × 0.2).

The Mindspan Elite also have better responses to less ideal values of certain biomarkers, very likely because they have a more robust biology that is more tolerant of a variety of stresses. For example, see the blood pressure graph below. Even at the low end of the range, people of the Mindspan Elite in Japan and Mediterranean Europe die from coronary heart disease (CHD) half as often as people of Mindspan Risk countries of the U.S. or northern Europe. As blood pressure values rise, the mortality rate rises much more gradually in these representative Mindspan Elite.

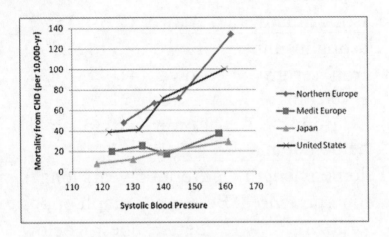

IDEAL BIOMARKERS

Given historical Mindspan Elite and Mindspan Risk biomarkers, and longevity biomarkers established through other research, here are biomarker ranges to shoot for.

IDEAL RANGES FOR KEY BIOMARKERS

Biomarker	Range
Cholesterol, total	170 to 190 mg/dL
— LDL	90 to 110 mg/dL
— HDL	45 to 70 mg/dL

Biomarker	Range
Triglycerides	Less than 120 mg/dL
C-reactive protein	Best is less than 0.5 mg/L; under 1 mg/L is okay
Fasting glucose	Less than 100 mg/dL
Fasting insulin	Less than 8 microIU/mL
Iron, serum ferritin	10 to 40 ng/ml
Iron, hemoglobin	12 to 13 g/dL
Telomere length	Longer than age group until age 65, then maintained at average of 50- to 55-year-olds
Body temperature	Lower is better
Blood pressure	Systolic 95 to 120, Diastolic 60 to 80
BMI	23 to 26 (Subtract up to 2 BMI units for small frame size; add up to 1 for largest)

Today your values might be far from these ideals, but apply the principles in this book and they are likely to start moving immediately toward better values. I suggest you get these tested soon, and then again in a few months. Once you are getting into the recommended ranges, you can test less frequently, but only if you stick with the plan presented in this book. (Which frankly is very easy, since the foods are easy to prepare and incredibly delicious!) Most of the values I recommend here are very close to standard ones you'll find elsewhere. (I recommend keeping biomarkers not listed here in the standard range, but check appendix B for more information and resources.) However, I suggest lower than normal triglyceride, C-reactive protein, and insulin values because I think the common range is too high because of poor diets. Some biomarkers vary with time of day, so if you measure your own blood pressure and body temperature, make sure you are consistent. Both blood pressure and body temperature in most people are lowest at night (during sleep) and highest in the afternoon.

As of today, recommendations for telomere length are essentially nonexistent, so my telomere length recommendation is on the cutting edge of science, but backed by solid research. You might not know the normal range for ferritin or hemoglobin, but if you do, you're probably surprised to see my low recommended range. There is no magic bullet for achieving extreme longevity and maximum mindspan, but after reading chapter 5, you'll begin to appreciate that the single most dangerous element in modern and Mindspan Risk diets is iron.

5.
IRON,
THE SHARPEST SWORD

The flame that burns twice as bright burns
half as long.

— Lao Tzu

Of all the dangerous double-edged swords,
iron cuts the deepest of all. The peril posed
by iron is unique among all dietary minerals.
It's the most abundant and potent oxidant in
the body, but your body doesn't have a way
to get rid of excess iron, unlike other minerals.

For most people, dietary iron might seem
reasonably easy to monitor and control, but
its ubiquity and puzzlingly positive reputation make this challenging. It is one of a
handful of nutrients that enjoy widespread
approval as a silver bullet. Low energy? No
need to get more and better sleep, take some
iron!

Many governments around the world now

recommend or even mandate its addition to foods, and more are in the process of doing so. Millions of people in developing countries benefit from these policies, since their foods are often deficient. But iron has a much darker side that has prompted an increasing number of scientists over the past few decades to warn of its dangers. Why the warnings, and what are the actual risks?

IRON AND OXYGEN: A DANGEROUS DUO

You can compare iron to a match in the presence of fuel and oxygen. In control, warmth and light are produced; out of control, the result is like a persistent, wind-driven wildfire. Or go back to our car analogy: dietary fats and sugars, like gasoline, are hydrocarbons that produce energy. Your body mixes this fuel with oxygen and then ignites it to create useful energy and heat. We need iron to carry oxygen throughout the body for this essential process.

But just as an older car rusts, so does your body. Its rust comes in the form of deposits of "garbage" — for example, hemosiderin, lipofuscin, and amyloid plaques in the brain that are primary drivers of Alzheimer's disease. Rust also comes in the form of "damage," such as oxidized components of cells and tissues (e.g., DNA and proteins), and iron is a primary driver in the creation of this garbage and damage. There are systems for garbage disposal and damage repair in the body, but they are imperfect and can get overwhelmed.

Your body creates compounds such as ferritin and transferrin, protein guardians that hold on to iron and protect valuable molecules within the body from its effects. Still, free iron occasionally escapes, and the higher the iron burden in your body, the greater the burden of accumulated garbage and damage over time, especially to brain neurons.

Many people are surprised to hear all this. They think of iron, like other micronutrients such as vitamin C and vitamin E, as purely beneficial. But three variables should guide how much iron you consume: gender, age, and genes. If you are male, be very careful with iron; you are probably getting far more in your diet than is safe. If you are older, do not think iron supplements will give you extra energy, and do not eat meat or other foods just to get extra iron (unless you have been diagnosed with iron-deficient anemia). Genes are also key. Some people absorb iron from food very efficiently, and since the body has no way to get rid of it, they are more likely to develop an iron-overload disorder, such as hemochromatosis and thalassemias.

Both hemochromatosis and thalassemias can shorten your life and cause symptoms such as extreme and chronic fatigue, diabetes, joint pain, impotence or low libido, bronze or gray color of the skin, heart arrhythmia, and depression.

Despite the common symptoms, sufferers were long overlooked until routine screening for blood iron biomarkers became more common in the U.S. during the 1980s and early 1990s. Unfortunately, a Medicare/Medicaid scandal in the late 1990s caused some of the more useful biomarkers like ferritin to be removed from standard panels (hemoglobin and hematocrit remain). As a result, there are many undiagnosed sufferers.

More men than women suffer the symptoms of hemochromatosis during middle age. However, after menopause, women carrying predisposing mutations rapidly accumulate excess iron stores and suffer the same range of maladies as men, including diabetes, heart disease, cancer, Alzheimer's disease and other dementias, Parkinson's disease, stroke, and more. The good news is that, except for the most serious cases, hemochromatosis is controllable to some degree through diet, phlebotomy (drawing blood), and iron chelation (a drug therapy that holds on to and shields iron, and helps remove it from your body).

People who live in areas with low iron dietary consumption don't suffer the same burden of hemochromatosis, showing that diet is important for those who carry predisposing gene variants. However, even if you don't carry one of these variants, it's important to remember that a poor diet can still lead to high blood iron and accelerated aging.

THIS IS YOUR BRAIN HIGH ON IRON

Certain parts of the brain and nervous system are especially sensitive to iron. In youth, iron is a critical nutrient for proper brain development. However, high body iron stores in adulthood — due to gene variants, diet, excessive supplementation, or a combination of all three — increase the risk of Alzheimer's disease, Parkinson's disease, ALS (Lou Gehrig's disease), stroke, and other diseases of the brain and nervous system. This is the AP rule at work: in youth we need lots of iron, but as we get older, these amounts become harmful.

The brain typically has a higher concentration of iron than any other metal. Specific brain regions affected by very different neurodegenerative diseases have one commonality: they show high levels of iron deposits.

In Parkinson's disease, the affected region is primarily the substantia nigra. In Alzheimer's disease, multiple regions are affected, including the hippocampus, the so-called librarian of the brain (because it files and retrieves stored memory information).

Men have a higher risk of Alzheimer's disease and other forms of dementia at younger ages than women — their risk is about five years younger. Increased brain iron plays a key role: up to the age of about sixty, women have an average ferritin level less than half that of men. As I explained earlier, this is because blood loss from menstruation keeps body iron stores low in women. After menopause, they gradually lose this protection, and in later years, women have levels of iron in the body and brain even greater than those found in men. Since women live much longer, they have a more than 50 percent higher risk of Alzheimer's disease. However, women who have undergone a premenopausal hysterectomy (and do not routinely lose blood iron) accumulate brain iron at the same rate as men (faster than women who continue to menstruate), and they develop dementia at a younger age.

Yet some still wonder about the primary causes of Alzheimer's disease and question whether reducing body iron by dietary means will reduce harm to the brain. But the evidence has been reasonably compelling for over fifty years, and has been growing in strength. Here is but a sample of the evidence. Studies on lab animals and people show that iron accumulates in their brains with advancing age. In the late 1950s, it was noted that people with hemorrhages or severe anemia (and hence low blood iron) have reduced brain iron deposits compared with people with normal iron levels. Animal studies show that high iron feeding increases body iron stores and shortens lifespan, and adding tea to the diet reduces body iron and increases lifespan. In late 2015, a study of people who ate a Mediterranean-style diet (characterized mainly by less meat and more fish) had larger brains and key brain structures and less atrophy than frequent meat eaters. The difference between the two groups that ate the most and least meat was equivalent to five years of brain aging. And of course there are the Mindspan Elite and their lower body iron stores and lower rates of Alzheimer's. Taken together, this evidence is very strong, but these studies don't show direct cause, as a clinical trial does. That's been done too. In 1991 the iron chelator drug deferoxamine* (which binds iron and renders it inactive) was shown to slow the progression of Alzheimer's disease. More recent studies show that this drug prevents Alzheimer's pathologies and memory loss in lab animals ingesting large amounts of supplemental iron. Now joining this collection of already compelling evidence are genetic links between iron and the disease.

GENES AND DEMENTIA

Research scientists have turned up many clues about the genetic regulators of overall human and brain longevity, but only two genes truly stand out, because they have by far the largest overall effects. Those genes are called APOE and APP. Variants of both cause Alzheimer's disease at an early age. Different variants extend lifespan and reduce Alzheimer's risk. Both genes are also influenced by diet and lifestyle, since they interact with iron, and amplify the effects of iron in the brain. While other genes play roles in longevity and mindspan, these are the two

* This drug (also called desferrioxamine) was injected into muscles and does not cross the blood-brain barrier, so depletion of body iron produced benefits, likely by reducing the amount of iron available for transport into the brain.

that warrant a much closer look.

Mindspan Gene 1: APOE

This gene — which has repeatedly been proven to have the most significant longevity effect of any gene — comes in three variant forms: e2, e3, and e4. Everyone carries two copies of the APOE gene, and each copy can be one of these three variants (each person has one of six possible combinations, which are e2/e2, e2/e3, e2/e4, e3/e3, e3/e4, and e4/e4). The e3 variant is most common (60 to 90 percent) in all populations around the world.

APOE's effects on longevity result from the harmful actions of the e4 variant and the moderately beneficial effects of the e2 variant (the e4 variant is greatly underrepresented in centenarians). The two most problematic duos are the e3/e4 combination, which typically increases risk for Alzheimer's disease by two to three times, and the e4/e4 combination, which increases risk by more than ten times.

In the United States, people with the e4/e4 genotype represent about 2 percent of the population, but 15 percent or more of all cases of Alzheimer's disease. Interestingly, some ethnicities, including people of recent African descent, appear to be largely protected from its negative effects. Even though Africans have the highest proportion of e4 carriers, they show low levels of Alzheimer's disease, and U.S. African American and Hispanic e4 carriers are at lower risk of dementia than U.S. Caucasians.

In addition to increasing dementia risk in most ethnicities, the e4 variant has also been linked to other health problems, including atherosclerosis, accelerated telomere shortening, and stroke.

Recent evidence has been building that implicates APOE in the transport of iron to the brain, and in mid-2015 the APOE and iron connection was elevated to the level of a near certainty. An international consortium of several Alzheimer's disease studies (the Alzheimer's Disease Neuroimaging Initiative) published the results of an over-seven-year study of three groups of people: non-demented, mild cognitive impairment (MCI), and Alzheimer's disease. They found that the cerebrospinal fluid (CSF) ferritin level predicted the degree of cognitive decline — higher ferritin led to faster decline and dementia. They further found that the APOE e4 variant was associated with higher CSF ferritin, more evidence that the e4 variant is responsible for raising the iron load in the brain and driving cellular damage, tissue loss, and plaque formation.

Mindspan Gene 2: APP

This gene for amyloid precursor protein (APP) causes the plaque (known as amyloid ß or amyloid beta) seen in brains afflicted with Alzheimer's disease. Research suggests that the job of APP in the brain is to protect cells and tissue from iron's oxidative damage.

Scientists discovered the APP gene in the 1980s while studying Down syndrome. The APP gene is on chromosome 21, which people with Down syndrome have in triplicate. Three copies of the APP gene lead to overproduction of APP and accelerated formation of amyloid plaques, which explains why many individuals with Down syndrome develop Alzheimer's as early as their thirties or forties.

The production of amyloid ß is also regulated by environmental factors. As mentioned in chapter 2, biology needs to be responsive to environmental conditions, so there are regulatory sensors and controls — similar to a thermostat — that provide an appropriate response. For example, genes associated with iron in the body are regulated at various levels by sensors that measure the presence of iron. In response, they turn production of the gene up or down, or exert control in other ways.

Out of 20,000-plus protein-coding genes in the human genome, fewer than 20 (1 gene in about 1,000) to date have been shown to be controlled by a specific system regulated by iron — called the iron-response element (IRE). In other words, this system is very rare and highly specific to the critical components in the body that regulate iron. One of these 1-in-1,000 genes is APP.

Here is how the IRE system works. As iron increases in a cell, it turns up production of the APP protein.* Other recent research indicates that the APP protein is responsible for exporting iron out of neurons. These clues, together with other evidence about APP, strongly support the idea that the job of APP in the brain is to protect cells and tissues from the oxidative potential of iron.

In 2012, Icelandic scientists discovered something else about the APP gene that revolutionized Alzheimer's research. Since the island of Iceland has relatively few people (about 320,000) and its gene pool is isolated,

---

* Copper also might contribute to Alzheimer's disease. APP also is stimulated by copper, but relative to iron, it is typically less abundant, a less powerful oxidant, and less worrisome.

its population is relatively easy to study. Analysis of genome data of many people showed that a small fraction who performed exceptionally well for their age group carried a specific variant of the APP gene (the name of the variant is A673T).* This variant provides approximately a full decade of protection against cognitive decline, and substantially longer life. Even more amazing and important for carriers of APOE e4, it seems to completely override the negative effects of the e4 variant![†]

Alas, this protective variant of the APP gene is extremely rare. So far it has been discovered only in Icelanders and their genetically nearest Scandinavian relatives, and is present in only about 1 in 200 of these people. Still, people of these countries are at highest risk for Alzheimer's disease — and they top the list of Mindspan Risk. The large degree of life extension and protection from cognitive decline due to this rare APP variant tell us that in these people, APP-regulated

---

* A673T indicates substitution of the alanine amino acid 673 of the APP protein with threonine.

† The genetic term for this ability to supersede the effects of another gene is epistasis, which roughly translates to "standing upon."

dementia is the single most important factor limiting their longevity and mindspans.

BAD GENES OR BAD ENVIRONMENT = ALZHEIMER'S DISEASE

We now have all the information we need to build a simple but sufficiently complete model of typical Alzheimer's disease to understand it and to greatly reduce the risk. Given the information we have, a few models are possible. The one presented here is based on a common view that a main role of APP is to protect the brain. The main genes involved in this simple model are APOE and APP, and the primary environmental trigger factor is iron. Here's a summary of the roles of iron, APOE, and APP:

- The process begins with either high levels of body iron stores, or excessive transport of iron to the brain by APOE e4 (or both, which is double trouble).
- This leads to increased production of the APP protein, in order to protect the cells and tissues of the brain.
- The excess iron acts like a lit match in your home, and APP like a small fire blanket. The IRE sensor on APP senses fire (iron) and turns up production of APP, which then smothers the excess

lit matches.

- A cleanup crew of special cells comes in and removes most of the mess, but a small bit of the blanket gets clipped off and left behind. This small bit is amyloid ß, the driver of plaque formation. The clipping of APP might serve no purpose; the clipping enzyme might serve another role in the cell, and the clipping of APP might simply be collateral damage.
- As fires break out, they are extinguished, but as the process continues, the blanket bits stack up. If there are few fires, then little APP is made and the accumulation of APP blanket bits is small.
- The A673T variant makes APP resistant to clipping, which slows production and aggregation of amyloid ß.
- As amyloid ß aggregates increase, functional brain cells are killed and displaced.
- The cleanup cells responsible for collecting and disposing of aggregates and other garbage are progressively overwhelmed. These cells replicate frequently to keep up with the burden, accelerating shortening of their telomeres. When their telomeres become critically short, they stop replicating

and functioning, and accumulation of the aggregates accelerates.

The costs of this process are at first negligible, but they add up over time, with serious effects showing up when someone reaches their seventies or eighties. This model reconciles two opposing views about APP and its role in the development of Alzheimer's disease. One view is that APP protects the brain against environmental assaults and damage, and an opposing view is that Alzheimer's disease is a pathological process unrelated to this protection, and instead is related to infection or inflammation. Applying the AP rule again, we see that the common variant of the APP gene both protects the brain *and* harms the brain through the long-term consequences of this mode of protection. And applying our other key rule, GENES + ENVIRONMENT = TRAIT, we have pegged dietary iron as the key environmental coconspirator. So in this case, COMMON APP VARIANT + HIGH IRON = ALZHEIMER'S DISEASE.

The rare, protective APP gene variant shows that improving the GENES part of the equation greatly reduces Alzheimer's risk. Reducing dietary iron improves the ENVIRONMENT part of the equation and also reduces Alzheimer's risk. This is *extremely important* because 99+ percent of us carry the common variant of APP, and our best option right now for reducing risk of Alzheimer's disease is to exert control through environmental regulators of risk.

MINDSPAN MAXIMIZER: NSAIDS

Aspirin, ibuprofen, and naproxen are three kinds of common over-the-counter non-steroidal anti-inflammatory drugs (NSAIDs). All three lower body temperature and reduce inflammation, and all have been shown to reduce the risk of Alzheimer's disease and other dementias by about 35 to 50 percent. Another type of painkiller, acetaminophen, appears to give no benefit, despite lowering body temperature and inflammation.

Certain NSAIDs appear to inhibit aggregation of the amyloid protein fragment that causes plaque formation in Alzheimer's disease. NSAIDs also have a significant side effect: gastrointestinal bleeding. This doesn't seem ideal, but this might actually help by reducing iron stores.

TOO MUCH OF A GOOD THING: HOW IRON IMPACTS YOUR HEALTH

Iron isn't just a factor in brain longevity but affects overall health and longevity too. Here is a brief overview of just some of the other top health hazards related to iron.

Lowered Immunity

One strong clue to the dangers of iron lies in the immune system. Microbial pathogens rely on iron for maintaining chronic infection. Your body fights back by maintaining control over this mineral through two iron-binding proteins: ferritin and transferrin.

Ferritin is a key member of your immune system's emergency response team. When your body senses the presence of a pathogen, it launches an immune response. It elevates body temperature to help kill the pathogen and increases the production of pro-inflammatory compounds in your immune system. This increased inflammation triggers ferritin to grab tightly on to iron, which in turn causes your body's serum iron level to go down. This is the same mechanism at work in obese people who have functional iron deficiency.

The reliance of microbes on iron explains why if you eat too much iron, you'll have more frequent, chronic infections. (This may be why back in ancient times bloodletting was so popular for many illnesses!) Similarly, eating less iron limits the growth of gut pathogens. This helps explain why GI infections increase and worsen in developing countries that have recently opted for iron supplementation.

Metabolic Dysfunction
French physician Armand Trousseau made a startling observation among some of his diabetic patients in 1865: their skin had turned an obvious bronze color. He dubbed the condition "bronze diabetes." Since then, research has shown a clear link between excess iron and impaired glucose tolerance and both type 1 and type 2 diabetes. If you want to reduce your risk immediately, consider donating blood. Donation decreases body iron stores and fasting insulin levels and increases insulin sensitivity, even if you're not diabetic. Of course, in addition to whatever other measures you might take in the short term, the ideal long-term solution to iron management is to follow the Mindspan Diet.

Cancer
Iron in food and supplements appears to be one of the most — if not the most — potent dietary drivers of increased cancer risk. In an

alarming study of over 300,000 people in Taiwan, cancer risk increased with increasing serum iron. Other, smaller studies also show increased risk of certain cancers with increasing body iron stores.

These population-based studies are backed up by other strong evidence. For example, increasing serum ferritin causes increased DNA damage. Another study found that across a wide range of vitamin and mineral supplements, only iron supplementation was associated with shorter telomere length. Alarmingly, the difference is equivalent to a minimum of several years of advanced biological age in users of iron supplements. Critically short telomeres destabilize chromosomes, greatly increasing cancer risk. Telomere length in white blood cells and other tissues is among the best predictors of overall longevity and cancer risk in tissues and organs throughout the body.

What about the objection that a substantial amount of this supplemental iron isn't absorbed? It is clear that some people do absorb enough to do damage, but even if it isn't absorbed, this excess iron has to go somewhere — and therein lies another problem. The "somewhere" is into your lower GI tract. Iron is often a limiting nutrient for microbial growth, and intake of more iron than the body can use or store is an invitation for trouble. Increased dietary iron has been associated with increased risk of colorectal cancer, one of the most deadly forms of cancer, whose incidence increases with the adoption of modern dietary practices.

Cardiovascular Disease

It's widely known that women live longer than men. Part of the reason is that men experience coronary heart disease, atherosclerosis, and other cardiovascular problems earlier than women.

In 1981, physician and research scientist Jerome Sullivan published the first explanation for why women in their thirties and forties almost totally escape the increasing risk of heart disease that plagues men of the same age. He suggested men's higher body iron was the cause, and menstruating women have a low risk until they stop losing iron monthly at the onset of menopause. Newer research suggests that part of the premenopausal benefit is due to estrogen, but not all. Here are some other factors implicating iron:

- Cardiovascular diseases and other diseases of affluence are rare among populations with low iron stores.

- People with high iron stores have shorter telomeres than people with lower iron stores. Short telomeres in heart muscle cells increase risk of a heart attack, and short telomeres in vascular cells increase risk of atherosclerosis severalfold.
- Atherosclerosis (plaque buildup in arteries) increases with increasing iron stores.
- Iron reduction through blood donation or diet improves vascular function and reduces plaque buildup.
- Serum ferritin and LDL cholesterol show a synergistic association with cardiovascular disease and mortality.
- Plaques have high iron levels — seventeen times higher than in normal vascular tissue.

The benefits of menstruation can be replicated by lowering body iron stores through lifestyle changes. High consumption of red meat ups iron stores, which explains why many studies have shown that a low-meat or vegetarian diet improves cardiovascular health. High-frequency blood donors also show significantly reduced body iron stores, decreased markers of vascular oxidative stress, and overall better vascular function when compared with people who rarely or never donate.

THE BIOAVAILABILITY PUZZLE

We often hear that spinach is loaded with iron, so if we need more iron in our diets we should eat more spinach (or eat less if trying to cut down on iron). But not so fast. Spinach is high in iron, but it is a poor source of iron for most people. How can that be? Spinach also has a compound called oxalate (or oxalic acid), which inhibits iron absorption. Most of the iron in spinach will likely just pass right through your gut.

There are many other similar compounds in a range of foods. These include phytates (in grains, walnuts, almonds, beans, lentils, and peas) and polyphenols (in tea, cocoa, coffee, walnuts, blackberries, raspberries, blueberries, and certain herbs, such as oregano and basil). Some herbal teas also have fairly high levels of polyphenols, including chamomile and mint teas. Grapes and wines also have polyphenols, and the amount is roughly predictable by color, with the darkest having the highest polyphenol content. Dietary fiber also inhibits absorption. Seaweeds commonly eaten in Japan have reasonable amounts of iron, but they too inhibit absorption.

Oxalates, phytates, polyphenols, and fiber can have different inhibitory effects on vitamins than on minerals, and all but fiber have little effect on vitamin absorption. All can strongly inhibit absorption of a range of minerals, including iron, calcium, zinc, copper, selenium, lead, and others. Certain of these inhibitory compounds are handled differently by different people. Some can be at least partly digested by the microbes in the gut, releasing the bound minerals. Much of this released cargo can't be absorbed, but some is. Overall, these effects greatly complicate determining how much mineral value is actually obtained in a meal containing these ingredients. The only way to know for certain how much iron you are absorbing is to get a blood test.

HOW TO PROTECT YOURSELF

It's easier to overload on iron than you might think: people who naturally accumulate excess iron or normal people who consume large excesses of dietary iron can accumulate very high body iron stores in a matter of weeks. Reduction of such stores can take years to reverse, even with the most aggressive measures, including dietary restrictions, routine blood draws, and chelation therapy. The key is not to build up iron in the first place. Here's how:

Limit Iron Intake

When you look at a nutritional label, you will often see the amount of iron in a food, which is shown as "% Daily Value." This is the percentage of the 18 milligrams government regulators suggest you consume every day to remain healthy. However, what the label doesn't say is that this value applies only to menstruating females and teenage males. The Daily Value for other adults is 8 milligrams. However, a more reasonable estimate of Daily Value for most people — especially those over the age of fifty — is 3 to 5 milligrams (depending on body size), but this is a rough estimate because bioavailability can be highly variable.

Read Food Labels

When you're buying packaged foods, check the ingredients list carefully. If it contains the word "enriched" (like white rice) and/or the words "ferric," "ferrous," or simply "iron," skip it.

Watch your water

Water drawn from old iron pipes can be high in iron, so let water run until cool and then bottle enough for several days' use. If you live in a town with high iron in the water, install a filter that works specifically to remove it.

Be Wary of Antioxidants and "Superfoods"

During my visits to the supermarket I often see food advertisements or labels stating how many antioxidants are jam-packed into a serving. Upon closer investigation, I sometimes see high iron levels — even added iron. To make matters worse, these products often include added vitamin C, which greatly increases iron absorption. Some studies have shown that antioxidant supplements (including vitamins) increase mortality. In the Framingham Heart Study, vitamin C intake is strongly associated with high body iron stores, including iron overload. Be aware of your iron intake and factors such as vitamin C that increase it, since the excessive and powerfully oxidizing iron will persist in your bloodstream long after the antioxidants are gone.

Beware of Rust as a Dye

While NSAIDs, including ibuprofen, can reduce the risk of dementia, choose your ibuprofen carefully! Generic ibuprofen is coated with iron oxide. This reddish-brown dye — yes, not just the color of rust, but actual rust! — can be found in the coatings of other pills and in foods too. The amount coating a typical ibuprofen or other similarly sized pill is generally less than 1 milligram. If you take a few per day, this can amount to over 2 milligrams of iron — or about a quarter of the recommended daily value for anyone other than a menstruating woman. You can rinse the dye off with water immediately before taking them. (Be careful and quick about it, because the rinsing might begin dissolving the pill.)

Avoid Smoking and Limit Alcohol

Alcohol and smoking both substantially increase the risk of breast cancer. Multiple studies have shown that these factors are especially potent in a person with high body iron stores. The theory is that iron promotes free radical generation through its interactions with alcohol and cigarette smoke. If you do drink, limit it to the equivalent of one to two glasses of wine a day, and maybe ten per week — and as with tea and coffee, drink red wine with food. Of course, adjust for your body size (if you are a small person, drink less).

Drink Tea and Coffee with Meals

Many publications have shown that tea and coffee reduce cardiovascular risks and overall death rates by lowering blood glucose and insulin. Many of these benefits have been attributed to caffeine, but pure caffeine administered to research volunteers results in worse glucose tolerance after a meal. A more likely explanation is that there's another compound in both tea and coffee that inhibits dietary iron absorption.

Measure Your Iron Biomarkers

Serum ferritin is a key biomarker that reflects the amount of iron stored in the body. The ranges of normal serum ferritin for men and women in the United States are shown below, as are the normal ranges for Japan. As you can see, there is a wide difference. Part of this difference is due to much more prevalent iron overload gene variants in the U.S., but an even bigger factor is diet. The upper end of these normal ranges provides no benefit and greatly increases the risk of dementias and neurodegenerative diseases. As you can see, the Japanese range, especially in men, while lower than in the United States, is still higher than ideal. While the normal range for Japanese women is good, aim for the lower half of this range (about 10 to 40 nanograms per milliliter) for maximum health benefits.

NORMAL RANGE OF FERRITIN IN THE U.S.

- For men, 24 to 336 nanograms per milliliter (standard units), or micrograms per liter (international units)
- For women, 11 to 307 nanograms per milliliter (standard units), or micrograms per liter (international units)

NORMAL RANGE OF FERRITIN IN JAPAN

- For men, 10 to 220 nanograms per milliliter (standard units), or micrograms per liter (international units)
- For women, 10 to 85 nanograms per milliliter (standard units), or micrograms per liter (international units)

IDEAL RANGE OF FERRITIN

- For men and women, 10 to 40 nanograms per milliliter (standard units), or micrograms per liter (international units). About 40 nanograms per milliliter is the measured average ferritin of Japanese women across all ages.

Unsurprisingly, people in the Mindspan

144

Elite have lower serum ferritin. As you'll recall from the previous discussion of biomarkers, the average ferritin level in men of Crete, Greece, was about half that of men in Zutphen, the Netherlands, and in Zutphen the risk of stroke and cancer is four times higher, diabetes is 70 percent higher, and heart attack is 50 percent higher. The Netherlands also has the unhappy distinction of being among the top ten countries in the world in Parkinson's mortality, and is near the top of the list in mortality from Alzheimer's disease and other dementias.

Is this genetics? Differences in lifestyles or diets? It's probably a combination of all three. But one thing is clear: average people with no obvious iron accumulation disorder can accumulate too much iron. That's why it's important to be proactive and test your ferritin levels.

YOUR MOVE: LIMIT AND TEST YOUR IRON

As mentioned in chapter 3, less meat, a moderate amount of cheese, less sugar, and more tea, coffee, and/or red wine are common features among diets of the Mindspan Elite. Here is something all have in common: they reduce absorption of dietary iron. Now that you are more sensitized to

---

the dangers of iron, you can take additional measures to reduce iron intake and to monitor your iron levels so that you don't have to guess if they are in the safe range.

When you look at a nutritional label you will often see the amount of iron in a food, which is shown as "% Daily Value." In other words, this is the percentage of the amount government regulators suggest you consume every day to remain healthy. But remember, what the label doesn't say is that this value applies only to menstruating women and teenage males. Eighteen milligrams is 100 percent for menstruating women, and 225 percent for other adults. Eight milligrams is 100 percent for most others, but even this is far too much.

However, because people absorb iron with varying efficiency and bioavailability can play a large role, the best strategy has two parts. First, be aware of the amount of iron in foods and limit your intake appropriately. Second, rather than guess about your body's iron stores, get them tested. Key biomarkers are serum iron, serum ferritin, hemoglobin, and total iron-binding capacity (TIBC). Unsaturated iron-binding capacity (UIBC) is another test that can substitute for TIBC. Be sure to keep the ferritin value in the low part of the normal range. Appendix B has full biomarker recommendations and resources. Contact your physician to ask about these tests, and for further information, visit mindspan diet.com.

■ ■ ■ ■

PART 2
TAKING
CONTROL

■ ■ ■ ■

Our bodies and minds are extremely adapt-
able, but not infinitely so. What you eat and
don't eat is crucial to achieving maximum
mindspan. In this section, you'll uncover
the ugly truth about modern carbs — how
they've been engineered to our detriment.
You'll learn the best and worst protein and
fat sources, using the diets of the Mindspan
Elite as your guide. You'll discover the X
factors in common foods and why people
who eat these in Mindspan Elite cuisines

around the world are leaner and healthier. This knowledge will help you to take control of your diet and give you a clear path to reach maximum mindspan.

6.
CRACKING THE MINDSPAN CODE

In a dark time, the eye begins to see.
— Theodore Roethke

Following the apparently alien transmission from chapter 3 attesting to the health benefits of refined carbs and "empty" calories, you might have felt more in the dark than ever about diet. But over the last three chapters you have begun to see — to see and understand how diet actually works in the real world. We now know that not all refined carbs are as evil as they are so often portrayed.

Despite their recent demonization, we need carbs to live. Our cells have an essential outer layer, the glycocalyx, composed of carbs. More important, the primary fuel used by most of our cells is the sugar glucose, the preferred cellular fuel for the body — especially for the brain.

Besides, vegetables are universally acknowledged to be great for us, and you've probably heard more than any other nutritional advice to eat more vegetables. With few exceptions, what macronutrient provides most of the energy in vegetables? The answer is carbs. Every mainstream vegetable except for the avocado (which is actually a fruit) is much higher in carbs than fat or protein, and most have essentially no fat. This list includes cucumbers, cauliflower, broccoli, potatoes, sweet potatoes, all squashes, tomatoes (also a fruit), and more. Even peas (actually a legume), which are touted as a high-protein vegetable, provide nearly three times as much energy from carbs as from protein.

We run into trouble only when we overload on the wrong kind of carbs — especially when we get too much too fast. What kind of trouble? You already know the answer: excess body fat and obesity, lethargy, metabolic syndrome, prediabetes, diabetes, and an increased risk of various other diseases.

Consider this. Daily food intake for a typical lean and active woman is about 2500 calories a day. How much excess over twenty years will it take for her to become obese? About 200 excess calories a day, maybe 250, right? Not even close. The truth is mind-boggling: if only 1 percent of her daily energy (25 calories at the start) is excess and being stored as body fat, in the course of twenty years she will gain 62 pounds of fat. With this small percentage of excess consumption between, say, ages twenty and forty, a woman whose ideal weight is 135 pounds would weigh nearly 200 pounds. Twenty-five calories is only about a quarter piece of bread!

Since this amount of food can go unnoticed so easily, is it any wonder so many are obese? It's easy to see that even a very small uncompensated increase or decrease in food intake, hunger or satiety, or energy expenditure can have profound long-term effects — if it occurs routinely. This is why it is critical to really understand how foods help regulate feelings of hunger and to identify which foods most potently increase or decrease these feelings — day in and day out, without your having to play food accountant at every meal.

Those in the Mindspan Elite tend to be leaner than average because their diet is based on starch of the right kind and within the appropriate context. This combination is a critical difference between healthy Mindspan Elite diets and unhealthy diets. In this chapter, you'll discover the key ways their cuisines tame the darker sides of carbs.

SLOW VERSUS FAST CARBS

As is always the case with food fads, some new jargon recently entered the food lexicon: "good carbs" and "bad carbs" (and even "net carbs"). One primary thing separates good carbs from bad carbs: the length of time between when the carb is eaten (or the moment it begins to enter the bloodstream) and when it reaches the peak level in the bloodstream. The less time this takes, the more dramatic the effect (usually bad) this carb has on your body. I prefer the terms "fast" and "slow," since your body's needs can change dramatically, and there are situations — such as during and after intense exercise — when fast carbs are good.

The standard way of measuring how a carbohydrate-containing food enters your bloodstream is through the glycemic index (GI). GI is a score of blood sugar level, and foods are ranked based on how they compare to a reference food (glucose or white bread). A food with a high GI raises blood glucose levels more than a food with a medium or low GI. Eating even a moderate amount of a high GI food can have consequences that reverberate for hours: it causes a rapid spike of glucose in the bloodstream that triggers the release of the hormone insulin.

Insulin is the key that unlocks and opens the doorways into cells so they can absorb glucose. As insulin is rapidly secreted into the bloodstream, glucose is rapidly taken up by cells. An insulin spike, as opposed to a slow and steady increase, often leads to an overcorrection, causing blood glucose and insulin levels to seesaw around a normal value. When glucose takes a sharp dip, this leads to feeling famished and fatigued (and an uncontrollable urge to plunder the vending machine). Unfortunately, this is a common occurrence with high GI carbs. When this takes place frequently over time, your regulatory systems become exhausted and stop functioning, which can lead to insulin resistance or metabolic syndrome, precursors to type 2 diabetes.

Not surprisingly, there are ethnic differences in how well the body handles carbs. Surprisingly, people of European ancestry handle starches and other carbs better than those of Asian ancestry, even though the latter lead the world in consumption of white rice. Europeans experience a lower GI from the same foods and a less pronounced insulin response than those in South Asia (India), and an even better response than those in eastern parts of Asia (China, Thailand, Vietnam, Cambodia, Japan, South Korea).

These numbers suggest that *everyone* should eat lower GI rice varieties (you can find a table of them on p. 140), and that people of European ancestry have physiologically evolved to handle substantial amounts of dietary carbs.

Some common refined carbs have very high GIs, which is why they get a bad rap in general. But whole grain foods, such as common whole wheat bread, are universally recommended over, say, pasta — despite having much higher typical GI values! Diet gurus add to this confusion by claiming that even good carbs increase the risk of diabetes. As this fog of confusion has spread, many frustrated and confused but health-conscious people have tossed all carbs collectively onto the nutritional trash heap.

Lost in this fog of confusion is the over-twenty-five-year-old knowledge that pasta and some common varieties of rice have GIs lower than typical whole grain foods, like whole wheat bread. Lost too is consistent scientific confirmation that carb-rich diets like those of the Mindspan Elite produce the lowest levels of all-cause mortality. Lost is the over-eighty-year-old knowledge that countries, regions, and individuals consuming the most carbs have the lowest levels of diabetes. The traditional flagship carb consumers have been Japan and Italy, leaders of the Mindspan Elite of today. It's no coincidence that as these people move toward modern Western diets and lifestyles, the incidence rates of type 2 diabetes in their countries have skyrocketed from very low levels nearly a century ago.

The truth is, diets rich in slow carbs produce the lowest levels of all-cause mortality, validating the historical diets of the Mindspan Elite.

THE DANGERS OF FAST CARBS

Diabetics need to control fast carbs very carefully because rapid digestion and absorption of these carbs can result in very high levels of blood glucose. But nondiabetics should also control fluxes of fast carbs, since excess blood glucose can promote gain of body fat, cause tissue damage, and increase your risk of type 2 diabetes.

Sugars in fast carbs can act as glue in your body, attaching to certain proteins like hemoglobin in the blood. These sugary glues are called advanced glycation end products (AGEs), and they're a leading contributor to aging by stiffening all organs and tissues. This process is very harmful — especially in the heart and vasculature, where stiffening can be deadly.

AGEs happen inside cells and outside

them. They occur in skin and are a primary cause of wrinkles. They happen in blood vessels and cause arterial stiffening. Your body has mechanisms to both prevent and repair them. However, frequent high levels of blood sugar overwhelm these mechanisms and allow for them to stick around permanently.

The foods encountered during almost all of primate and human evolution were the low GI foods — and smaller portions — of the very distant past. Imagine the process of hunting and gathering a variety of foods and the slow, methodical consumption of food that must have taken place over the course of a physically demanding day. Contrast that to today's large meals packed with high GI and iron-heavy carbs. The overall load on your system is unprecedented. Diabetics with severely uncontrolled blood glucose actually age more rapidly than other people: their skin wrinkles prematurely and diseases of old age manifest early and progress more quickly. Obese people die early of many types of disorders normally seen in older people (heart disease, stroke, cancer).

Reducing blood glucose spikes has many benefits:

- Increased mental and physical stamina and energy

- Decreased body fat
- Slower biological aging and more youthful appearance
- Reduced mood swings

Blood sugar spikes also cause damage to skin and other tissues in nondiabetics. If you have poorly controlled blood glucose, a low GI diet probably would make you look younger over time. That obvious damage to your skin is also happening inside your body, and reducing it will likely make you healthier and make you feel more energetic. As if those benefits aren't enough, your digestion is likely to improve, and you'll feel better and look less puffy and bloated.

All of these benefits combined might lead to a greatly enhanced mood, but there are other reasons for the improvement. The crash you feel after a high-calorie meal — especially one high in fast carbs — can lead to sugar cravings and postprandial depression, which is a fancy way of describing the lethargic state that can follow a meal. Excessive fast carb intake simply exacerbates this feeling of lethargy. Even if you aren't managing a weight problem, avoiding this energy crash and its underlying causes will greatly improve your long-term health and quality of life.

THE BIRTH OF METALLO-CARBZILLA

The words "enriched" and "fortified" have the ring of health promotion to them. Indeed, food marketers often trumpet a product's enriched or fortified status. In the U.S. today, for example, about half of dietary iron is obtained through fortified grain products.

There is no doubt that some refined grain products are poor food choices and have negative health effects aside from iron enrichment. But because of added iron, most of what you think you know about refined carbs is wrong. Iron fortification of flour began in the U.S. and the U.K. in the early 1940s, and the largest studies of vegetarian diets have been in these countries. The result is that iron fortification has undermined the benefits of vegetarian diets in people who eat typical amounts of refined grain foods, and therefore has greatly perverted epidemiological deductions about disease risk and mortality in vegetarians. Similar confusions have arisen about nonvegetarian carb consumption.

In the last chapter I mentioned an important study showing that eating a more Mediterranean-style diet is associated with larger brain structures and overall brain size. The most significant of all associations was low meat, but contrary to consistent findings in Mediterranean countries, this study indicated a negative effect of grains.* I am not surprised by this. Why? Because these people reside in the United States, and most of the grain products they have access to are iron-enriched fast carbs. Their rice is not the rice of the Japanese Mindspan Elite, and their wheat is probably mostly breads and breakfast cereals overloaded with iron. Even their pasta is very different from the favored carb of the Mediterranean Riviera regions, and the difference is iron.

Most people think carbs cause diabetes, but iron is a bigger risk factor for the development of diabetes and triggers an even greater insulin release than low GI carbs. Insulin response (per gram of food) for red meat is almost double that of fish — and surprisingly, *more than double that of pasta*! So excess iron is the hidden risk for diabetes in your diet, not good carbs or gluten.

WHAT ABOUT GLUTEN?

Gluten is a mixture of proteins found in wheat, barley, and some other grains. There is a current anti-gluten mania sweep-

---

* The result was not statistically significant, possibly because the study was not large enough.

ing the world. I even see "Gluten-Free!" labels on foods that have never contained gluten, like nuts and oils.

Gluten is a serious problem, but only for a very small number of people. The actual prevalence of celiac disease — an autoimmune condition in which gluten causes potentially life-threatening intestinal damage — is less than 1 percent of people, according to one recent multi-center study of over 13,000 people. But now some diet gurus claim that gluten is poisoning everyone, and they blame it for everything from joint pain to weight gain to forgetfulness — and even Alzheimer's disease. But aside from the small percentage of people with celiac disease, the evidence is very flimsy.

I believe people when they complain that their bodies, brains, and guts are in trouble. But the answer for most of them is not a gluten-free diet. Always bear in mind that the Mindspan Elite of both Japan and the Mediterranean eat lots of wheat. What they don't eat is iron-enriched grains. Iron is a proven driver of gut inflammation, infection, and even cancer — and overload exerts these effects on everyone, not just a small minority with an autoimmune disease. If you live in a country that enriches most wheat with iron, I am not surprised that eliminating wheat from your diet makes your gut feel better. Try eating wheat products free of enriched iron, and if you still feel discomfort, get tested for celiac disease.

One of the troubling elements of the anti-gluten campaign is that a problem is being created where none exists for most people. Those who don't have gluten sensitivity but believe they do are looking for alternatives to wheat-containing foods, and many of these foods are far worse than the wheat-based versions. Gluten-free pastas made of rice, brown rice, and various other grains often have glycemic index scores far higher than standard semolina wheat pasta. Some of the GI values I have seen are over 100, and even some of the whole grain pastas are nearly that high. This is reminiscent of the trans fat debacle. A small problem has been blown into a much bigger one because of the hyperbolic claims of a few extremists. Plus, the focus on gluten distracts us from the actual, much bigger problem of iron.

Iron fortification of foods is done with the best of intentions, but it is clear that low but sufficient iron poses no clear health risk to adults. As mentioned in chapter 4, in 2006 about 50 percent of Japanese women of childbearing age were iron deficient (serum ferritin less than 20 ng/mL) — the highest rate of all developed countries. This appears to be cause for serious concern, and some scientists still fret about iron deficiency in Japanese women. But this level isn't a concern, it has set the standard! It is truly amazing that there's a complete disconnect between this apparently alarming statistic and the fact that Japanese women are the longest-lived people in the world!

The current overload of nutritional iron began in developed countries in the middle of the twentieth century. By 1950, many European countries and most of the U.S. states had adopted laws that mandated iron enrichment of cereal flour and breads. The troubling truth is that these decisions were based on Depression era data, and by the time these laws were enacted, the average diet in many of these countries already contained excessive iron because of high postwar meat consumption.

The problem with current iron-enriched grain products is that the iron is absorbed rapidly with large amounts of monosaccharide sugars from the breakdown of the starch in the grain. This is a toxic and completely unnatural combination that produces unprecedented stresses on your body, especially your vasculature and your pancreas, which regulates insulin and glucose.

Sweden and Denmark led the enrichment campaign and instituted mandatory iron-enrichment programs even before the U.S. and U.K. The small size and relative homogeneity of these countries allows them to move more quickly on such issues than their larger Western counterparts. Why is this important to recognize? Because, based on abundant iron in modern diets, extensive scientific evidence, and a better understanding of the risks and benefits of iron enrichment, both countries have repealed their iron-enrichment programs and mandates.

Here is the status of iron fortification of grain products, as of mid-2015:

- Eighty-two countries have enacted legislation to fortify wheat flour (only Australia doesn't mandate iron fortification).
- Thirteen countries have enacted legislation to fortify corn products.
- Six countries have enacted legislation to fortify rice.
- The United States is the only country in the world that mandates iron fortifi-

cation of *all three* (wheat flour, corn products, and rice).

- Costa Rica mandates fortification of all three grains with various nutrients, but does not currently fortify rice with iron.
- About 30 percent of wheat flour worldwide is fortified.
- About 50 percent of maize flour worldwide is fortified.
- About 1 percent of rice worldwide is fortified.

These policies probably help some people in developing countries, but in developed countries, the problem is out of control; there is a massive iron glut! Common breakfast cereals contain wildly excessive amounts of iron: one serving of enriched farina contains about 50 percent of the RDI of iron, one serving of Grape-Nuts contains about 90 percent of the Percent Daily Value (PDV), and Product 19 and Total contain 100 percent of the PDV (18 milligrams) per serving of 100 calories.

By any measure, this amount of iron is excessive and unnecessary in a balanced diet. But here's what's more shocking. As mentioned in the previous chapter, the Percent Daily Value of iron listed on food labels in the U.S. (18 milligrams per 2,000 calories) is for menstruating women. Estimated need for men and nonmenstruating women is 8 milligrams. If maximum mindspan is the goal, evidence strongly supports about half this value, or 4 milligrams (about 3 to 5 milligrams, depending on body mass). Redoing the calculation for these adults, using the government's numbers and a diet of 2500 calories per day, a 200-calorie serving of one of these high-iron cereals provides 450 percent of iron in about 8 percent of daily calories, an over-56-fold excess. Using my estimated iron requirement, some breakfast cereals have over a hundred times the appropriate amount of iron!

On a personal note, I find it very troubling that one of these cereals with toxic doses of iron was my grandmother's everyday staple for breakfast. As her dementia progressed, I once saw her begin to pour some of this cereal into her evening glass of sherry before I stopped her. At the time, I had no idea of the dangers of these foods. She had been eating this cereal for many years before her dementia became evident, and at the time, its high iron content was almost universally believed to be a cornerstone of good health and vitality. Now this toxic concoction is suspect number one in her demise.

The problems of such excesses aren't limited to adults. Most infant formulas contain more iron than is found in breast milk — some up to ten times the amount, which explains why formula-fed babies have significantly higher body iron stores and suffer more frequent infections and sudden infant death syndrome (SIDS).

WHAT ABOUT WHOLE GRAINS?

As first discussed in chapter 3, leaders of the biomedical and nutritional mainstream credit the cardiovascular and longevity benefits of Mediterranean cuisines to whole grains. This is the pinnacle of mainstream scientific mythmaking.

Until the past few years, many inhabitants of PACA, Liguria, Piedmont, and Sardinia had rarely seen whole wheat pasta — and it is still rare. Most Piedmontese would recognize brown rice — but only because they are the leading grower of rice in Europe, not because they eat much of it. Essentially all of the rice consumed in these cuisines is milled white rice. What about the Spanish, French, Greek, and Italian breads over the past decades? Almost all white.

A seed of grain like rice or wheat is naturally encased in a hard and fibrous outer husk or hull. This is removed for eating, but the whole grain is otherwise intact. The cohesion, density, and fiber of intact or partially intact grain slows the digestive process and food absorption in the small intestine.

Finely grinding grain diminishes this effect. Finely ground whole wheat bread and white bread cause an about equal rise in blood sugar. The primary difference between most whole grain foods and refined grain foods is that whole grain foods retain more of the fibrous bran and germ. Most commercial whole grain foods are made of flours ground so small that most potential health benefits are lost, and the remainder are questionable, especially since this fine grinding exposes the natural grain oils to more rapid oxidation.

In contrast, a grain like white rice or pearled barley isn't a whole grain because the outer bran and germ have been removed. These grains consist of the intact starchy endosperm, which remains dense and cohesive. Many types of intact white rice and pearled barley have much lower GIs than foods made of whole grain flours, such as whole wheat bread. Pasta is made of ground durum wheat, but after it is ground, it is reaggregated into a dense and cohesive form, similar to intact rice (the pasta called orzo is even shaped like rice). Couscous is a similarly reaggregated, dense, and cohesive form of durum wheat.

The bottom line is that so-called whole grains are not automatically good for you, and some "refined" grains like low GI white rice and pearled barley are better for you than many whole grains.

The same is true for healthful Asian cuisines. Japanese and Okinawan cuisines are supposedly anchored by whole grains and sweet potatoes, respectively. But Japanese would be extremely perplexed by such a claim, since most of the rice they eat is white. And Okinawans traded their sweet potato staple for white rice over sixty years ago. For the past fifty years, sweet potatoes have provided only a tiny fraction (about 1 percent) of their food energy. Still, this raises an important question. Are whole grain foods better or worse for health than the best refined grains, like pasta and rice? We don't know; we only know for certain that the mindspan leaders of the world eat the latter.

Nevertheless, I agree with leading Paleo food researcher Loren Cordain that there are problems with whole grains. Grains are a plant's reproductive material, so plants have evolved protections against their consumption, such as toxins and antinutrients. These include saponins (detergent-like compounds that can cause leakage of the gut), phytates, lectins, and other toxins. Whole grains have them in abundance: they are highly concentrated in the outer bran, germ, and husk (a.k.a. hull), because they have the greatest shielding effect there, like a suit of armor.

Scientists who study animals that eat lots of grasses and grains, such as cows, sheep, and buffalo, observe them moving from one food type to seek others, even if there is abundant food of one type. The theory is that they have evolved instincts to minimize the ingestion of specific toxins in whatever they have been eating. Take a lesson from these critters: the most common whole grain foods are poor choices and should be avoided almost as avidly as poor refined grain foods, like air-filled white sandwich bread enriched with iron.

In the U.S., typical whole wheat bread is a high glycemic index, air-filled, brownish, but otherwise excellent imitation of white sandwich bread. Sure, it has more fiber, and it has phytates that reduce absorption of the naturally high iron content. But wheat bran and insoluble fiber can actually worsen constipation and irritable bowel syndrome (IBS) symptoms. Whole wheat also has easily oxidized fats, which are often supplemented with oxidized canola or soybean oils. Add some preservatives and high-fructose corn syrup, and you've got the food people eat as a recommended staple in their pseudo-Mediterranean diets.

Compare this to traditional white breads made with starter, al dente pasta, and the best types of white rice — all of which have far lower glycemic indexes and are very low in iron. Plus, essentially all of the fats have been removed, which allows for the addition of fresh fats and oils, like cheese or olive oil.

I happen to love morning oatmeal (although I mix it with at least half white rice or barley), fresh whole wheat or rye bread, buckwheat noodles, and certain other whole grain foods — but our preferences and beliefs must take a backseat to facts. And here are the facts: the Mindspan Elite have validated records for longevity and mindspan, and they have reached these pinnacles by eating mostly refined grain foods.

THE BEST CARBS: LIGIR CARBS

To repeat: the best carbs are those eaten by people of the Mindspan Elite. These are typically low iron and glycemic index (GI) refined carbs. You can remember these key properties by the acronym LIGIR (pronounced like "tiger"). Base most of your meals on LIGIR carbs.

In addition to this proven longevity performance, here are a few points to keep in mind about the best refined grain foods (not enriched with iron) versus whole grain foods:

- "Whole wheat" bread that doesn't say it is 100 percent whole wheat is often a mixture of whole wheat and iron-enriched white flour.
- Relative to refined grains, whole grains reduce vitamin D levels in the body and inhibit absorption of minerals, including magnesium, calcium, zinc, and selenium (as well as iron). It is currently unknown why or how whole grains reduce blood levels of vitamin D.
- Arsenic is found in the bran of some rice. The worst offender: brown rice. Your safest option: parboiled white rice, which has a third less arsenic than regular white and less than half of brown.

- Low GI white rice has among the lowest GI values, even in type 2 diabetics. Barley also has a very low GI.
- Relative to refined grains, whole grains have higher levels of oxidizable fats. These fats have a nonideal balance of omega-6 to omega-3 fats, as detailed in the next chapter. Oats are among the worst. The high fat content of oats can become oxidized, emitting a rancid odor. Brown rice has about half the fat but the same problem. Barley has a better fat balance, and even the whole grain has about a third the fat of whole grain oats. Pearled barley has half the fat of the whole grain. White rice has the least fat.
- The vast majority of grain toxins and antinutrients are found in the outer bran and germ of the grain seed. For example, wheat germ agglutinin (WGA) is highly concentrated only in the germ and is not present in the starchy endosperm. WGA has been reported to cause a wide range of health problems. A "whole grain" such as whole wheat or brown rice has the outer husk removed but contains the bran and germ — and the toxins — while refined wheat flour or white rice consists only of the

starchy endosperm and little or none of the seed toxins.

- Many breakfast cereals made with whole grains are overloaded with iron (refined grain breakfast cereals are too). Always avoid these foods. They are marketed as health foods, but the truth is, they are the polar opposite.
- Constipation is the most common GI disorder. Bran and insoluble fiber from grains can actually worsen constipation and IBS symptoms.

YOUR MOVE: MORE AND BETTER CARBS

Eat more carb-rich foods, especially low glycemic index grains and starches. About 45 to 60 percent of your dietary energy should come from good carbs — mostly from vegetables and LIGIR carbs. Excellent LIGIR carb-rich foods include high-amylose white rice (especially parboiled or converted rice, but not enriched with iron), sweet potatoes, pasta, beans, lentils, peas, chickpeas, and hummus.

Here are more tips for making good choices:

1. Select carbs that do not have added iron. Most white rice and wheat prod-

---

ucts sold in Mindspan Elite countries and regions do not have added iron, while those sold in the U.S. and certain other countries do. Look for the word "enriched" and the words "ferric," "ferrous," or simply "iron" on the ingredients list, and avoid these foods. Be aware that grain products at restaurants are often enriched with iron, so always check.

2. Select low glycemic index (GI) foods. Certain grain foods have excellent properties that give them a low GI score.

3. Certain starches can undergo conversion into healthier forms that are partially or even totally resistant to digestion. Grains and starches with high amylose content, such as basmati or other common types of long-grain rice, are especially good at this transformation.

4. Certain preparation methods promote conversion of starches into indigestible form. Steaming or boiling followed by cooling and refrigeration help boost levels of digestion-resistant

starches. Parboiled rice (also called converted rice) has among the lowest GI scores because it is precooked and then cooled and dried prior to sale.

MANAGE YOUR CARBS

It's not just what types of carbs you eat, it's how you consume them. One key to slowing and reducing sugar spikes is slowness itself. Many Mindspan Elite regions are known for traditions of leisurely meals. Research shows that people who eat more slowly typically eat less, are less hungry, and weigh less than people who eat quickly. Exercise also blunts blood sugar spikes, so if you're physically active (which these cultures are), your physiology can more easily handle incoming sugars.

Traditional meals in Japan are methodical and unhurried. Japanese have a traditional saying, *"Hara hachi bun me"* (or *"Hara hachi bu"*), which translates as "Eat until you are 80 percent full." The idea isn't to eat less than you need, but that your mind takes time to sense the fullness of your belly. Mediterranean meals are famous for their carefree pace and rich social component (two to three hours for a leisurely lunch and siesta). You might not have that much time for a midday break, but stretch out the duration between the first and last bites, and enjoy the moment.

It also makes a difference how the meal is prepared. When cooked appropriately (not overdone and soggy) and not chewed extensively, pasta and rice have dense starch structures that are digested slowly. Many types of rice eaten in countries like Japan, such as Koshihikari or basmati, are high in a starch called amylose, which slows the rate of digestion.

Japanese and Mediterraneans also have another way of slowing down their carbs: they often eat them later in a meal. It sounds somewhat strange to a Westerner, but there is a set order to a traditional Japanese meal. A minimal traditional meal has four primary components: soup (usually miso), rice, pickles, and green tea; the meal almost invariably begins with the soup. More complex and formal meals will include other dishes (vegetables, fish, meat), also in a set order, but all are bookended by soup at the beginning and rice, pickles, and green tea at the end.

Mediterraneans have more variability, but they too have traditional order to their meals. Soups, salads, cheese, and pickled finger foods like olives are often eaten prior to the main meal. Antipasti and hors d'oeuvres are the Italian and French terms for pre-meal foods, and most English speakers know them because these pre-meal servings are firmly established components of these cuisines. Taking a cue from these Mindspan Elite traditions, I eat plenty of LIGIR carbs, but I generally precede them with other foods, like soup, salad (with vinegar), cheese, olives, and a small amount of fish (especially pickled herring and sardines). I suggest you likewise follow their example, and you will find recipes and suggestions for them in chapter 12.

So, unlike what happens in research labs, carbs are almost always eaten in particular ways, and along with other foods that help reduce GI levels. Protein, fats, high salt, and certain kinds and amounts of fiber can all slow carb digestion and absorption into the bloodstream.

WHAT DOES SALT HAVE TO DO WITH ALL OF THIS?

Despite their current mindspan dominance, the Japanese were longevity laggards during the first half of the twentieth century: they were in about the middle of the international pack for life expectancy, and their stroke rates were over twenty times higher than they are today. What happened to cause such an enormous change? It resulted from the simple reduction of a common ingredient: salt.

The first countrywide measurements of dietary salt were made in Japan during the 1950s. One thing immediately stood out: Japanese salt intake was off the charts, especially in the north, where some measurements showed consumption of over 11,000 milligrams of sodium per day (which translates to over 28 grams, or an ounce of salt for a person under 150 pounds!). At the time, the link between salt intake and stroke was unknown.

By the 1960s, researchers realized there was a link between salt, blood pressure, and stroke. The Japanese began a countrywide effort to reduce salt consumption. As they cut back on dietary salt, the rate of stroke deaths fell precipitously. Salt intake remains high throughout Japan (over 5,000 mg of sodium a day) and is still higher in northern regions — which helps explain why there's a gradient of longevity in the south. Nevertheless, a curious thing happened as salt levels dropped: type 2 diabetes increased.

Japanese and other scientists have discovered that high salt intake lowers the GI of food and enhances insulin action. I don't recommend using salt as a means to lower GI; there are much more healthful ways to accomplish the same result. Vinegar and other food ingredients in Japanese cuisines substitute for high salt to blunt carb-driven spikes in blood sugar (we'll learn more about these in chapter 9). Japanese in the prefecture of Okinawa are among the longest-lived Japanese, and in their rise to the greatest longevity in Japan — and the entire world — they used the least salt among all Japanese.

Plus, Okinawans are located far to the south of the rest of Japan and have hotter weather. This gives them two other advantages over mainland Japanese. First, they traditionally have lost more sodium (and iron, calcium, and other minerals) through sweating, which further reduces the risk associated with salt intake. Second, they drink more water and tea throughout the day than mainlanders, further reducing the negative effects of salt and other minerals. Hot weather is also a feature of other Mindspan Elite regions. Sweat loss of salt and other minerals like iron might be a reason why, and it might be one reason that exercise is beneficial.

MAXIMIZING MINDSPAN WITH OTHER ASIAN CUISINES

At some point during the discussion of Japanese and Okinawan longevity and foods, you might have wondered if other Asian foods have a similar longevity effect. After all, there are some clear similarities, and Chinese food is more similar to Japanese food than to Western foods. While Japanese cuisine is commonly grouped together with other Asian cuisines and is superficially similar, and like other Asian cuisines it also uses white rice as a staple, there are substantial differences.

One difference is the food order I mentioned above. Traditional Japanese meals are orderly, and a basic meal consists of a beginning, a middle, and an end, and four largely invariant components (soup, rice, pickled vegetables, and green tea). Other Asian cuisines feature these components too, but they aren't presented in essentially invariant order, or typically as ceremoniously.

DIET-DRIVEN MINDSPAN EROSION IN OKINAWA

Among all countries of the world, Japan is the longevity and mindspan leader, with the highest longevity found in the southern prefecture of Okinawa. This area's longevity advantage is remarkable: it has three times the concentration of currently living supercentenarians as the second best prefecture!

Since the 1970s, Okinawa had led Japan and the rest of the world in overall longevity and in concentration of centenarians — but then something changed. First, overall longevity fell precipitously. In 1995 Okinawa was still number one in life expectancy among forty-seven Japanese prefectures. Only five years later, it had fallen into the bottom half. In 2009 Okinawa still was number one in centenarians, but then in 2010 it dropped to second place. In 2011 it dropped to third, then eighth, and in 2014 it was announced that Okinawa had dropped to eleventh place among all prefectures.

How did this center of extreme longevity fall so far, so fast? What was happening to people in their nineties to reduce their chance of making it to age one hundred? There were two major and related changes that drove this decline: the growth of fast food and meat consumption. In the second half of the twentieth century, Okinawa has hosted the largest U.S. military concentration in Asia. Western fast food came along for the ride, and over the recent past Okinawa has accumulated the highest concentration of fast-food establishments in all of Japan. Those growing up with this trend have paid the price.

A related trend is that Okinawans transitioned from eating only about 10 pounds of meat per person per year in the mid-1950s to eating about 120 pounds per person in the mid-1990s. In that forty-year stretch, they went from eating the least meat in Japan to eating the most — by far. I don't think it is surprising that this massive increase in fast food and meat consumption immediately preceded the loss of their unrivaled status at the peak of Japanese longevity.

The moral of the story? Their genes didn't change — but their diets did, providing yet another clear and powerful demonstration that what you eat is critical to health and longevity.

Other differences are the foods and macronutrient compositions. Compared to, say, most Chinese cuisines, Japanese food features more fermented foods and fish, less fat and oil, and much less meat (Chinese eat much more pork). Therefore, the intake of animal fat and protein is substantially higher in China, and this way of eating is accompanied by higher iron intake.

Traditional Okinawan cuisine has similarities to the cuisines of both Japan and China (especially nearby Fujian). It has essential features of Chinese food that make it simpler to prepare and eat than Japanese cuisine (Chinese-like stir-fries are very popular), but it shares the orderly and ceremonial qualities of Japanese meals. Importantly, Okinawans traditionally begin each meal with a soup of fermented foods, just like other Japanese.

Before the Okinawan diet became excessively Westernized, the macronutrient profile of their diet was similar to that of the overall Japanese diet. Although their food is similar to Chinese, they eat much less meat, even at the higher levels they reached after 1990. Taken together, these facts tell us that the entirety of Japanese cuisine and traditional eating is not required for maximizing longevity and mindspan, and that other Asian cuisines will likely produce similarly impressive outcomes by incorporating a few key advantages. These components are very important to the longevity effects of Japanese cuisine. Slow rate, specific order (soup first, carbs later), and composition of the foods in a Japanese meal substantially slow digestion, producing a gradual impact on the body and a sustained feeling of fullness and satiety.

7.

FAT FRIENDS AND FOES

All I really need is love, but a little
chocolate now and then doesn't hurt!
— Lucy from "Peanuts"

The very word "fat" elicits strong emotions. It conjures up so many negative connotations about people that it transcends the realm of nutrition. Fat — the "F word" of many a dieter's lexicon — is associated with poor health, laziness, low energy, lack of self-discipline, and worse. But over the last decade, dietary fat has made an amazing comeback. It's no longer viewed as the dietary devil. In fact, most types (including the much villainized saturated fat) are now viewed as being truly essential components of a healthy diet. But the different types can be so confusing you may feel like you need a Ph.D. in biochemistry to sort it all out. Here's a breakdown of the essentials.

ESSENTIAL FATTY ACIDS (EFAs): A PRIMER

Some fats are not only good for us, they are indispensable for life. Essential fatty acids (EFAs) must be eaten in the diet or our bodies cannot function. We get our dietary EFAs from plants and microscopic marine life. Even the EFAs in animal protein come indirectly from these sources: for example, EFAs in fish are made by phytoplankton at the bottom of the food chain.

All EFAs are types of polyunsaturated fatty acids (PUFAs). There are two general types: omega-6 and omega-3 (also called n-6 and n-3).

The three main types of omega-3 fatty acids are eicosapentaenoic acid (EPA) and docosahexaenoic acid (DHA), found in fish and shellfish, and alpha-linolenic acid (α-LA), the primary omega-3s in plants. Of the three, DHA and EPA (dubbed "fish FAs") are probably most important. DHA makes up your brain's cellular membranes, and both DHA and EPA are also involved in regulating your body's immune and inflammatory responses. These types of omega-3s are associated with lower risk of cognitive decline and dementias. Adequate DHA is important for everyone, but especially expectant and nursing mothers, since breast milk DHA is an essential brain-building nutrient. (This is why breast-fed babies have more DHA in their brains than formula-fed babies.)

Ideally, for DHA plus EPA, you want to consume about 200 milligrams per day per 100 pounds of body weight (so a 150-pound man, for example, should get about 300 milligrams per day). Research shows more probably doesn't help and may even hurt you: fish oil supplementation of only 1.3 grams per day of DHA plus EPA among people with cardiac defibrillators caused an increase in defibrillation events.

You can also get EPA and DHA from certain types of fortified eggs. Hens fed fish meal, special algae, or their normal feed supplemented with fish oils produce eggs with moderate EPA and DHA content. Recently, scientists have succeeded in moving genes for synthesis of fish FAs into a plant. They're currently able to produce only small amounts, but it probably won't be long before you're able to start getting your daily dose of fish oil from plants. For many reasons, including the wonderful flavors, I suggest you get your DHA and EPA from eating fish, seafood, and eggs, but supplements will do in a pinch. Lacto-ovo vegetarians can get some DHA and EPA from eggs. Vegans should investigate DHA and EPA supplements made from algae.

RETHINKING THE RATIO

Ideally, you should be getting about equal amounts of omega-6 and omega-3 in your diet. Some scientists estimate that the diets of our evolutionary ancestors had an omega-6 to omega-3 ratio of anywhere between 1 to 1 and 4 to 1, compared with today's typical Western diets, which often exceed 10 to 1 — a result of too much omega-6 (through whole grains and oils and indirectly through grain-fed farm animals), and too little omega-3 (through seafood and shellfish). By comparison, the ratio in the current Japanese diet is about 4 to 1, which is in this acceptable range.

This imbalance is thought to be a primary contributor to inflammation, heart and cardiovascular diseases, and even cancers and psychological disorders. While a small amount of shorter omega-3 can be converted to DHA and EPA, this conversion is inhibited by omega-6. Given these issues, it isn't surprising that a lower (better) omega-6 to omega-3 ratio is associated with better health and biomarkers, such as longer telomeres. So even though omega-3 intakes in Mediterranean countries are roughly the same as in the U.S. and other Western countries, they eat less omega-6, and consequently their diets have lower omega-6 to omega-3 ratios.

One example is a common food item: the chicken egg. The omega-6 to omega-3 ratio in typical Western supermarket eggs is over tenfold higher than the omega-6 to omega-3 ratio in eggs produced in Greece and many Mediterranean countries. These differences are due to the food eaten by the hens. *Since the omega-6 to omega-3 balance is important to health, long term, we need an alternative to feeding our food-producing animals such an unbalanced diet.* Right now, when you're grocery shopping, look for eggs that have the USDA certified organic label, which means they must come from eggs that are free-range.

MINDSPAN ELITE PREFERRED FAT SOURCES

What are the amounts and primary food sources of Japanese and Mediterranean Mindspan Elite dietary fat?* The top fat sources for Japanese and Mediterraneans are listed in the table opposite.

---

* Composite data, primarily from the Food and Agriculture Organization (FAO) of the United Nations, representing a fifty-year average, from 1961 to 2011.

Japanese (55 to 70 grams per day)

Canola oil (including mustard-seed and rapeseed oil)	17%
Soybean oil	15%
Fish and seafood	11%
Meat, excluding poultry	9%
Dairy	7%
Eggs	7%
Soybeans	5%
Grains	5%
Poultry	3%
TOTAL, vegetable fat	57%
TOTAL, animal fat	43%

Mediterraneans (54★ to 130 grams per day)

Olive oil	25%
Meat, excluding poultry	15%
Dairy, excluding butter	13%
Soybean oil	8%

★ Fat intake of traditional diet of Sardinian shepherds.

Animal fats	6%
Butter	5%
Sunflower-seed oil	5%
Poultry	3%
Eggs	2.5%
TOTAL, vegetable fat	56%
TOTAL, animal fat	44%

THE DANGERS OF IRON PLUS PUFAS — AND THE ADVANTAGE OF BEING SINGLE

While omega-3 polyunsaturated fatty acids (PUFAs) have a good reputation, they aren't squeaky-clean. Some good scientific studies have linked high intake of omega-3 fats to a variety of health problems. A likely culprit is oxidation.

If you know something about art, then you might know that oil paints are made by combining casein, a protein from milk, together with linseed oil (also called flaxseed oil), which is rich in omega-3 fat. When these are mixed together in the presence of oxygen, the combination quickly forms a very hard polymer. The multiple reactive groups on the PUFA (think "poly") each react with a part of a protein. The polymer is an interlocking network of these connections.

Similar reactions take place between the proteins in the body and PUFAs, and they are driven by oxidation. This may help explain why PUFAs have been implicated in airway inflammation (the lungs are a site of the body rich in oxygen and iron) as well as in other ailments such as cancer. Since oxidation is the enemy of the PUFA, high body stores of iron very likely contribute to any negative effects of PUFAs.

Mediterranean Mindspan Elite consume copious amounts of olive oil, an ingredient that has earned a worldwide reputation as a pillar of healthful *and* flavorful Mediterranean eating. People just plain love olive oil. There are various theories on why olive oil is so healthful. Some think it is the colorful polyphenolic compounds, which probably have antimicrobial properties. Others credit olive oil's high monounsaturated fatty acid (MUFA) content.

Unlike PUFAs, MUFAs have only one (mono) chemical group that can be oxidized, so they can't form a network or polymer of oxidized links, as PUFAs can. If you tried to make paint with olive oil instead of linseed oil, it would never set. MUFAs are similarly less reactive in your body. So maybe the thing that makes MUFAs so great isn't so much what they are, but what they are not.

In other words, look at MUFA-rich oils another way. Essentially all calories in oils come from MUFAs, PUFAs, and saturated fatty acids (SFAs), so another way of saying that olive oil is MUFA-rich is to say it is low in saturated fats and PUFAs — particularly certain omega-6 fats. When we look at the Mindspan Elite, it looks like there is an optimal level of PUFAs, and any more or less is not good.

The Japanese consume much less fat than Mediterraneans, but their total PUFA consumption is about the same, and their omega-6 to omega-3 balance is good (about 4 to 1), thanks to their high canola, fish, and soy consumption. So the large difference between Japanese and Mediterranean fat consumption comes mostly from MUFAs. This is a defining feature of olive oil: like LIGIR carbs, it is a nearly ideal source of energy, and it is low in minerals like iron.

It's a much different story, however, when the difference in fat intake comes along with iron. As mentioned earlier, the Okinawans were Mindspan champs from the 1970s to about 2000, thanks to their traditional cuisine. But their fat intake gradually crept up, from about 6 percent mid-century to almost a third (29 percent) by the early 1980s. This higher fat intake wasn't so alarming — it was only slightly higher than other Japanese cuisines, and much lower than some Mindspan Elite Mediterraneans, such as the Greeks of Ikaria. What was problematic about the Okinawan fat increase was that it came mostly from meat (and, of course, its high iron content). As a result, around the year 2000, Okinawa began lagging life expectancy increases relative to other Japanese.

The important thing to note here is that the range of fat intakes that support excellent health and world-leading mindspan can range from under 10 percent to well over 40 percent of calories. Just make sure that most fat comes largely free of iron, the amount and balance of PUFAs are right, and other macronutrient choices are good ones. This is why olive oil is a better choice than almost any other fat.

As you consider the healthful properties of olive oil, bear in mind that people of the Italian and French Rivieras eat less fat than their fellow French and Italians and other Mediterraneans. In his excellent book *Flavors of the Riviera,* food researcher Colman Andrews writes: "Even olive oil, the very fuel of Mediterranean life, has been used only sparingly in these parts." While I don't consider the generous amounts of olive oil they use as "sparing," other experts on the region generally agree that people in these parts have traditionally eaten less olive oil and other fat than is widely believed.

Regional Mediterranean consumption of less fish and fat generally — and olive oil in particular — comes as a great surprise to many people. Still, olive oil is a main source of dietary fat in the Rivieras. And we can be sure that olive oil can power a person to centenarian status and beyond. Mindspan Elite men of Ikaria, Greece, get about half of their dietary energy from fat, and most of it is in the form of olive oil.

STILL IMPERFECT: SATURATED FATS

The current dogma of the medical establishment is that saturated fats — found in foods like butter, cheese, lard, tallow, red meat, and poultry — increase the risk of heart and cardiovascular disease. But this claim is simply not supported by strong evidence.

This theory was turned on its head in 2004, when Harvard epidemiologists found that postmenopausal women with heart disease who ate the most saturated fat showed a low level of plaque buildup in their arteries. Those who ate more carbs — particularly those with a high glycemic index — showed more. So did those women who replaced other fats, including saturated fats, with

PUFAs. A year earlier, a group of Australian scientists showed that consumption of 100 grams of high-fat Camembert cheese, added to an otherwise low-fat diet, did not raise cholesterol levels. Even more evidence: cardiovascular diseases in the United States began declining around 1950 and experienced a steep decline between 1965 and 1995, a time when the amount of saturated fat consumption was fairly stable.

Perhaps the most famous pro-saturated-fat example of all is the so-called French paradox: the French have a high intake of overall fat and saturated fat but relatively low body weight and heart disease. This paradox continues to confound nutritional scientists and epidemiologists because it contradicts two of their favorite dogmas: high fat intake causes obesity and high saturated fat intake causes heart disease.

People in northern and central France actually eat less meat than many other Westerners. It's their full-fat dairy consumption that makes them really stand out: they are the world's number one consumers of milk fat, and second in the world's consumption of both cheese and butter. On average, each person eats seventeen pounds of butter per year, about four times as much as the average American!* Overall, the consumption of saturated dairy fat in France is about double that in the United States.

The French paradox involves both dietary and genetic factors. From the Mediterranean and moving northward, there is increasing heart disease, which coincides with an increasing ability to digest lactose and increasing milk consumption. Most Mediterraneans cannot digest lactose, so when they do eat lactose, they don't absorb the highly reactive galactose sugar into the bloodstream. We'll revisit this point in chapter 9, but it is very likely that lactose is a contributing factor to low Mediterranean heart disease.

From southern Europe northward, there is also an increase in the harmful APOE e4 gene variant, meat consumption, and body iron stores. These factors also keep heart disease lowest in southern France and other parts of southern Europe. So even though saturated fat raises LDL, which has health risks, it is only one of many factors.

But don't go slathering butter on a bowl of

---

* But French butter isn't like the butter most people know. Many are taken a little aback by the mildly tart flavor of some traditional French butters. The tartness is due to lactic acid, which comes from the use of cream from fermented milk.

lard with bacon sprinkles just yet. Enter the Lyon Diet Heart Study to help sort this out. This was a landmark study conducted in the late 1980s and 1990s on people in the city of Lyon in southern France. People who had already suffered one heart attack were split into a control group, which was allowed to continue a "normal" French diet, and an experimental group, the members of which were asked to emphasize Mediterranean aspects of the southern French diet.

Those on the Mediterranean arm of the study ate a diet low in saturated and polyunsaturated fat and high in monounsaturated fat and fiber: more bread, fruit, olive oil, and canola oil margarine and less meat, butter, cream, and cholesterol. Relative to the control group, these people suffered about a third of the recurrent heart attacks and half of the cardiac events of the control group over four years.

These trials show that Mediterranean-style eating can offer dramatic benefits, even to people who already incorporate some of these elements in their routine diets. And the diet's combination of lower omega-6 and iron closely conforms to the Mindspan Elite's dietary formula.

The conflicting evidence about the health effects of saturated fats and PUFAs is in large part explained by the oxidation states of PUFAs and LDL. Once again, much of the blame falls squarely on iron. Since common saturated fats (from land animals) raise LDL, and genetic evidence tells us that this promotes heart disease, eat it in moderation. But first address the primary problem of excessive dietary iron.

THE STILL BAD FAT

The trans fat tale is one of the most recent and high-profile failures of both the food industry and nutritionists. For most of the twentieth century margarine was produced by a process called hydrogenation (and partial hydrogenation). This process makes liquid oils stiffen into a spread, more like butter. Partial hydrogenation also created a new kind of fat — a synthetic trans fat. Margarine producers looking to expand their business developed an advertising approach around the dangers of saturated fats, absent evidence that trans-fat-based margarines were any better. Some nutritionists jumped on the bandwagon and many consumers were persuaded to make the switch, only to find much later that the switch hurt more than it helped.

The problem with trans fat is that it raises LDL at least as much as saturated fat, and although the role of HDL is uncertain, trans fat lowers it. In other words, it's all bad. As with other fats, excess iron and oxidation make a bad situation far worse. Still, eliminate synthetic trans fats from your diet, period. Since manufacturers have reduced serving sizes in an effort to hide trans fat content, you'll have to play detective yourself. Read nutrition labels and don't buy any products with partially hydrogenated oils.

THE REAL SKINNY ON NUTS AND OILS

Your two staples when it comes to cooking should be olive oil and canola oil,* both of which have high MUFA content, and canola has a good balance of omega-3 and omega-6. Try to use less soybean oil, and minimize "vegetable" oils such as corn, common safflower, and sunflower, which all have much higher levels of omega-6 EFAs. Here are some other tips:

- Buy cold-pressed canola oil, which has been pressed to release its oil and processed at lower temperatures. Many supermarket varieties of canola oil are not cold-pressed but instead are hydrogenated to prevent the PUFAs from

* If you are sensitive or allergic to nuts and seeds, stick with olive oil.

oxidizing.

- Always store canola, soybean, and flax-seed oils and walnuts, pecans, and other high-omega nuts in a sealed airtight container, preferably in the refrigerator. This will help prevent oxidation.

My top choice of nuts to snack on are walnuts, pecans, macadamia nuts, hazelnuts, and almonds. They've got a good balance of omega-3 to omega-6, are rich in MUFAs, and should be included in a varied diet. These are all nuts with lower iron and a high ratio of MUFA to saturated fat. When you eat others, make sure you're also consuming foods high in alpha-linolenic acid, like flaxseed or canola oil. Some other good alpha-linolenic acid balancing foods include flaxseeds, beans (navy, black, kidney), kale, and purslane, a green leafy vegetable eaten in Greece by both people and farm animals. But in general, stick with the MUFAs and moderate the PUFAs.

MAKING THE CHANGE, STARTING TODAY

You may have been able to get away with a diet high in bad fats such as oxidized polyunsaturated fats or trans fats for some time now, but don't be fooled: eventually they will start to have a real impact on your health. Why is this? Why do the bad effects take time to emerge, and why do they take some time to undo? It is easy to see how this works, using our car analogy.

Dietary fat is fuel, just like gasoline in a car's gas tank. And just like a gas tank, your body fat is a reservoir for storing fuel. Since your heart is the primary organ in your body that uses fat as fuel, think of your heart as your body's engine. Now imagine eating a meal with lots of bad fat. The amount of dietary fat from any single meal that is stored as body fat is only a small fraction of the amount of body fat, and the amount of bad fat is diluted by whatever fat you have eaten in the past. This is just like putting a bit of bad gasoline in your car. Imagine that your car has 95/100ths of a tank of decent gasoline to which you add a small amount of bad gasoline. Your car probably will run fine . . . at first.

But imagine that you do this repeatedly. Sometimes you get some good gasoline and sometimes you get bad gasoline. It might take a while, but at some point the car is going to run badly, and over time the engine might be ruined. Keep this analogy in mind when you eat foods rich in oxidized polyunsaturated fatty acids and trans fats.

Also keep in mind that the reverse situation is true. If you have been eating bad fats, they will be stored in your body as fuel for some time. Don't think you can start eating healthier fats and go out and run a marathon a week later without risk. You will need to go through weeks of diluting them and replacing them with good fats — especially if you have large amounts of excess body fat from years of poor eating. Always bear in mind both sides of this coin, and eat today for your best possible future.

YOUR MOVE: EAT THE RIGHT FATS

1. Go fish. It has long been known that fish is brain food: it's filled with DHA and EPA, omega-3 fatty acids that build up brain membranes. Eat a few small to moderate servings of fish a week: anchovies, wild salmon, and herring are all good choices. If you are vegetarian or vegan, consider a DHA and EPA supplement made from algae.

2. Opt for olive oil and canola oil. For certain recipes where olive oil isn't ideal because of its rich flavor, use canola oil, which should be stored in the refrigerator.

3. Aim for at least 2 grams of alpha-linolenic acid in your diet daily. Good sources include flaxseeds, soybeans, pumpkin seeds, and walnuts, as well as canola, soybean, and flaxseed oil.

4. Be selective with saturated fats. Even though those who live in central and northern France eat a lot of butter and have low to moderate levels of heart disease, I don't recommend that everyone increase their intake of butter and animal fat to match the French. Nevertheless, cheese, cream, sour cream, butter, and other lactose-free dairy is fine in moderation and has minimal ill effects in the context of a healthful diet. The most healthful sources of saturated fat are nuts (especially cashews), coconut and coconut milk, cocoa butter, cocoa, and dark chocolate (all low sugar).

5. Eliminate trans fats from your diet. Don't be fooled by a product that says zero grams trans fat — it can have up to 0.5 gram per serving, which, if you have two to three helpings, can really

add up. Read nutrition labels and don't buy products with hydrogenated or partially hydrogenated oils.

8.
SOLVING THE PROTEIN PART OF THE PUZZLE

Since the 1970s, followers of the high-protein, low-carb approach have claimed with increasing insistence that their way is the route to optimal health. There are many problems with this claim, but one really stands out: throughout their rise to the pinnacle of longevity and mindspan, the Mindspan Elite have had low overall and animal protein intake. Even more scandalous, the main source of their dietary energy is carbs. I know that in the prevailing climate, this sounds like heresy, but as you'll discover in this chapter, research shows it's a key to maximizing mindspan.

PROTEIN'S COMPLEX ROLE
Strict calorie restriction (CR) doesn't provide the same benefits in people as it does in lab animals. A primary reason might be our outsize brains and their fatty composition. It seems that we need some body fat to buffer

the effects of CR on our brains, especially when we get older. A bit of body fat also provides energy reserves when an unforeseen problem crops up, like a lengthy disability or illness. But there is a way to both maintain a protective amount of body fat and reap some of the benefits of CR: by adopting a low-protein diet.

Research shows that animals raised on low-protein diets live longer than animals eating diets with typical amounts of protein. They also live almost as long as animals eating strict CR diets. In the early 1990s, scientists discovered that the key was limiting essential amino acids (amino acids your body can't make) like tryptophan or methionine.

Methionine is a key regulator in protein production, as well as processes involved with sulfur metabolism and B vitamins. Since your body can't make methionine, these processes are slowed when it's in short supply.

Animals on methionine-restricted diets aren't bone-thin, like their counterparts on full CR. They eat about as much as fully fed animals in a control group, but are smaller and leaner. Later in life, the methionine-restricted animals stay closer to the same size and weight while the control animals shrink, and about 90 percent of them remain healthy and alive at the time 50 percent of the fully fed animals have died.

We need to take great care in applying these and other results from animal studies to ourselves, partly because of our biological differences, but also because the food used in these animal studies is so crummy.

In an earlier chapter I mentioned that these animals are fed a sugar-cookie diet. The glycemic index and load of this diet are through the roof. Although animals live longer on protein- or methionine-restricted diets, the main weakness of these studies is the low quality of the remaining food. Reducing protein in this food increases the proportion of sugar and starch, thus increasing the already sky-high GI. If the lost protein or methionine were replaced by good food, then the life-extension benefits probably would be even greater. Yet even with such diets, low methionine shows a range of benefits, and high dietary methionine increases oxidative stress, damages cellular DNA, and disrupts the body's ability to regulate blood sugar, insulin, and fat metabolism.

Vegetarian diets, which have low methionine content, improve biomarkers, like total and LDL cholesterol. Simply adding methionine undermines these benefits. Other research on real-world diets shows that *animal protein is as great a disease risk factor as ani-*

mal fat. The China Study, a well-known study done in the 1980s, found that dietary protein intake is a primary determinant of diseases in later life, including cardiovascular diseases and cancers. A 2006 Finnish study followed middle-aged men for fourteen years and found that those with the highest methionine intake had a twofold higher risk of heart attack. But the elevated risk of disease that results from excess animal protein is old news. Research from the mid-1960s shows that people of countries with good health and low diabetes eat typically "Eastern" diets "relatively lower in protein (particularly animal protein), fat, and animal fat. A high proportion of calories is derived from carbohydrate, particularly from rice."

RED MEAT, RED HERRING

Low intake of animal products — especially red meat — has long been associated with lower levels of heart disease, cancer, and diabetes, but for decades the focus has been almost exclusively on animal fats, especially saturated fat. It's true that regular high intake of saturated animal fat negatively impacts cholesterol.*

---

* The impressive protection against heart disease

However, the French paradox (high French consumption of non-meat animal fat yet low levels of cardiovascular diseases) challenges the singular focus on saturated fat and suggests it is somewhat of a red herring. When we look more closely, we find that red meat undermines health in at least three other ways:

- It has more iron than most plant sources, and the type of iron found in meat (heme iron) is absorbed more efficiently than iron in plant sources. Remember that LDL cholesterol is most dangerous when oxidized — and that increases with high amounts of iron.
- Even worse, heme iron has a synergistic effect on the absorption of plant sources of iron. That means it increases your body's absorption of *all* dietary iron.
- Meat is high in all essential amino acids, which might be harmful rather than beneficial.

---

offered by certain variants of the gene PCSK9 (through reduction of LDL cholesterol) shows that this is one way in which red meat increases cardiovascular diseases.

From the 1970s through the early 2000s, low-carb diets were the sole domain of diet gurus. But over the past decade or so, low-carb diets have gained some mainstream traction. Low-carb diets are recommended for two things: weight loss and management of insulin and glucose disorders (metabolic syndrome, prediabetes, type 2 diabetes). But are they effective?

Studies of weight loss are mixed. Some very good studies show the benefits of low-carb regimens, and some show the benefits of reduced-fat diets. One of the most rigorous studies to date showed that fat restriction produces more weight loss. But there is no reason to be confused by these apparently conflicting results because the differences found by the best studies are very small.

Many studies show that higher-fat diets help with insulin and glucose disorders. I don't doubt the results of these studies, but they have some serious problems. First and foremost, most of them have been done in countries (like the U.S.) where carbs are mostly of poor quality and are widely enriched with iron. Even in these hot spots of crummy carbs, iron is a bigger risk factor for diabetes than carbs.

This highlights a critical point about the difference between low-carb diets: some suggest replacing carbs with healthful fats, and others make no special distinction, allowing — and even encouraging — large amounts of meat. The latter greatly increases iron intake and is dangerous for your long-term health. It also undermines health in the short term — especially if you are at risk for diabetes.

If you have a glucose/insulin disorder, strictly limit iron and high GI carbs. Also, opt for amounts of MUFA-rich fats (like olive oil) at the higher end of the preferred range (around 40 to 45 percent of calories) until your iron, glucose, and insulin are under control.

Relatively low animal protein intake is a shared dietary attribute among Mindspan Elite regions and subcultures, including the pescatarian and vegetarian Seventh-day Adventists of Loma Linda, California. Seventh-day Adventists typically don't smoke or drink alcohol, many maintain a low-meat diet, and a substantial fraction are vegetarians of various kinds (some eat fish or eggs or dairy). A smaller percentage are heavier meat eaters, and relative to their vegetarian brethren, they suffer two to three times the rate of dementia.

THE PROTEIN PREFERENCES OF THE MINDSPAN ELITE

Now that you've learned all of this, you're probably not surprised to discover that the Mindspan Elite consume less overall protein and far less animal protein than the Mindspan Risk, with a ratio of plant to animal protein of about fifty-fifty. (All plant foods have protein, but examples of common sources of plant protein are beans, rice, pasta, other grain foods, and vegetables.) That's key, because animal protein typically contains several times the amount of methionine found in moderate methionine foods like lentils, rice, and wheat, staple foods of the Mindspan Elite. While it's difficult to calculate an exact number, the Mindspan Risk's traditional methionine consumption is at least double that of the Mindspan Elite.

Overall, the Mindspan Elite typically get anywhere from 11 to 16 percent of their total daily calories from protein. Historically, this range was 9 to 14 percent, which was mostly plant-based protein.

Mindspan Elite eat about a third less protein than the Mindspan Risk populations, and about half the animal protein. Here's a breakdown of their top protein sources (sources with lower values than the smallest shown are not listed).*

Japanese (90 grams per day)

Grains (mostly white rice)	28%
Fish and seafood	25%
Soybeans	10%
Meat, excluding poultry	8%
Dairy	7%
Eggs	6%
Vegetables	5%
Poultry	4%
TOTAL, animal protein (46 grams)	51%
TOTAL, plant protein (44 grams)	49%

* Data primarily from the Food and Agriculture Organization (FAO) of the United Nations, representing a fifty-year average, from 1961 to 2011.

Mediterraneans (102 grams per day)

Grains (mostly refined wheat)	37%
Meat, excluding poultry	17%
Dairy	15%
Poultry	6%
Fish and seafood	6%
Vegetables	4%
Eggs	3.5%
Beans and pulses	3%
TOTAL, animal protein (50 grams)	49%
TOTAL, plant protein (52 grams)	51%

Mindspan Risk (140 grams per day)

TOTAL, animal protein (92 grams)	66%
TOTAL, plant protein (48 grams)	34%

Mindspan Elite protein sources are also among the top foods low in iron but high in other important minerals, such as magnesium, selenium, and calcium. They're also rich in compounds that inhibit iron absorption, such as the protein phosvitin, found in egg whites. Dairy has calcium, which inhibits both heme and non-heme iron (and is the only inhibitor of the former). Typical plant sources of protein, such as soybeans, grains (both rice and wheat), greens, herbs, and vegetables also inhibit iron absorption in various other ways.

Back now to the Okinawans, but with a focus on protein. In the early 1950s, they got less than 1 percent of their calories from meat, and about 1 percent from fish (a quarter of the amount eaten by mainland Japanese). Most of their protein was from plant sources. But they gradually began to eat more meat (mostly pork) and fish, and by the early 1980s protein had increased from about 9 percent of total calories to about 15 percent.

That was still a pretty low number, but that wasn't the main problem. The issue was they had gone from a diet that was primarily plant protein to one with vastly more animal protein. They were getting a lot more methionine and much more iron. They also became more sedentary and quickly gained weight. Sounds like the standard Western formula for disease. As a result, recent generations of Okinawans are fatter and sicker and have fallen from the pinnacle of human longevity and mindspan.

I was surprised that most Japanese and Mediterranean dietary protein comes from grain, but I was even more surprised that Mediterraneans don't eat much fish. Most people I've told this to are shocked, but the Mediterranean Sea is not rich with fish and seafood. It produces a moderate amount and this limits consumption. In fact, Ligurians import a substantial amount of their fish. Mediterranean Mindspan Elite consume about 1 to 1.5 percent of their calories from fish and seafood, whereas Japanese consume over 5 percent. Average consumption in the U.S. is under 1 percent. Seventh-day Adventist pescatarians eat an amount midway between the Japanese and the U.S. average, and they live the longest among all Seventh-day Adventists.

Only 6 percent of Japanese eat fish twice or more per day, and this figure was even lower in the past. In other words, nearly 95 percent of Japanese eat fish once or less per day, and this is usually a small amount (as a flavoring or garnish). Nicoyans of Costa Rica also eat only moderate amounts of fish and seafood. While fish consumption is moderate among many of the Mindspan Elite, it is routine.

Get most of your dietary protein from foods low in iron. A primary difference between Mindspan Elite and Mindspan Risk cuisines is that the former eat far less meat. Compared to plant sources of protein, meat has substantial amounts of heme iron, which is not only absorbed efficiently but increases the absorption of non-heme iron from all foods.

About 10 to 15 percent of your dietary energy should come from protein. The remaining 45 to 60 percent should come from good carbs, and 25 to 40 percent from healthful fats. If you eat meat and fish, stay closer to a 10 to 12 percent range of protein, and if you eat mostly vegetarian, stay in the 14 to 15 percent range. As you can see, the carb to fat ratio spans a large range, and this is fine as long as you eat good carbs and good fats, but keep protein intake on the low side.

If benefits like those seen in lab animals apply to people, CR-like benefits of methionine restriction are lost with high consumption of meat (and other sources of animal protein). Limit them, especially red meat, as much as possible.

Emulate the Mindspan Elite and get at

least half of your protein from plant sources like grains, rice, beans, and vegetables — and even more if you enjoy eating vegetarian or vegan. If you can't shake the omnivore impulse, moderate intakes of certain sources of animal protein low in iron (like eggs and cheese) are good additions to the diet. Their inhibition of iron absorption at least partly counterbalances their higher methionine.

At the beginning of this chapter I suggested it is scandalous in the current anti-carb climate that the main source of Mindspan Elite dietary energy is carbs, and that their favored carbs are refined. But this news is all the more shocking because these high-carb foods are also the main source of their protein. I knew that Mindspan Elite diets are rich in grains, but once again, I admit that I was amazed to discover that most of their dietary protein comes from grain — especially the Mediterranean figure of 37 percent protein from grain.

Something else also surprised me: the high dairy protein intake in Japan — about 7 percent of all protein. Mediterranean dairy consumption is also very high. However, there are clearly established genetic differences between the Mindspan Elite and Mindspan Risk that cause very different responses to dairy, as I'll explain in the next chapter. I think these differences and how they influence mindspan will surprise you.

9.
X Factors — The Last Piece of the Puzzle

Most diets and food pyramids focus only on carbs, fats, and protein, claiming they are the only sources of food energy. Some diet gurus insist that fat is responsible for obesity, but more recently we've heard from many more that weight gain is all about carbs. Some expert scientists counter that only total food energy matters (an oft-heard mantra from this group is "A calorie is a calorie is a calorie"). Now we know one thing for certain: *All of these claims are wrong.* Why? Many reasons; but to start with, they ignore the role of other crucial players in the diet, especially X factors.

We touched briefly on X factors back in chapter 2: these mysterious agents are the products of fermentation, the process by which microbes metabolize food and release energy. In ancient times fermentation was regarded as a divine or mystical process. It changed foods into tangy, pungent, and fizzy concoctions that tingled the tongue and even altered perceptions. (The roots of the word "ale," a common fermented beverage of ancient times, mean sorcery, magic, and intoxication.) The tingle, the tang, and the tipsy are X factors at work.

First and foremost, X factors are fuel for your body, just like carbs, fats, and protein, but they have some unique and powerful properties not shared by these other macronutrients. There are two reasons I call them X factors. One is that they typically don't appear on diet pyramids or expert lists of calorie sources. The other is that many fermented foods contain a wide array of such factors (some foods contain over a hundred), their amounts are variable, and the identities and amounts of each in any given dish or bite of food are simply unknown. Here are some of the best-known and most abundant X factors.

- Short-chain fatty acids (SCFAs): Some key SCFAs in our diets are lactic, butyric, acetic, and propionic. Lactic acid is responsible for the tartness of yogurt, sour cream, sourdough bread, buttermilk, and many cheeses. Butyric acid gives old butter a distinctive aroma and flavor, and dilute acetic acid is vinegar.

223

- Alcohol: A main source of X factor calories is alcohol, also known as ethanol. At about 7 calories per gram, the caloric content of ethanol is between carbs and protein (both have about 4 calories per gram) and fat (about 9 calories per gram).

A normal diet will provide a substantial amount of your daily fuel energy as X factors. But X factors do more than just provide fuel: even small amounts cause pronounced physiological changes in your body. Just a couple of teaspoons of vinegar or a slice of sourdough bread will slow overall digestion and absorption of sugar into the bloodstream — blunting potential blood sugar spikes. But as you'll see in the next section, it isn't absolutely necessary to consume X factors to get these benefits. In partnership with our tiny friends in our guts, we can summon these X factors from within.

MEET THE MICROBIOME

The gut microbiome, the collection of microbes residing in your gut, has many amazing and mysterious properties. One of the most amazing is that it produces food energy that's transported out of the gut to fuel tissues of the body. In other words, these microscopic critters are paying you rent by feeding you — mostly in the form of X factors like acetate, lactate, butyrate, and propionate. These compounds provide up to 8 percent of all dietary energy in a typical diet (even more in very high fermentable fiber diets). This doesn't sound like a lot, but they exert important large effects beyond just slowing digestion and blunting blood sugar spikes. X factors (either eaten or produced by the microbiome) influence appetite, overall metabolism, blood glucose, insulin, and the risk of metabolic syndrome and diabetes. But this is just scratching the surface of their mysterious powers.

One of their most astonishing powers is that they have the ability to regulate body weight. Scientists discovered this by transferring the gut microbes from obese animals to lab animals whose own microbes had been cleaned out with antibiotics. The result? The recipient animal gained weight. Yet animals that receive transfers of gut microbes from a lean animal's microbiome don't gain weight. These animals all eat the same amount of food, so weight gain boils down to whether the microbes came from an obese or lean donor.

Here are a few things to keep in mind about feeding your gut microbiome to keep your partnership a happy one. First, all food fermented by the microbiome — and, therefore, the source of all X factors produced by the microbiome — is carbs. Second, iron-fortified foods are bad for your microbiome. Excess food iron increases disease-causing (pathogenic) microbes in the gut. This may help explain why it's associated with various GI disorders and diseases, including colon cancer, the second most deadly cancer in the United States and many other developed countries. We've known for years that people with lower GI disorders like Crohn's disease have microbiomes that differ substantially from those of people with healthy guts. They also have different diets. Many sufferers have anemia because they limit iron-containing foods, probably intuitively, because the iron increases their symptoms and suffering.

TWO SOURCES OF X FACTORS

There are two ways that X factors fuel our bodies: they can be eaten in the form of *fermented* foods (for example, vinegar), or they can be produced in our bodies from *fermentable* foods. X factors obtained by either path provide a range of benefits. So treat your microbiome with respect and feed it well. Eat foods rich in fermentable carbs.*

The Best Fermentable Foods

Mindspan Elite diets are rich in foods loaded with fermentable carbs. Top foods include greens, grains, vegetables, leeks, garlic, onions, and beans. Liguria and neighboring areas have a favored collection of greens called preboggion, and Greek Mindspan Elite have a similar collection called horta. Chicory is a standard ingredient in both of these; its leaves provide good fiber, but its roots are a much richer source of the fiber called inulin. Belgian endive and radicchio are cultivated chicory. Leeks, garlic, and onions are also favored, and they are likewise rich in fermentable fibers. Beans are great, but just make sure you purchase canned beans with no added salt, and don't rinse them, since the thick liquid is loaded with fermentable carbs. (If unrinsed beans are too hard on your gut, pour off some of the liquid and eat it with other foods like vegetables or rice.)

You might be wondering why refined carbs are an acceptable food within Mindspan Elite cuisines if they are simply fiber-free ver-

* Another term for some of the most beneficial portions of this fermentable stuff is prebiotic.

sions of the whole grain. If we strip off the fiber, don't we eliminate or greatly reduce fermentation and its benefits?

The surprising answer is that starches in all grains can take on a molecular structure that's resistant to digestion, becoming what's known as resistant starch. This may not sound good, but it's actually good for you and your microbiome, because even though you can't digest resistant starch, your microbiome can. It is essentially the conversion of some of the starch in food into the equivalent of fermentable fiber. Resistant starch content ranges from about 3 to 4 percent for rice to about 10 percent or slightly higher for wheat and oats. Starches in other well-known starchy foods like potatoes, peas, plantains, bananas, and many more can also become digestion resistant.

The resistant starch content of certain grains depends in part on how the grain is prepared and stored. The easiest way is to boil or steam the grain and then let it cool. The good news is that reheating doesn't completely undo the process, and in fact cycles of heating and cooling produce increasing amounts of resistant starch. It is common and traditional in Japan, for example, to make a large amount of rice and store most of it for later meals, so most of their meals over the last century have likely been high in resistant starch.

Legumes are even higher in resistant starch than most grains. Chickpeas (garbanzo beans) are a staple in Liguria, and are also a favorite in Spain, Sardinia, and Greece. In emerging mindspan-leading countries in the Americas, exemplified by Costa Rica, people eat very large amounts of beans and other legumes, including for breakfast. Nicoyans and other Costa Ricans also regularly eat other foods very high in resistant starch, like fried plantains.

Some whole grains provide good amounts of fermentable fiber. Oats are especially rich, but refined barley has about the same amount plus additional non-fermentable fiber. White rice has little fiber, but when cooked and cooled, it can form substantial amounts of digestion-resistant starch, as can barley. Both are good sources of fuel for your microbiome.

X Factors in Your Diet

X factors are also present in many flavorful foods. Vinegar is a wonderful addition to many foods, and like salt, it enhances other flavors. Sourdough bread, yogurt, and many cheeses would taste flat without the tang of lactic acid. And wine, beer, and other spirits add substantial ethanol calories to many diets. Fermentation of these X factors doesn't take place in your gut. It happens under controlled conditions at the countless bakeries, cheese makers, wineries, breweries, and vinegar producers who make the food you eat.

There are many more fermented ingredients and foods in the cuisines of the Mindspan Elite. Not only are fermented foods common in traditional healthful cuisines, but it's also common and traditional to believe they are a key to good health and long life. In Mediterranean cuisines, bread, wine, beer and ale, vinegar, cheese, and yogurt are everyday foods. (The Italians and French lead the world in consumption of vinegar and wine, respectively.) In traditional Japanese cuisine, miso, soy sauce, rice vinegar, sake, and fermented vegetables (pickles) and fish (for example, dashi) are ubiquitous.

Miso, a fermented soybean product, and dashi form the base of various soups eaten at every Japanese meal of the day, including breakfast. Soy sauce, rice vinegar, and sake are indispensable flavorings in daily meals, which usually include pickled vegetables (one or more vegetables in a brine of salt which is either fermented or contains added fermentation products, such as vinegar and/ or alcohol). Pickled vegetables are less common in Okinawan cuisine, but they eat lots of vinegared seaweed, and like other Japanese, they start every meal with soup, typically miso and dashi.

THE SECOND-MEAL EFFECT

One widely known property of certain fibers is to slow digestion of starches and sugars, which slows absorption of sugars into the bloodstream. A lesser known but even more remarkable property is they not only reduce sugar spikes at the time they are eaten, but also have this effect the next time you eat, even if they are not eaten with the second meal!

This property is called the second-meal effect, but this name fails to capture its extended power since research has shown that it can exert beneficial effects even the next day! This is an incredibly important attribute of X factors, and it has been known for over twenty years. It is mind-boggling that such an important effect has been known to a small number of academic researchers for so many years but has been unknown to the public — even while the low-carb craze was rising to prominence.

The second-meal effect has been at work round the clock for many decades in people of the Mindspan Elite. When every meal has this effect on the next one, the body falls into a comfortable groove of handling each carb-rich meal with ease. Combine an active life with eating right and the second-meal effect, and sugar and insulin spikes and crashes will occur very rarely, if ever. Mindspan Elite folk are leaner than those in other developed countries, and control over blood sugar and insulin spikes — and, therefore, hunger — is a primary reason for this.

YOUR MOVE: EAT FERMENTED FOODS

Eat fermented foods to further tame your carbs. Vinegar is a common ingredient throughout leading Mindspan Elite cuisines, and you should consider including it in small amounts routinely in your diet. Also make other fermented foods a regular part of your meals.

Fermented foods like vinegar slow the transit of foods through the digestive tract. These foods also promote a second-meal effect, slowing digestion at the next meal. But be careful, since straight vinegar is acidic and too much can harm delicate tissues and the enamel on your teeth. Mixing a small amount of vinegar with food will reduce its acidity and make it safe for consumption.

Recall from chapter 6 that salt blunts blood sugar spikes. Vinegar and other fermented foods do this too, and they have two clear advantages over salt: (1) they don't raise blood pressure, as salt does; (2) they exert a beneficial second-meal effect, and salt does not. Like salt, vinegar enhances flavor. A small amount of vinegar goes a long way toward making food more flavorful and more healthful.

Taken together, common X factors provide in excess of 20 percent of daily energy to Mindspan Elite diets of the world, at least twice that found in countries (like the U.S.) that suffer from high levels of diabetes, obesity, and dementia in later years. You're probably wondering why this difference is so large, and whether the Mindspan Elite have some secret advantage or stealth source of X factors. They do. The good news is that you can get an equal or even greater advantage, but you have to know how.

DAIRY AND THE STEALTH X FACTORS OF THE MINDSPAN ELITE

Unlike Mindspan Risk populations, Mindspan Elite tend to get most of their dairy from fermented foods such as cheese and yogurt, rather than milk.* So they get lots of X factors (like lactic acid) in their foods. Mediterraneans in particular get far more dairy X factors than Mindspan Risk. Many also consume a fair amount of milk and lactose. However, there's a crucial difference in the fate of their lactose: they're mostly lactose intolerant, or lactose non-digesters (LCT−), while the vast majority of Mindspan Risk are lactose digesters (LCT+).† Why is this important? Because when a typical person of the Mindspan Elite eats lactose, they don't digest it, their gut microbes do.

This means most Mindspan Elite don't ab-

---

* According to a 1999 study by the Foreign Agricultural Service of the U.S. Department of Agriculture (USDA), the highest per capita consumers of cheese were Greece, France, and Italy, in descending order. The Greeks ate about 52 pounds of cheese annually — about two-fifths more than in the United States, and more than twice that of the U.K.

† About 99 percent of Japanese (and over 95 percent of other Southeast Asians) and 50 to 70 percent of Mediterraneans can't digest lactose, while the same is true of only about 10 to 15 percent of Americans and Brits, under 20 percent of northern French, and less than 10 percent of Scandinavians.

sorb about 35 percent of the calories in whole milk, all of which are sugar — half of which is the troublesome sugar galactose. A cup of milk contains about 10 to 12 grams of lactose, which must be broken down to be absorbed. When an LCT– person consumes lactose, what happens to it? It moves through the gastrointestinal tract and gets fed to his microbiome to make X factors. To gut microbes, it is food just like dietary fiber or resistant starch. LCT+ people, on the other hand, don't get these benefits and instead absorb galactose into the bloodstream.

This is a serious problem. Galactose is highly reactive and rapidly forms advanced glycation end products (AGEs). It is more dangerous than any other common sugar — but only if the lactose is digested, liberating the highly reactive galactose for absorption into the bloodstream.

We talked about the French paradox in chapter 7 — the fact that the French consume high amounts of saturated fat (mostly from dairy) but have low rates of heart disease. This pattern is largely explained by lactose consumption and the ability to digest it. As you move northward from the Mediterranean, there's increasing heart disease. This pattern coincides perfectly with increasing milk consumption and an increasing ability to digest lactose (LCT+). Mediterranean dairy is like other full-fat dairy: it is typically high in saturated fat. Their consumption of lots of dairy doesn't seem to impact them and increase the risk of heart and other diseases. The simplest explanation is that many of them can't digest lactose.

Other research also shows that Mindspan Elite who consume dairy actually have lower rates of disease. In one Italian study of yogurt consumption, those who were most protected from heart disease consumed a cup of yogurt per day. The amount of lactose in this one cup provides the majority of Italians who are LCT− with about 11 grams of fermentable sugar — over half of the entire daily intake of fiber, and about double the 5 grams of fermentable fiber consumed daily by Americans!

Similarly, Japanese consume an average of about a cup of milk a day, from which they probably derive over 10 grams of fermentable fiber in the form of lactose — also double the amount of fermentable fiber in Western diets. A study of Japanese and Okinawan elderly and centenarians showed that older people who drank more milk were more likely to survive into older age. We now know from modern genetics that virtually none of them are able to digest lactose.

These facts help solve a long-standing mystery. The Japanese eat little fruit and only moderate amounts of vegetables and get only about 2 grams of fiber daily from their beloved soybeans. But unlike other nations with low fiber intake (like the Mindspan Risk), the Japanese have low levels of colon cancer. Naturally, nutritionists have long puzzled over this anomaly. Lactose is a big part of the answer, but in addition to this 11 grams of fermentable sugar, rice provides a whopping dose of digestion-resistant starch, which likely exceeds this amount. Even if it is only half this amount, the total fermentable carbs provided by only lactose and rice together at least doubles the total fermentable fiber in Western diets. Mystery solved!

But most in Mindspan Risk populations don't enjoy this benefit — *and* they bear the cost of highly reactive galactose permeating their bodies. Per capita annual consumption of milk in the U.S. is about 100 kilograms, which means that the average person consumes 4.5 kilograms of lactose (about 10 pounds) every year! And that's only from drinking milk. It's also found in many other common foods, as you can see in the following table.

LACTOSE IN FOODS

Food	Serving Size	Lactose (grams)
condensed milk	1 cup	30
Evaporated milk	1 cup	27
Yogurt (nonfat)	1 cup	15
Yogurt (low-fat)	1 cup	14
Skim plus milk	1 cup	16
Low-fat or nonfat milk	1 cup	12 to 14
Whole milk	1 cup	11
Yogurt (full-fat)	1 cup	11
Buttermilk	1 cup	11
Greek yogurt (nonfat)	1 cup	3
Frozen yogurt	1/2 cup	7
Ice cream	1/2 cup	6
Ricotta cheese	1/2 cup	3 to 5
Cottage cheese	1/2 cup	3
Half-and-half	1/4 cup	2
Light cream	1/4 cup	2
Whipping cream	1/4 cup	1
Heavy cream	1/4 cup	1
American cheese	1 ounce	2

Food	Serving Size	Lactose (grams)
Mozzarella cheese	1 ounce	0.5 to 1
Cream cheese	1 ounce	0.5 to 1
Most hard cheeses	1 ounce	Negligible to 1
Butter	1 tablespoon	Negligible

People in the United States (and others who are LCT+) eat yogurt because they hear about studies showing that yogurt has health benefits, like the Italian yogurt study cited above. But most Mindspan Elite are protected against the ill effects of lactose (milk sugar), even if they do consume milk or incompletely fermented dairy like yogurt. This is very important, because galactose has been linked to a range of health problems, including cataracts, diabetes, and cancer.

For the rest of us non–Mindspan Elite, here are some tips about dairy:

• If you can digest lactose, don't drink milk. I know it sounds strange and counterintuitive, but research suggests milk (particularly galactose) is a cause of cardiovascular diseases and possibly dementias. If you are of northern or western European descent, avoid liquid milk (cow's, goat's, sheep's, etc.) and products made from milk, like ice cream. Hard cheese, butter, cream, sour cream, and other dairy products lacking lactose are fine in moderation.

- If you are not sure of your LCT status, avoid milk and other lactose-containing dairy like ice cream, buttermilk, and even yogurt.
- If you're lactose intolerant (LCT−), you may have given up dairy because of the gut pain and belly distention consuming it causes you. And you may have switched to lactose-free products. But that's a mistake! These products don't get rid of galactose; they only break lactose down into glucose and galactose monosaccharides, which can then be absorbed into the bloodstream and have the same harmful effects.
- Don't overdo the cheese, regardless of your LCT status. There might be risks to high levels of cheese intake. I suggest you follow the example of Mediterranean Mindspan Elite and eat flavorful cheeses in moderation. But always be aware that traditional Mediterranean cheeses come from free-range animals

and have a higher omega-3 to omega-6 ratio. Therefore, look for grass-fed cheeses.

- Don't take calcium supplements. Several studies link them to atherosclerosis. You do need vitamin D, however, so make sure you get 400 IU through an occasional supplement — more often if you are indoors a lot.

YOUR MOVE: SUPPORT YOUR MICROBIOME

Eat fermentable carbs to help your microbiome produce X factors. X factors can be obtained in food directly, or your gut microbiome can manufacture X factors in your gut, which they share with you. X factors from either source help you to tame carbs and make them beneficial.

Eat more fermentable carb-rich foods. Good examples are chicory leaves and roots, lettuce, leeks, garlic, onions, a wide range of beans, barley (pearled), and parboiled or specially prepared white rice.

If you can't digest lactose and don't feel sick from doing so, feel free to consume milk and other dairy. If you can digest lactose, eat other sources of fermentable carbs.

If you are able to digest lactose, consider adding a prebiotic (such as fructooligosaccharides or lactulose), or a fermentable fiber supplement (such as psyllium) to your diet. Irrespective of your ability to digest lactose, eat fiber-rich beans, legumes, and veggies to feed your microbiome. If you eat substantial amounts of red meat, replace most or all of it with these low-iron, highly fermentable carb foods.

ANOTHER X FACTOR ADVANTAGE: ALCOHOL

Mediterraneans hold the title for the highest per capita wine consumption in the world. The French lead the pack, downing 1.25 liters per week (about 1 small glass per day, mostly red wine), with the Italians close behind at 1.1 liters. Consumption still varies across the region — the French consume 50 percent more than Greeks, who consume less than drinkers in the U.S. and U.K., for example — but alcohol is still an important X factor. Countries with the highest combined intake of fermented dairy and alcohol have the lowest levels of obesity (about 10 to 25 percent), while those with the lowest intake have the highest levels of obesity (anywhere from 30 to over 45 percent). In other words, high countrywide intake of fermentation products is associated with roughly half the obesity rate of countries with low intake.

The way in which Mediterraneans imbibe is probably just as important as how much they drink: alcohol is typically red wine and is more regular and moderate than in the U.S. and western European countries. Even though their overall intake is higher (about 10 percent of total daily calories), they binge-drink less, and alcohol is paired with a meal.* They also consume substantial amounts of fermentable carbs from fruits, vegetables, beans, legumes, grains, and dairy, and their pasta has digestion-resistant starch, which is another source of X factor fuels produced by the microbiome.

Mindspan Elite who can't digest lactose (almost all Japanese and most Mediterranean Europeans) get up to 30 percent of their daily calories from fermented products such as alcohol, fiber, and resistant starches from vegetables, fruits, and grains as well as milk and yogurt. This is about double the value for the U.S. or U.K.

* The Japanese drink much less alcohol than most Mediterraneans, but their diets are rich in other nonalcoholic fermented foods and fish.

If you don't drink alcohol, however, there's no need to start; there are plenty of other ways to make sure you get X factors into your diet. Ironically, the refined carbs vilified in our culture as simply empty calories are, for the Mindspan Elite, primary food for the production of X factors by the microbiome. The overall diets, typical leanness, and record longevity and mindspans of the Mindspan Elite provide strong evidence that X factors are among the most powerful regulators of hunger and contributors to overall health.

■ ■ ■ ■

PART 3
IN CONTROL WITH THE
MINDSPAN DIET

YOUR ACTION PLAN, MEALS,
AND RECIPES

■ ■ ■ ■

You've digested a lot over the last nine chapters. You now know the meaning of mindspan, and you have become aware that environments are at least as important as genes in shaping traits, and that our needs change dramatically as we get older. We reviewed the commonalities of Mindspan Elite traditional diets. You discovered the dangers lurking in everyday foods, and how this problem becomes magnified as you age. Perhaps most important, you discovered the most healthful sources of carbs, fat, and protein, and what foods to avoid. Now comes the really rewarding and fun part: how to implement the Mindspan Diet in your own life. I'll give you a list of household pantry staples you should stock up on, practical advice on incorporating healthful Mindspan eating, and of course, plenty of recipes based on the favorite foods of the Mindspan Elite!

10.
THE MINDSPAN DIET
IN ACTION

Furious activity is no substitute for
understanding.
— H. H. Williams

When I started my journey to eat healthfully,
I thought it would be easy because I knew
who to emulate: the people with the greatest
mental and overall longevity in the world. I
compiled a short mental list of Mindspan
Elite, starting with the two populations
widely recognized for their spectacular
health, long lives, and world-leading mindspans: the Japanese and the Mediterraneans.

However, as recounted in the first pages of
this book, my first attempt at emulating these
Mindspan Elite eating habits went poorly. I
did most things according to my superficial
understanding at the time. Only when I dug
deeper did I discover that many olive oils in
the United States are not pure, and that even

those approved as 100 percent pure extra virgin, there are important differences. Some are much closer to authentic Mediterranean olive oils. In short, look for ones that are cold-pressed, and the more opaque and dark green they are, the better.

As I upped my dark chocolate and red wine, I got more headaches, and it took some trial and error to learn which types and brands I can eat safely. I was also eating far too much milk and yogurt. Since I am able to digest lactose, I wasn't benefiting from lactose as a fiber; instead, I was toxifying myself by absorbing dangerous amounts of galactose. Along with this off-limits dairy, I ate cheese and butter to excess, which raised my total and LDL cholesterol above the ideal range. This wouldn't have been so bad, but I had yet to fully comprehend the dangers of iron.

Eventually I discovered that there are significant differences between pastas and breads produced in Mindspan Elite regions of the Mediterranean and those in the United States — even those breads that appear to be artisanal or rustic. There are multiple small ones, like the use of a starter culture or the semolina flour content, but the main difference is iron enrichment. None of the Mindspan Elite Mediterranean regions produce pasta, bread, rice, or other grain products enriched with iron. Like many people in the United States and other developed countries who think they are eating authentic Mediterranean, I was poisoning myself with supplemental iron. Now I have traded most of my butter for high-quality olive oils produced in Mindspan Elite countries. Because of lactose, I never drink milk or eat yogurt, but I enjoy moderate amounts of hard cheeses because they are essentially lactose-free. I eat even more pasta and rice but carefully avoid iron-enriched grain products. And I make most of my own bread. Typically, organic flours, pasta, and breads do not have added iron, so first I look for organic; then I check the ingredients to make sure there is no added iron. I finally feel good and my cholesterol and other biomarkers are in the ideal range.

As you introduce key changes to your diet and lifestyle, aim high! Don't imagine that the average mindspan of the Mindspan Elite is the best you can achieve. I believe even the Japanese and Mediterranean averages could be better if they lowered their intake of iron. Many dietary and other environmental factors contribute small amounts to mindspan, but iron is clearly the single most important factor.

AN ENRICHING EXPERIENCE

The deeper I dug along many rich veins of information about Alzheimer's disease and other dementias, the more I found iron. All the evidence about iron makes sense once we apply our two key rules: GENES + ENVIRONMENT = TRAIT, and the AP rule. The latter (see page 88) tells us that actions of genes that are beneficial for reproduction in early life can harm us in the post-reproductive phase of life. The same is true for environmental factors (such as dietary iron), because they interact with genes (like APP) to establish a trait, like good cognitive function — or on the flip side, Alzheimer's disease.

THE ANTI-IRON AGE

Iron is a critical nutrient for proper functioning of the body and mind, but I can't emphasize enough that most adults in developed countries get far too much of it. Japanese women have the lowest iron levels in the developed world, the longest lives, and low rates of Alzheimer's disease. But like women in other countries, their body iron stores increase after menopause, so, by limiting iron, even they should be able to reduce their risk of Alzheimer's disease and live even longer.

The most recent research indicates that Alzheimer's disease is a close second to cancer as a cause of death in developed nations. Excess iron contributes to cancer and other leading causes of death. Therefore, as developed nations begin to understand and control these large excesses of dietary iron, typical longevity and mindspan will continue to grow.

I am still surprised by some of the truths I uncovered in my research. I am amazed that white rice and pasta are so frequently derided, despite being the dietary bedrock of cultures with the greatest longevity records in human history. But this is understandable once you realize that refined carbs in countries where most biomedical research is done have been engineered into killers. You can't physically *see* the difference between non-enriched and iron-enriched rice, wheat, or corn, but the latter not only contain excessive amounts of absorbable iron but are engineered to be the fastest carbs in the West. (FYI: The United States is the only country in the world that enriches all three with iron.) Most of the research on the dangers of refined carbs has been done on people who eat

251

these superfast, iron-loaded carbs. Is it any surprise, then, that folks who eat them get sick?

THE REAL, SIMPLE MINDSPAN DIET

My own fumbling, research, and tinkering to arrive at the Mindspan Diet is your great good fortune. In fact, despite the complexity of some of the underlying science, the plan itself is simple. Below is a dietary top ten list of critical items for reaching maximum mindspan. This list is followed by five other important lifestyle factors to boost mindspan. Some of these weren't covered in detail in the body of the book, like meditation, sleep, and exercise, but they work together with the dietary improvements to benefit all areas of your life. I have also included a Mindspan Diet cheat sheet of these ten recommendations at the end of the book — tear them out and tape them to your fridge or kitchen cabinet!

1. Limit iron. If you are an adult man or a woman past the age of menopause, you should measure your body iron stores and recalibrate your iron intake. The Daily Value of iron listed on nutrition labels is calibrated for male teens and menstruating women. If you

252

don't fall in either of these categories, you need to divide the Daily Value by 4. Be especially wary of breakfast cereals. You should watch your iron and ferritin levels, and try to keep them at the low end of normal (have them tested at least annually; see appendix B for more information). Unless your test results indicate you are iron-deficient anemic or you have noticeable symptoms, you should not take iron supplements. If you drink tap water and have older metal supply pipes, let the water run until clean and cold, and then fill clean bottles for immediate use and storage. If you now cook in cast-iron cookware, stop. Also consider donating blood.

2. Limit red meat. Red meat is the primary dietary source of bioavailable iron (heme iron), and is high in the amino acid methionine. Heme iron synergistically promotes absorption of non-heme iron. The best nutrition for mental longevity is a mostly vegetarian diet, with little or no red meat. Preferred primary protein sources are, in descending order, grains, legumes, and vegetables > fish > eggs and cheese > poultry > red meat.

3. Slow down. Japanese and Mediterranean foods and eating styles ease the body into digestion. Start a meal with X factors and a low glycemic index soup and salad. Place healthful carbs in the second half of the meal.

4. Eat good carbs and good fats. Mindspan champs of the world eat lots of healthful carbs. Get most of your carbs from vegetables and LIGIR (low iron and glycemic index refined) carbs, pasta, white rice (preferably parboiled or converted), and sourdough bread. Following point 1 above, be very wary of iron enrichment of grain products. Mindspan Elite also eat a good balance of omega-3 and omega-6 fats. Good carbs should be about 45 to 60 percent of the diet, and good fats about 25 to 40 percent. If you have metabolic syndrome or prediabetes, limit iron even more strictly and eat on the higher end of this fat range until your blood glucose and insulin normalize. With low body iron stores, you'll greatly reduce your risk of diabetes, and you won't have to fear saturated fats and PUFAs — but limit animal saturated fats if your LDL is higher than 110 mg/dL.

5. Ditch the milk (if you can digest lactose). Do not consume milk and minimize ice cream, yogurt, cottage cheese, and other milk products that contain substantial amounts of lactose (milk sugar). Cheese, cream, sour cream, butter, and other dairy products with trace amounts of lactose are fine in moderation for most people. It might sound counterintuitive, but only consume lactose if you cannot digest it, which allows it to be metabolized by microbes in the gut.

6. Feed your brain. Mindspan leaders of the world eat more fish and seafood than most others, but most don't overdo it. Japanese eat a fair amount of fish, but 95 percent eat fish once or less a day. They especially avoid eating large quantities in a single meal, which is more typical among the Mindspan Risk. Eat a few small to moderate servings of fish a week. I eat a bite-size piece of pickled herring about once a day on average, and I also eat a dish with sardines or anchovies at least once a week. These kinds of smaller fish typically have low levels of mercury, and they are favorites among the Mindspan Elite. If you are vegetarian or

vegan, take a DHA and EPA supplement made from algae.

7. Drink coffee, tea, or red wine *with meals*. Extreme mindspan is found in various cultures around the world, and they all drink coffee, tea, and/or red wine with meals. These beverages inhibit the absorption of iron (and other minerals, so don't overdo it). Relative to tea, coffee, cocoa, and other common inhibitors, red wine is a weak inhibitor of iron absorption. But other forms of alcohol actually promote iron absorption, so it is a better choice overall. Its higher inhibitory activity explains why it is more beneficial for lifespan and mindspan than other types of alcohol.

8. Drink alcohol in moderation. If you drink alcohol, limit yourself to two drinks a day (less if you are small) and spread out your drinking. Red wine is best; drink it slowly with meals. If you don't drink, don't start.

9. Limit sugar. Cut back on table sugar, and when choosing between a sweet fruit and a non-sweet one (squash, tomato, cucumber, bell pepper, etc.), choose the latter. The problem isn't the carbs; it is fructose, a primary in-

gredient in table sugar and fruits.

10. **Take B and D vitamins.** Take a B vitamin supplement (containing at least folic acid or folate, B6, B12, and niacin) and a vitamin D supplement, at least occasionally. Take vitamin D more often if you spend most of your days indoors. Unless you are under the care of an accredited healthcare provider treating you for a deficiency detected by testing, there is no reason to take megadoses of these or any other supplement. Look for a high-quality supplement that provides 100 percent of the Percent Daily Value. The only purpose of a B complex that provides thousands of percent of B vitamins is to make colorful urine.

Other important factors:

11. **Quiet your mind.** Take at least a few minutes during your day to do this. Another term for this is meditation, which has clear benefits for body and mind. There is much speculation about why this is good for you and your brain, but the simple answer is that we don't really know why, we just know that study after study shows

benefits.

12. Move! Mindspan Elite are active people. Many have been farmers or shepherds or have otherwise been active for most of their lives. And longer telomeres are associated with multiple different kinds of routine exercise. The lesson? Don't sit immobile for hours on end. Exercise routinely in moderation, but stay active. Set a goal to exercise vigorously two to four days a week. Get a rest day in between exercise days. Sweat is an effective way to reduce body iron stores, and it is the only known natural approach to accelerate this process.

13. Get enough sleep. The Mediterraneans have it right with their lengthy midafternoon siestas. Good and sufficient sleep is essential for a long life and for proper mental functioning. Naps are great if you can manage to get them. Studies have found an association between short sleep duration (less than five hours a night) and both higher mortality and shorter telomere length (older biological age). Make sure that you get between six and a half hours and eight hours a night, and that you feel rested.

14. Stay sharp. Many research studies show that learning new, interesting, and challenging information is key to staying mentally sharp by building what scientists call cognitive reserve.
15. Reduce inflammation. If you have a choice of painkillers, consider an NSAID, such as aspirin or ibuprofen. Consult your doctor about these medicines, as they have clear risks of bleeding and other side effects.

FOODS TO EAT AT MANY OR MOST MEALS

- Vegetables
- Leafy greens and herbs such as leaf lettuce, chicory, kale, borage, seaweed, kelp, spinach, mint, chervil, cilantro, parsley, basil, oregano, thyme, etc.
- Legumes
- LIGIR carbs: pasta or high-amylose white rice (preferably parboiled or converted) boiled or steamed, stored in your fridge, and then reheated for immediate use
- Vinegar and other fermented foods
- Rustic, dense, and chewy sourdough breads
- Coffee or tea (caffeinated or herbal, but

not decaf tea) *with meals*
- Olive oil and nuts

FOODS TO EAT IN MODERATION

- Fish and other seafood. Try to get at least 2 percent of your calories from fish and seafood. Emphasize smaller, fattier fish, low in mercury. Examples are herring, sardines, and anchovies.
- Rustic, dense, and chewy breads (non-sourdough)
- Fruits; emphasize non-sweet ones such as tomatoes
- Cheese and other non-lactose-containing dairy
- Eggs
- Canola oil
- If you are *unable to digest lactose,* you can consume moderate amounts of liquid milk and other dairy foods that contain liquid milk and milk sugar (lactose, sweetened condensed milk).

FOODS TO EAT LESS

- Poultry and other sources of animal protein
- Added sugar, sugary beverages, and other sources of large and concentrated quantities of sugar

Foods to Avoid

- Red meat (beef, lamb, pork, etc.). Reduce dramatically or eliminate altogether. One standout commonality of all Mindspan Elite is that meat plays a small role in their traditional cuisines.
- If you are *able to digest lactose,* avoid liquid milk and other dairy foods that contain liquid milk and milk sugar (lactose, sweetened condensed milk).
- High glycemic index carbs (most commercial white and whole wheat breads), especially in the absence of counteracting X factors
- Deep-fried foods, especially those fried in an unknown oil when eating out

Foods for Men and Nonmenstruating Women *Never* to Consume

- Iron-enriched foods. Especially avoid super-enriched breakfast cereals (both hot and cold). Also avoid enriched white flour, crackers, commercial white breads, white rice, most grits and farina, pizza, pasta, tortillas, muffins, cookies, cakes and cake mixes, and the list goes on and on. Look for the words "enriched," "iron," "ferrous," and "ferric." The most confusing of all is "reduced iron." This does not indicate less iron; it is a form of iron that is added to food.

These general guidelines are incorporated into the recipes in chapter 12.

THE FOODS AND MEALS

The foods and recipes that form the core of the Mindspan Diet are disproportionately Mediterranean, with a special focus on cuisines of the French and Italian Rivieras. Key ingredients for these cuisines are readily available, and Italian food is easy to prepare and is already a favorite food style in the United States and many other countries. Other dishes are inspired by foods from other traditional Mindspan Elite cuisines, including those of Japan, Sardinia, Greece, Spain, and Costa Rica.

There are also traditional Japanese and other Asian recipes, but many Japanese ingredients are difficult to find and Japanese dishes are more difficult to make than those from the Rivieras. But don't be concerned about this. Recall that Okinawan food is similar to Chinese food, but it is eaten in a Japanese style. So the key to maximizing mindspan is not Japanese food per se, but the overall nature of the food and the way it is eaten (slowly, starting with X factors and then carbs). This is shown clearly by the commonalities of and differences between Japanese and other Mindspan Elite cuisines. If you can't find seaweed or kelp or work it into a meal, then use leaf lettuce, basil, borage, spinach, thyme, sage, kale, parsley, cilantro, or one of many other excellent greens or herbs. And remember, tea and coffee serve a similar nutritional purpose.

Traditional Okinawan cuisine and outstanding longevity and mindspans teach us an important lesson. They show us that Chinese or other Asian foods made of the right ingredients, and prepared and eaten appropriately, produce longevity results equivalent to those of Japanese cuisine. The same is true for other foods, but there are invariant essentials: minimal red meat; initial soups and appetizers featuring X factor foods (fermented and fermentable); LIGIR carbs, usually in the form of pasta or white rice; and so on. The Chinese cuisine that most informs Okinawan cuisine is Fujian. Fujian foods have been described as light but still flavorful, highlighting rather than masking flavors of the ingredients. Fujian cuisine is also known for soup at most meals. It's a lot like Japanese, but easier to cook.

Cuisines of the Mediterranean Rivieras are fattier than those of Japan and Okinawa, but they have lower overall fat and animal fat content than other French and Mediterranean cuisines. One thing we've all heard about Mediterraneans is true of Rivierans: most of the added fat in their food is olive oil. When I first began eating Mediterranean style for my health, I thought the mindspan leaders of the French Riviera ate plenty of butter and cream, like the other French. They don't. Jacques Médecin's classic book on traditional Niçoise cuisine shows that very clearly. Recipe after recipe features copious quantities of olive oil, with only occasional butter or cream and even less milk. Recipe books of traditional Ligurian cuisine feature even less butter and cream and little or no milk. The Mindspan Diet Mediterranean-style recipes are based on these traditional cuisines, together with features they share in common with Japan, but in some meals with a nod to the Japanese preference for slightly lower-fat meals. This is the core of the Mindspan Diet recipes and meals.

Turn the page — and *buon appetito*!

11.
STOCKING UP

Reading through *The Mindspan Diet*, you might have been wondering if the recipes would require mostly exotic ingredients or mysterious cooking gear and techniques. Well, good news: the answer on all counts is no! All recipes can be prepared with minimal and standard equipment and techniques. You're probably already very familiar with most of the ingredients required for the Mindspan Diet recipes; most are basic kitchen staples. Just keep in mind that the selected ingredients are important for maximizing mindspan (sorry, no substitutes)! Here's what you need to get started:

Water. Always use good water for everything, including making pasta, rice, and bread. Run the tap until the water is as cold as it will get, and then fill several large storage bottles. Since indoor plumbing (especially older plumbing) is often made of iron and copper piping, it's worth installing an iron removal filter. Automatic ice makers can also be a problem because they make ice from water standing in pipes. Instead, make ice in trays with good water.

Herbs and spices. Use fresh herbs when possible. Rosemary, basil, and sage in particular take on a different flavor when dried, and rosemary becomes difficult to re-hydrate. Other herbs to have on hand are thyme, bay leaves, and marjoram or oregano (these last two are related; oregano is slightly stronger). Essential spices are black pepper, crushed red pepper flakes, turmeric or curry powder, granular garlic powder (try to use fresh when possible; don't get the fine pow-der — it clumps), and, of course, salt.

GRAINS

Organic grains. You should opt for them whenever possible, since they don't have added iron, unlike most grain products in the United States and many other countries. The list includes bread, flour, pasta, torti-llas, crackers, breakfast cereals, and just about every other grain product. You still need to read nutrition labels: be especially careful of the phrase "reduced iron." This is a type of iron additive.

Non-enriched flour. Unless semolina flour, whole wheat flour, or other flour is specified, use white, unbleached, non-enriched flour. Make absolutely sure the flour you are using is not enriched with iron.

Pasta. This must be prepped the right way. Pasta is so versatile that it can be used as a main course or side dish. It can be served as the base for a deeply flavorful sauce, or it can be eaten with just a sprinkling of herbs and a bit of olive oil or butter. Just follow the lead of many traditional Mediterranean Riviera cuisines to make this dish as flavorful — and healthful — as possible. As with other grain products, look for organic varieties to avoid iron enrichment, which is nearly ubiquitous in the United States and many other countries.

- Always cook pasta only until it is al dente (firm).
- Consider using the dry varieties instead of fresh pasta, a standard in Liguria and in other regions of Mediterranean Mindspan Elite. Dry pasta is also very convenient, and if it's good quality, it tastes wonderful. (For these reasons, most of the pasta recipes are for sauces alone.)

- Watch portion size! About 7 ounces (200 grams) of pasta per person is appropriate for a main course. Adjust the amounts for smaller and larger people, or if you want to lose weight.

Low to moderate GI white rice. Just make absolutely sure the rice you are using is not enriched with iron (some of your safest bets are imported Japanese, Indian, Brazilian, and Thai rices). You'll have to do some sleuthing to make sure, by reading the nutrition label. The typical range of iron in non-enriched rice is 0 to 2 percent of the Daily Value in about 150 calories, compared to iron-enriched rice, which tends to have a value of 6 to 8 percent. Making surplus rice and pasta to store in the fridge is not only very convenient but also increases the content of digestion-resistant starch. See the section on Rice, Pasta, and Barley for directions on how to make the best ready rice and pasta.

THE BEST RICE AND PASTA CHOICES

The total number of rice varieties is so large nobody knows for certain how many there are, but a commonly quoted figure is 40,000. Therefore rice can vary a lot in certain properties, aside from flavor and texture. Two of the most important for your health are glycemic index (GI) and amylose content (AC); the latter is the key to the formation of digestion-resistant starch (RS). RS content depends on both amylose content and preparation method.

In general, choose rice and pasta with low GI values, although the GI of the overall meal is more important. Certain acceptable and specialty carb choices depend on your level of activity and the other foods in a meal. For example, Japonica rice in Japan typically has only medium amounts of amylose, but when it is prepared properly and eaten within the right context, the GI can be low. Use the table on the next page as a general guide to choosing the best types of rice and pasta. A GI below 55 is low (best); 55 to 75 is medium (acceptable); above 75 is high; 100 and above is akin to an injection of glucose directly into your bloodstream. I prefer a mix of about 1/2 to 2/3 long-grain rice (generally parboiled) and 1/3 to 1/2 Japonica rice. This results in a GI in the low to mid-40s.

Food	GI	AC%*
Best choices		
Parboiled (a.k.a. converted) long-grain white rice	30–50	22–28%
Basmati white rice	50–65	22–26%
Parboiled medium-amylose rice **(Thai jasmine)**	50–60	15–18%
long-grain Brown rice	40–50	22–26%
Wheat pasta **(semolina, not whole wheat)**	45–60	25–30%
Couscous **(semolina, not whole wheat)**	60–70	25–30%
Acceptable choices		
Japonica white rice **(Japan, e.g., Koshihikari)**	50–75	15–18%

* Relative AC (amylose content) percentages shown here are as typically reported.

Japonica brown rice	50–70	15–18%
Calrose brown rice **(U.S. Japonica)**	75–85	14–17%
Calrose white rice **(U.S. Japonica)**	82–86	14–17%

Specialty uses

Jasmine white rice	70–110	13–18%
Parboiled waxy (glutinous) rice	70–90	0–2%
Waxy (glutinous) rice	75–100	0–2%
Brown rice pasta	80–90	variable %

Barley. Like rice, barley is versatile and flavorful. Even though pearled barley is refined, like white rice, it has a lot more fiber. Much of the barley fiber is distributed throughout the starchy endosperm, whereas most rice fiber is in the outer bran and germ that are removed in the production of white rice. This is a primary reason barley has a lower glycemic index than most rice — and just about all other grains. Pearled barley typically takes at least 40 minutes to cook, but quick-cook varieties take just 10 to 15 minutes. Immediately after you purchase the barley, open the container and make sure it doesn't smell rancid. If it does, return it to the store. I prepare barley just as I do rice (the Japanese way): I rinse it with several changes of clean water prior to cooking.

Oats. Oats have a high content of polyunsaturated fatty acids (PUFAs) for a grain, and rolled or quick-cook oats can become rancid quickly. Always give oats the sniff test, just as with barley. Oats are also high in iron, but the majority is not bioavailable and shouldn't be absorbed. For these reasons, I suggest you eat a serving at most two or three times a week, and mix your oats with a majority of rice, which is a low PUFA grain. Even better, replace your oatmeal with pearled barley, or a barley and rice mix.

Home-baked bread. Most rustic and artisan breads are made with iron-enriched flour and should be avoided. Unfortunately, traditional rustic breads made with non-enriched white flour are very hard to find. I make my own breads, and I've provided some basic bread recipes so that you can do the same (it's not as daunting as it seems!). I also make my own pickled vegetables. They are so good I prefer them to any commercial alternative. Recipes for both can be found in the Homemade Staples section.

Bread machines make baking bread almost automatic, but the results often lack the denser, chewier texture of slowly digested breads. This is partly due to the use of yeast rather than starter, the amount of gluten, and the type of flour. To make a denser, chewier bread, use starter, added gluten, and/or some semolina flour. The recipes tell you how to do this. Also add some cooked vegetables, like pumpkin, which adds to the texture and nutritional value.

If you don't fancy making your own bread and prefer to ask your local baker to make breads for you, be careful. Every one of the many so-called artisanal bakeries I've ever visited in the United States uses iron-enriched flour, so be sure to check. If you'd like to coax your baker into making truly traditional bread without added iron, here's a strategy I recommend: purchase some non-enriched flour and give him or her a gift of the flour and this book, with an explanation about the absence of added iron in traditional Mediterranean baked goods.

As discussed earlier in the book, I don't agree with people going on a gluten-free diet unless they have an actual diagnosis of celiac disease. If you're considering it for health reasons, I would suggest keeping an open mind and giving the Mindspan Diet a chance. I predict after a couple of weeks of enjoying its wide array of foods — including those that contain gluten — your gut will be happier, and you'll be thinking and feeling better. If you eat wheat free of added iron and still have a problem, get tested for celiac disease.

If you must go gluten-free, then there are many healthy and delicious foods that are a natural part of the Mindspan Diet, such as beans; seeds and nuts; animal proteins such as eggs, meat, fish, and poultry; fruits and vegetables; and rice. You can pair any gluten-free pasta with one of the many sauces found in this recipe section.

X FACTOR AND RELATED FOODS

Vinegars. A variety of flavorful vinegars are available at many grocers. White vinegar works fine for most recipes, but try red wine, rice, apple cider, pear-infused, and authentic balsamic vinegar (not the typical caramel-colored white vinegar).

Soy sauce. Purchase and use soy sauce made of fermented soybeans. Avoid synthetic or imitation soy sauce made with hydrolyzed protein and caramel color.

Milk, dairy, and lactose. If your inability to digest lactose has been confirmed by a genetic test, feel free to consume moderate amounts of milk and lactose-containing foods — for example, milk in your tea or coffee. Sweetened condensed milk is almost pure lactose. Use it as a sweetener and to feed your microbiome for X factors. If you are able to digest lactose, avoid milk and lactose, and see the next section on beans for alternative food sources for your microbiome. Irrespective of your lactose status, feel free to consume moderate amounts of butter, sour cream (try reduced-fat), heavy cream, and hard cheeses; all are essentially lactose-free.

OILS AND NUTS
Canola oil. Canola oil is the primary oil in the Japanese diet. I follow their example and use canola oil for low-temperature sautéing and a variety of other uses, including some salad dressings. Always purchase cold-

pressed canola oil in amounts you can use in two months or less, and keep it in the refrigerator.

Olive oil. There is a wide range of olive oils available on the market, made from many different kinds of olives. I use olive oil from Italy, Greece, Spain (or a mixture of these), or California. The European oils have proven health benefits. For sautéing, frying, and high temperature roasting, I use light olive oil, which smokes and burns at a higher temperature than extra virgin olive oil. However, for most recipes, I use cold-pressed extra virgin olive oil.

Nuts. Top choices are macadamia nuts, pecans, walnuts, and almonds. Roasted soybeans and peanuts aren't nuts, but they're nutlike and make good snacks. Nuts have substantial PUFAs, so give them a sniff test when you first purchase them — especially the pecans and walnuts, which go rancid quickly.

PROTEINS
Sardines, anchovies, and pickled herring. Sardines and anchovies are small fish, and herring are only a bit larger (small herring are often sold as sardines), placing them

lower on the mercury accumulation food chain than larger fish, such as tuna. All are rich in the very long chain omega-3 fats, DHA and EPA. All three can be purchased fresh, but canned sardines and anchovies and jarred pickled herring are extremely convenient. All three make great snacks, although a small amount of salty anchovy goes a long way.

Beans. I always purchase salt-free canned beans. They are far more convenient and cook much more quickly than dried or fresh beans. There are two reasons I get salt-free beans: it allows me to use less salt, and I can use the thick liquid in the can. This liquid is rich in fructooligosaccharides, perfect fuel for the microbiome. Either don't rinse the beans and use the liquid along with the beans in a recipe or drain part or all of the liquid into a container and use it in recipes as desired. Careful, this is fairly powerful stuff, and too much can cause bloating and gas.

Tofu. Many kinds of tofu are available. For soups and to use as egg replacements (about 3 ounces of tofu per egg), use soft or silken tofu. For stir-fry dishes, try firmer tofu. To store tofu, drain, remove from the package, place in a container with a secure lid, rinse with clean water, add water to about halfway up the tofu block, fasten the lid securely, and refrigerate.

THINKING ABOUT MEALS — THE BIG PICTURE

Meals of the Mindspan Diet are based upon the Japanese tradition of the interchangeability of breakfast, lunch, and dinner foods. Still, most of us have grown accustomed to certain kinds of foods for different meals, so special breakfast food recipes are provided.

Pre-Breakfast and Breakfast

Start the day right with X factors, fermented foods that help you achieve maximum mindspan, such as miso or pickled herring.

Lunch and Dinner

Keep on track and end the day right with X factors such as bread, vinegar, cheese, yogurt, soy sauce, rice vinegar, or fermented vegetables (pickles). Remember, X factors and foods rich in fermentable fibers and digestion-resistant starches provide a second-meal effect that carries over into the next day, getting your body into a healthy and comfortable groove.

12.
MINDSPAN RECIPES

Japanese and Mediterranean folk have dietary advantages that many of us don't have, but that are easy to get. Their meals typically come slowly in a series of courses, setting the stage for healthy maintenance of blood sugar. The world-leading longevity and mindspans of mainland Japanese and Okinawan people show that their traditional ways work. But despite both populations being Japanese, their cuisines are very different. Still, there are a few key similarities. One is that breakfast, lunch, and dinner are preceded by soup, and another is that breakfast consists of the same foods as those that are eaten at lunch and dinner.

The meals in the Mindspan Diet follow this basic orderliness. Every meal begins with a pre-meal. Even if we are unused to these Japanese-inspired traditions or don't eat the exact foods they do, the rest of us can mimic and even improve upon these advantages

with meal management. The most important step in this process is to, like the Japanese, prepare your body to manage the
coming meal's food, and to establish within
your physiology a robust second-meal effect
that carries over to every subsequent meal.

Recall that the Mindspan Elite minimize
the glycemic index of their foods by the use
of salt and fermented foods like vinegar, but
high salt is a health risk and has no second-
meal effect. I suggest you use a bit less salt
and a bit more vinegar. Many recipes in this
book don't specify an amount of salt, but
you should always keep in mind this simple
rule. The recipes that do specify salt amount
follow the formula.

To maximize the second-meal effect, you
should precede every meal with a small pre-
lude dish containing some X factors, like
miso (fermented soy) and vinegar. It is beneficial to do this with all meals, but at the
first meal of the day, your body has experienced its longest fasting state of the daily
cycle. You are "breaking the fast," and this is
the way to do it right.

PRE-BREAKFAST

Breaking the overnight fast starts with what I call pre-breakfast. This is the most important pre-meal of all, since it follows the longest fasting period of the day. Your body needs to ease into daily meals and not be assaulted by a massive surge of fat or sugar into the bloodstream.

I usually make about one cup of broth, with about half a teaspoon of concentrated miso paste, a bit of dashi, and a teaspoon of vinegar. A simpler version for most people is to use the brine (and fish, if desired) from a jar of pickled herring instead of the dashi and vinegar. For variation, I season it with black pepper, scallions, chives, garlic, or another herb or spice, and sometimes I'll add mushrooms, and I often accompany the miso with one or two small pieces of pickled herring or quail eggs (these can be purchased canned in some supermarkets), or some other Japanese treat. Occasionally I combine my pre-breakfast soup with my green tea by simply mixing some green tea flakes into my soup. Not only does this taste good but it reduces the complexity of the morning routine when you are in a rush. I have my pre-breakfast while I'm making breakfast.

Prior to various meals of the day, I sometimes eat a homemade pickled cucumber. Commercially available pickles work too, but they aren't as good and I replace about half of the overly salty brine with homemade brine containing less salt and more vinegar and other spices. (The recipe for homemade pickling brine is in the Homemade Staples section.)

It isn't difficult to like these savory foods for lunch or dinner, but some people can't get used to the idea of having them for breakfast. Try them first thing in the morning, but if you simply can't get used to the Japanese-style versions, find a broth you like and prepare about a cup with about a teaspoon of vinegar. You can use that as a pre-breakfast, then eat your breakfast more slowly. If you are always pressed for time in the morning, try having pre-breakfast before you shower and dress, then eat breakfast.

Pre-Breakfast Miso Soup

This flavorful pre-meal soup is my standard, and its flavor can be altered with many tasty additions, including tofu, scallions and other onions, vegetables, and a wide variety of mushrooms. A small amount of vinegar establishes a strong second-meal effect and intensifies the flavor, without the high salt content of traditional miso soup. Miso can be difficult to find, and dashi is even tougher. One teaspoon of soy sauce can substitute for miso in a pinch, and try replacing the dashi with water and 1 tablespoon of brine from a jar of pickled herring, plus one or two small herring pieces.

Servings: 1

1 cup dashi or kombu dashi (see recipes on pp. 331 and 330) or water
1 teaspoon vinegar
1/2 to 1 tablespoon miso paste (depending on salt content and flavor desired)

1. Pour the dashi, kombu dashi, or water and the vinegar in a saucepan and heat on high until about to boil. Then reduce heat and simmer on medium low. Add the miso and stir vigorously until all the miso is dissolved. This can also be prepared in a micro-wave oven.

2. Serve in a mug or bowl with a soupspoon.

OPTIONAL: Try replacing the dashi with water and 1 tablespoon brine from a jar of pickled herring, plus one or two herring pieces. As you stir the miso into the boiling water, the herring will disintegrate, making a rich herring broth. Try adding tofu; shiitake, shimeji, or enoki mushrooms; and scallions or chives, or a bit of sardine or anchovy. Stir in some green tea flakes for a healthful and simple pre-breakfast combo soup and tea.

Breakfast

The recipes in this section will appeal to Western palates, but they can be eaten at any meal of the day. Likewise, any of the recipes in the other sections can be eaten for breakfast. For example, try the Okinawan egg and tofu-based stir-fry (chanpuru) dishes.

Even though most of these breakfast recipes are quick to make, try to eat them slowly or in stages so that you don't overeat, and always precede them with a pre-breakfast. As with all meals, drink green or black tea or regular or decaffeinated coffee with your meal. As discussed in chapter 11, feel free to use milk or other lactose-containing dairy in your tea or coffee — but only if a genetic test confirms that you are unable to digest lactose. If you are able to digest it, find a lactose-free alternative like heavy cream, or coconut or soy creamer.

COSTA RICAN GALLO PINTO

Gallo pinto can be made in large batches (lasting a few days), which can be stored in the refrigerator, reheated as needed, and eaten at any meal. Costa Ricans have a special salsa, Salsa Lizano, that they put on their gallo pinto, but Blue Zones author Dan Buettner writes that even to Costa Ricans, Worcestershire sauce is an acceptable substitute. For a tasty East meets West variant, use soy sauce instead of salt.

Servings: 1

1 teaspoon olive or canola oil
1/2 cup water
1/2 to 2/3 cup beans (black, pinto, kidney, etc.)
1 teaspoon vinegar
1/4 teaspoon cumin
Black pepper to taste
1 small garlic clove, minced (optional)
1 to 1 1/2 cups precooked rice
Squeeze of lime juice
Salt or soy sauce to taste

In a medium saucepan, cook for 5 minutes on medium heat the oil, water, beans, vinegar, cumin, pepper, and garlic, if desired. Reduce the heat to low, add the rice, and heat until very warm but not boiling (to preserve the resistant starch content of the rice). Season with lime juice, salt or soy sauce, and pepper.

OPTIONAL: Top with salsa, hot sauce, avocado slices, and/or a bit of sour cream. Try adding 1/3 cup diced cooked vegetables (onion, bell pepper, zucchini, etc.). Also try topping with freshly chopped cilantro.

QUICK BARLEY AND RICE

Like rice, barley is incredibly versatile and great at any meal, including breakfast. They work well together, too — the result being a dish with more Asian flair.

Servings: 1

1/3 cup quick-cook pearled barley
1 to 3 teaspoons vinegar
2 teaspoons sugar (optional)
2/3 cup precooked rice
Salt to taste

Place barley into a 2-cup measuring cup and rinse a few minutes with several changes of water. Add water to the barley, up to the 1 1/4-cup level. Add vinegar, and sugar, if desired. Pour the water and barley into a small saucepan, stir, and cook for 10 to 12 minutes over medium heat. Mix the cooked barley with the precooked rice and heat for an additional minute. Cover and remove from heat, then let stand 3 minutes. Season with salt.

OPTIONAL: For a rich custardy flavor, try stirring an egg into the barley and water prior to cooking.

X Factor Oatmeal and Rice

I love oatmeal for breakfast, especially a hot bowl of it on a cold day. It also happens to be a favorite breakfast of Seventh-day Adventists, members of the Mindspan Elite by way of *National Geographic*'s Blue Zone status. But remember, don't eat a serving more than two to three times a week. Use low glycemic index old-fashioned oats and *never* use presweetened and iron-enriched single-serving packages of oatmeal! This recipe can be prepared in the microwave, but beware of boilover. This recipe contains a small amount of vinegar in the cooking water. Putting it into the water allows the vinegar to penetrate the oat grain, reducing the tart flavor. A little sugar nicely counters the tartness of the vinegar, creating a mild sweet-and-sour flavor.

Servings: 1

2/3 cup water
1 to 2 teaspoons vinegar
2 teaspoons sugar (optional)
1/4 cup old-fashioned oatmeal
1 cup precooked rice
Salt to taste

Add water, vinegar, sugar if desired, and oatmeal to a small saucepan, mix, and cook for 5 minutes on medium heat. Stir in the rice and continue heating. Cover, remove from heat, and let stand 3 minutes. Season with salt.

OPTIONAL: For a rich custardy flavor, try stirring an egg into the oatmeal and water prior to cooking. Try adding some cinnamon, apple, peach, or other fruit. If you feel like getting experimental with some prebiotics to fuel X factor production by your microbiome, stir in a bit of inulin or fructooligosaccharides. Try starting off with a small amount of inulin, or 1 tablespoon of liquid from a can of beans. The thick liquid in a salt-free can of beans is rich in fuel for your microbiome.

EGG CONGEE (RICE PORRIDGE)

Congee is a staple across Southeast Asia, commonly eaten by both mainland Japanese and Okinawans. Without the egg, the glycemic index can be too high, but cooking with the egg and vinegar brings the GI down into the acceptable range. Most people find that 1 teaspoon of vinegar adds no discernible flavor, so start with 1 teaspoon and then try increasing to 2 teaspoons. For a vegan option, instead of the egg you can use an equivalent amount or more of tofu, broken into small pieces. For maximum X factor impact, try the optional prebiotics (see below).

Servings: 1

2/3 cup water
1 teaspoon canola oil
1 cup precooked rice
1 large egg, beaten, or about 3 ounces tofu,
     preferably silken
1 to 2 teaspoons vinegar

1. Add water, oil, rice, egg or tofu, and vinegar to a medium saucepan over medium heat, and mix well. Turn the heat to low, cover, and cook for 10 minutes, stirring occasionally. (If you are in a hurry, you can

pulverize some of the rice with a fork, reducing the time it takes to get a porridge.) Use less water if you want a thicker porridge or more water for a thinner porridge, but too much water or overcooking will raise the GI unacceptably.

2. This congee is great as a savory or sweet dish. I prefer it savory, and eat it with a bit of salt and black pepper.

OPTIONAL: For variety in flavor and texture, and to mix a bit of Mediterranean with Asian for breakfast, you can mix your rice porridge with a bit of coarse semolina (farina) and sufficient water to hydrate it. Add 1/3 cup of fresh berries or fruit cut into 1/2-inch cubes. Try chunks of apple, peach, nectarine, plum, or apricot. Frozen berries also work well. Also feel free to top with some walnut, pecan, or other nut pieces. If you feel like getting experimental, try the prebiotic option described on page 291. Also feel free to stir in a teaspoon of psyllium husk and about 2 tablespoons of water. Any of these options will be beneficial for your microbiome and your X factors.

PUM-CRAN TOAST

Lightly toast a thick slice of pumpkin semolina bread (see recipe on p. 419) or high-quality organic sourdough bread from a local bakery, and drizzle with extra virgin olive oil.

OPTION FOR VEGANS: Spread with high-quality fruit jam or preserves.

OPTION FOR NONVEGANS: Spread with small amount of butter and high-quality fruit jam or preserves. Or add 1 scrambled or poached egg or a slice of cheese to your toast.

VEGGIE OMELET

Servings: 1

1/3 cup diced vegetables (bell pepper, zucchini, or both)
2 tablespoons diced onion
5 medium fresh white or brown mushrooms, sliced
1 teaspoon olive oil or high-oleic safflower oil
1 teaspoon butter
2 large eggs
1 ounce Cheddar, Monterey Jack, or other hard cheese

Sauté vegetables, onion, and mushrooms in oil and butter until all are tender, about 12 minutes; this time can be cut in half by pre-cooking the vegetables in a microwave for 2 to 3 minutes. Add eggs and cook until firm. Place cheese on top of the eggs and then fold in half, into a semicircle.

OPTIONAL: Layer with thin avocado slices or scallions. Top with hot sauce or salsa.

SOUTH OF THE BORDER
BREAKFAST BURRITO

The omelet on page 295 makes a great breakfast burrito filling. Instead of creating an omelet, simply stir in the eggs to cook and then use a spatula to fill a flour tortilla. Fold bottom end of tortilla up over filling about one inch and then roll in sides to form a nice burrito shape. Top with avocado, salsa, scallions, cilantro, a dollop of sour cream, and/or lime juice, and eat with a fork and knife. If you prefer to eat as a wrap, apply the toppings before folding tortilla.

SALADS AND STARTERS

ANTIPASTI/HORS D'OEUVRES

A plate of antipasti (Italy) or hors d'oeuvres (France) can be served to a party of many guests, but a few of these ingredients can be enjoyed before a meal on your own. Most of the foods in this list can be purchased ready to eat, challenging the notion of unhealthful premade foods. Watch the salt content, especially of the artichoke hearts, olives, mushrooms, cheeses, and meats, and heed the standard warning about iron in crackers and bread. Artichoke hearts in oil are best; those in brine typically have far too much salt to be eaten alone.

Servings: varies per number of people

Bell peppers
Mixed olives
Marinated mushrooms (jarred or canned)
Cheeses
Artichoke hearts (jarred or canned in oil)
Prosciutto and salami
Crackers and small disks of baguette
Cherry tomatoes
Sardines (canned)
Extra virgin olive oil for dipping
Olive oil vinaigrette (see recipe below)

1. Wash the peppers, cut away the stems, and remove the ribs and seeds. Slice into strips.

2. Arrange all ingredients on a cutting board or platter, along with a glass of wine or refreshing mint or jasmine green tea.

OPTIONAL: Try adding a bit of crushed or roasted garlic or crushed red pepper flakes to the dipping oil.

OPTIONAL: For a MediterAsian-style appetizer and presentation, serve peppers, tomatoes, sardines, thinly sliced carrot sticks, and blanched peapods or sugar snap peas with a dipping bowl of Japanese ginger dressing (see recipe on p. 302).

CLASSIC OLIVE OIL VINAIGRETTE

This classic vinaigrette and its simple variations go great with virtually any salad. Most vinegars will work fine, but red wine vinegar is the top choice.

Servings: 4

1/3 cup extra virgin olive oil
3 tablespoons red wine vinegar
1 teaspoon oregano
1 garlic clove, finely chopped or pressed
1/2 teaspoon salt
Black pepper to taste

1. Mix all ingredients together with a food processor or in bowl.
2. Serve over a mixed green salad or with raw vegetables.

OPTIONAL: For a creamy vinaigrette dressing, simply mix together a 2 to 1 ratio of dressing to mayonnaise, and add about 1 additional teaspoon of vinegar for every 2 tablespoons of dressing. For a garlic vinaigrette dressing, add 1 or even 2 additional cloves of finely chopped or pressed garlic. For Greek salad dressing, instead of 3 tablespoons of red wine vinegar, use 1 1/2 tablespoons of vinegar and 1 1/2 tablespoons of lemon juice.

JAPANESE GINGER DRESSING

This salad staple boasts X factors such as soy sauce and apple cider vinegar and has PUFA-balanced canola oil as its base. (You can use soybean oil instead, but the PUFA balance is not as good.)

Servings: 6

1/4 cup canola oil
2 tablespoons soy sauce
2 tablespoons apple cider vinegar
2 tablespoons finely chopped scallion (or other onion)
2 tablespoons finely chopped celery
1 tablespoon finely chopped gingerroot
1 teaspoon lime juice
Black pepper to taste

1. Mix all ingredients together with a food processor or in bowl.
2. Serve over a mixed green salad or with raw vegetables.

GREEN SALAD

A green salad is a flavorful staple of all Mediterranean Mindspan Elite cuisines. Try different lettuces. A top choice is red leaf lettuce with occasional additions of watercress. Healthful and tasty salads can be as simple as some lettuce and dressing, or marvelously complex, with over a dozen ingredients. The core of this recipe makes for a simple mixed green side or main salad. The options span a wide spectrum of flavorful ingredients.

Servings: 2 large or 4 small side salads

1 or 2 bunches lettuce (to make 2 cups shredded)
1 large tomato
1/2 large cucumber, peeled and sliced
1/2 small red, orange, or yellow pepper, sliced
A few slices of sweet or red onion
Olive oil vinaigrette (see recipe on p. 300)

Rinse lettuce leaves well and dry (preferably in a salad spinner). Shred to make 2 cups. Cut tomato in sections and remove seeds, if desired. Place lettuce in a medium salad bowl, pour the vinaigrette over it and toss, then arrange the other ingredients on top.

OPTIONAL: For variety, try adding steamed asparagus or another vegetable (either raw or cooked), including sliced carrots and small bits of cauliflower. Good cold additions are anchovies, olives, capers, marinated mushrooms, raisins, walnut pieces, pecans, berries, and a cheese of your choice. For variety in greens, try green leaf lettuce or romaine, with minor additions of spinach, chicory, escarole, borage, purslane, mint, arugula/rocket, watercress, or sorrel.

MAIN COURSE OPTION: To make this salad a main course for lunch, per person add a sliced hard-boiled egg and 1/2 cup kidney beans, and serve with some herbed rice or pasta on the side.

GREEK SALAD

Greek salad is a classic, and this salad is a large starter or a main meal, with some additions. Try this with a firm lettuce, such as romaine.

Servings: 2

4 to 6 slices red onion
2 cups shredded lettuce
1 large plum tomato
1/2 large cucumber, peeled and sliced
1/2 small green pepper, chopped
1/2 small red pepper, chopped
1/4 cup chopped kalamata or black olives
1/3 cup crumbled feta cheese (may also be cut into small bite-size chunks)
Greek salad dressing (see optional recipe on p. 300–1)

1. Soak onion slices in a bowl of ice water for 10 minutes to reduce the intensity of the flavor. Then dry the rings and cut in half. Combine all ingredients except for the feta cheese and dressing in a medium salad bowl. Pour 2 servings of salad dressing onto the salad and toss to mix. Place the feta cheese on top of the salad.
2. Serve with a slice of sourdough bread and

olive oil for dipping.

OPTIONAL: Try with red or green leaf lettuce.

GOAT CHEESE AND PEAR TORTA

Goat cheese is low in lactose and is fermented, which makes it an ideal choice for this Italian starter staple. But you can also experiment with different kinds of cheese and fruit or preserves. One great alternative is blue cheese instead of goat cheese, or figs or fig jam instead of cooked pear. If you use fig jam, don't cook it in the pan; simply spread it on the torta.

Servings: 2

2 teaspoons extra virgin olive oil
1/2 teaspoon fresh rosemary
2 teaspoons pear vinegar or vinegar of choice
1 small shallot, halved and sliced
1 small pear, cored and cut into 1/4-inch slices
1 medium to large tortilla
1 ounce goat cheese
Freshly ground black pepper to taste

1. Add olive oil to a medium skillet over medium-low heat, then add rosemary, vinegar, shallot, and pear and cook 10 minutes or until both the pear and the shallot are tender and the shallot is translucent. Meanwhile, cover tortilla with small bits or a thin smear of goat cheese. Once the shallot and pear mixture is done, place it on the tortilla evenly, heat in an oven or toaster oven at 350°F for a few minutes, cut into 6 to 8 slices, and top with freshly ground pepper.

2. Serve with salad or other appetizers, such as olives or antipasti.

OPTIONAL: Drizzle the top of the finished torta with a balsamic vinegar reduction, which you can purchase in fine food and cooking stores (don't use balsamic vinegar simply dyed with caramel color).

Chickpea and Fava bean Tapenade

This is a great mindspan starter for vegans. If you'd rather have a nonvegetarian Mediterranean option, mash into the bean mixture one 2-ounce can of anchovies, or anchovies and capers, in olive oil. If you have trouble finding fava beans, it's fine to substitute lima beans.

Servings: 4 to 6

1 15-ounce can fava beans, drained
1 15-ounce can chickpeas (garbanzo beans), drained
1 cup water
1 tablespoon extra virgin olive oil
1 tablespoon vinegar of choice
2 teaspoons lemon juice
1 heaping teaspoon chopped capers
8 medium olives, finely chopped
1 garlic clove, chopped or pressed
1 tablespoon finely chopped fresh mint
1 tablespoon finely chopped fresh parsley
1/4 teaspoon crushed red pepper flakes, or dash of hot sauce
Salt and black pepper to taste

1. In a saucepan, covered, cook fava beans and chickpeas in water for 10 minutes. Pour

the beans and chickpeas into a medium mixing bowl and mash with a fork until a uniform paste is achieved (a food processor can be used instead). Stir in the remaining ingredients.

2. Serve with raw vegetables, crackers, or toasted bread.

MEDI BRUSCHETTA TOPPING

While many traditional Mediterranean bru-
schettas contain mozzarella, feta, or goat
cheese, I don't think these are necessary
thanks to the sharp flavors of these vegetarian ingredients. Again, this is a great vegan
option, and it's so versatile it can go with
anything — raw vegetables, crackers, even
toasted bread. Nevertheless, if you're feeling deprived of your favorite cheese, by all
means, add it in!

Servings: 2 to 4

2 large sun-dried tomatoes
1 small zucchini, finely diced and cooked
1 tablespoon extra virgin olive oil
2 plum tomatoes, diced
1 tablespoon vinegar of choice
8 medium olives, chopped
1 heaping teaspoon chopped capers
1/2 cup finely chopped sweet onions
2 garlic cloves, chopped or pressed
1 small carrot, peeled and shredded
1 tablespoon finely chopped fresh basil
1/4 teaspoon crushed red pepper flakes
Salt and black pepper to taste

Rehydrate the sun-dried tomatoes in a small container or mug with 3 to 4 volumes of hot water. A microwave accelerates the process. (You can also cook the chopped zucchini at the same time in the microwave.) Mix the other ingredients in a small mixing bowl. After the sun-dried tomatoes are fully hydrated, mince them and stir them into the final topping mix.

Provençal Couscous Salad

This classic couscous salad is made with seasonal ingredients available in many Mediterranean countries. It is served cold or at room temperature. The Greek tabbouleh salad recipe following is made from all the same ingredients by simply substituting bulgur wheat for the couscous. Variations of either can be made by adding black or kalamata olives, chopped red onion, or capers.

Servings: 6 to 8

3 medium tomatoes
1 teaspoon salt
1 cup uncooked couscous
2 tablespoons extra virgin olive oil
1 1/4 cups water
2 tablespoons white wine vinegar
1/4 cup lemon juice
2 cups minced fresh parsley
3 cups minced fresh mint
A few grinds of black pepper

Chop tomatoes, place in a colander in the sink or inside a large bowl, add 1/2 teaspoon of the salt, and mix well. Let drain for 30 minutes. In a large mixing bowl, add couscous and olive oil, and mix until the oil is well distributed. Boil water and add to the couscous and oil mixture. Stir and fluff with a fork. Let cool for 15 minutes, then stir in vinegar, lemon juice, parsley, mint, and remaining 1/2 teaspoon salt. Finally, stir in the drained tomatoes and pepper.

GREEK TABBOULEH SALAD

This dish is recent to Greece but is consistent with general mindspan dietary guidelines. This salad is essentially identical to the Provençal couscous salad on page 313, except for the use of bulgur wheat instead of couscous.

Servings: 6 to 8

3 medium tomatoes
1 teaspoon salt
1 cup bulgur wheat
2 tablespoons extra virgin olive oil
1 1/4 cups water
2 tablespoons white wine vinegar
1/4 cup lemon juice
2 cups minced fresh parsley
3 cups minced fresh mint
A few grinds of fresh black pepper

Chop tomatoes, place in a colander in the sink or inside a large bowl, add 1/2 teaspoon of the salt, and mix well. Let drain for 30 minutes. In a large mixing bowl, add bulgur and olive oil, and mix until the oil is well distributed. Boil water and add to the bulgur and oil mixture. Stir and fluff with a fork.

Let cool for 15 minutes, then stir in vinegar, lemon juice, parsley, mint, and remaining 1/2 teaspoon salt. Finally, stir in the drained tomatoes and pepper.

OPTIONAL: Tabbouleh made according to this recipe is vegan, but small bits or squares of feta cheese (about 1/4 cup) can be added for a more authentic Greek flavor. Try adding olives, chopped red onion, or capers.

SOUPS AND STEWS

ZUCCHINI SOUP (OR PUMPKIN SOUP)

This smooth soup boasts the ability to appear and taste creamy without any cream! If you'd like to pump up the flavor or simply try a variation, you can always grate cheese on top, or stir in a dollop of sour cream or crème fraîche.

Servings: 4

5 small to medium zucchini (or 1 1/2 pounds pumpkin)
1 1/2 tablespoons extra virgin olive oil
2 medium onions, chopped
1 garlic clove, chopped or pressed
2 1/2 cups chicken or vegetable broth
1 large tomato, peeled, chopped, and seeds removed
1 teaspoon sage (fresh if possible)
1/2 teaspoon black pepper
1 cup precooked rice

1. This soup can be prepared by first shredding the zucchini in a food processor, or by chopping the zucchini into small pieces, cooking the soup, and then passing it through a food mill or pureeing with a food processor, blender, or hand blender. The goal is to make the zucchini creamy, not chunky. If using a food mill, add the rice only after the soup is passed through the mill.

2. Heat olive oil in a large frying pan over medium heat and add chopped onions. Cook onions until translucent (about 6 to 8 minutes). Add garlic and zucchini and sauté for about 5 minutes. Add broth, tomato, sage, and pepper and cook on low to medium heat for 25 minutes. If the soup isn't creamy, it can be passed through a food mill. After milling or before serving, return to the pan, add the cooked rice, and heat for 5 minutes.

CREAMY TOMATO SOUP

The ultimate childhood comfort food, this grown-up version has a fraction of the calories and sodium content and gets most of its flavor from fresh vegetables and seasonings. If you've got kids, they'll love it too.

Servings: 4

1 medium onion, chopped
1 large garlic clove, minced or pressed
2 tablespoons extra virgin olive oil
1 tablespoon butter
3 tablespoons flour
6 large tomatoes, or 1 28-ounce can diced tomatoes
3 cups low-sodium chicken or vegetable broth
3/4 cup chopped carrots
1 small bay leaf
1 teaspoon dried thyme, or 1 sprig fresh thyme
1 tablespoon finely chopped fresh dill
A few leaves fresh basil, chopped (about 1 tablespoon)
Salt and black pepper to taste

Add the onions and garlic to the olive oil and

butter in a large stockpot, and cook over medium-low heat until the onions are soft and light golden. Stir in the flour and cook for 2 minutes. Add the tomatoes, broth, carrots, bay leaf, and thyme and cook for 30 minutes on low heat, stirring occasionally. Add the dill and basil, mix well, and cook for an additional 10 minutes. Take the soup from heat and remove the bay leaf and thyme sprig, if using. Using a hand blender or food processor, puree the soup. Season with salt and pepper.

KALE AND CANNELLINI SOUP

The beans give this soup a rich, hearty texture, canceling out the need for animal protein (or cream). You can always add a couple of ounces of diced ham for a more stick-to-your-ribs option.

Servings: 4

1 tablespoon olive oil
1 large onion, chopped
1 garlic clove, pressed or minced
1 bunch kale (about 12 ounces), ribs
  removed
  and chopped
4 cups chicken or vegetable broth
1 15-ounce can cannellini beans
2 ounces ham, diced (optional)
Salt and black pepper to taste

Heat olive oil in a large stockpot, add onions and garlic, and cook until slightly brown but not burnt. Place the kale and broth in the pot, and cook covered for 15 minutes. Add beans and ham, if desired, and cook for an additional 5 to 10 minutes. Season with salt and pepper.

ONION AND GARLIC SOUP

This combination of onion and garlic (a healthier twist on French onion soup) is milder than it sounds and should scare only vampires. Try various kinds and combinations of onions.

Servings: 4

6 large onions
6 garlic cloves
1 tablespoon olive oil
3 cups beef or vegetable broth
Black pepper to taste
1/4 cup white wine
2 tablespoons soy sauce
1 teaspoon Worcestershire sauce
1 to 2 ounces of a flavorful hard cheese
   (e.g., asiago), grated

Slice onions and garlic and sauté in olive oil until translucent but not brown or burnt. Put broth in a 2-quart saucepan and add the sautéed onions and garlic. While the soup is simmering, add pepper, wine, soy sauce, and Worcestershire sauce. Stir occasionally for 10 minutes. Remove from heat and transfer mixture to serving crocks or bowls. Top with cheese.

OPTIONAL: After topping with cheese, bake uncovered for 10 to 15 minutes at 275°F. If you're in a rush, forget baking; just break off a small piece of country sourdough and go — slowly! — to town.

ROASTED TOMATO AND BEAN SOUP

The flavor of the roasted tomatoes makes this soup special. It lies somewhere between that of sun-dried tomatoes and excellent tomato paste, but it has a slight smokiness. The roasted tomatoes are the key ingredient. Nevertheless, if you are pressed for time, you can use rehydrated sun-dried tomatoes for a slightly different but excellent flavor.

Servings: 4

6 large tomatoes
3 tablespoons olive oil
1 large onion, chopped
3 garlic cloves, minced or pressed
1 tablespoon butter
2 tablespoons flour
3 cups chicken or vegetable broth
1 teaspoon chopped rosemary
1 teaspoon chopped sage
1 teaspoon chopped oregano
1 15-ounce can navy beans or cannellini
  beans
Salt and black pepper to taste

1. Slice tomatoes into 4 equal circular pieces each and place in a single layer in a glass baking dish coated with 2 tablespoons of the

olive oil. Roast at 425°F for 30 minutes, turn the slices over, and roast an additional 30 minutes.

2. While the tomatoes are roasting, prepare the soup. Add onions and garlic to remaining 1 tablespoon olive oil in a medium stockpot, and cook until slightly brown but not burnt. Push the onion-garlic mixture to the side and make the roux in the center of the pan: add butter to the pan and whisk in the flour over medium heat until thickened and slightly brown. Add broth, herbs, and beans. Once the tomatoes are roasted and dry, but not desiccated, add them to the soup and cook for an additional 15 minutes, stirring occasionally. Season with salt and pepper.

MEDITERRANEAN MUSHROOM STEW

This wonderful meatless stew is a great family dish! It's also delicious with a small amount of beef. (Not everyone needs an iron-restricted diet, especially younger women.) This recipe calls for a bouquet garni, which usually means a bunch of parsley, a sprig of thyme, and a bay leaf, either tied together or in a cooking bag. I suggest extra thyme for this recipe; try 3 sprigs.

Servings: 6

2 tablespoons extra light olive oil
1 pound stew beef, cut into 1-inch cubes (optional)
4 garlic cloves
3 tablespoons extra virgin olive oil
2 medium onions, peeled and quartered
6 large carrots, peeled and chopped, or 1/2 pound baby carrots
1 celery stalk, chopped
1 bouquet garni
1 tablespoon butter
1/4 cup flour
4 cups low-sodium vegetable or beef broth, or water
3 tomatoes, diced, or 1 15-ounce can

crushed or diced tomatoes

2 cups dry red wine

1/2 pound green peas (frozen are fine)

1 pound small potatoes, cut into bite-size chunks

2 pounds fresh mushrooms (1 pound if using beef), cut into chunks

Chopped parsley

1. Add the extra light olive oil to a large stockpot.

2. If you're using beef, heat the stockpot on medium-high heat. Once the oil is hot, add beef and cook over high heat until all pieces are browned. Remove from heat.

3. Smash the garlic cloves by pushing down on them with the side of a large kitchen knife, and remove the papery outer skin. In a large skillet, add 2 tablespoons of the extra virgin olive oil, onions, garlic, carrots, celery, and bouquet garni, and cook until the garlic and onions are golden. Place the stockpot over medium heat (if meat is included, push the meat to the side, away from the heat) and add remaining 1 tablespoon extra virgin olive oil and the butter to the empty portion of the pot, and stir in the flour a bit at a time to make a roux. Once the flour has thickened, stir in broth, tomatoes, wine, peas, potatoes, mushrooms, and sautéed vegetables and bouquet garni. Simmer on low heat for 3 to 4 hours. Remove the bouquet garni before serving.

4. Top with a garnish of parsley. This is a meal in itself and requires no side dishes or rice, but it goes well with a bit of rice.

OPTIONAL: For a Japanese infusion, you can use shiitake mushrooms.

KOMBU DASHI (VEGETARIAN DASHI)

This broth is the main ingredient in the fish dashi on the next page, and it is a great base for making vegetarian miso soup.

2 cups water
10 to 12 square inches (for example, 2
   inches by 5 inches) kombu (dried kelp)

Add the water to a stockpot. Rinse kelp with cold tap water and add to the water. Stir and turn the heat to high. Just as the water begins to boil, turn the heat to low. Let kombu remain in the water for 2 minutes, then remove.

DASHI (FISH DASHI)

This broth forms the basis of many Japanese soups and recipes. Good instant dashi can be found in some Asian food stores, but watch out for the MSG, since most have it. It is also easy to make fresh. This recipe uses fewer bonito flakes than many authentic Japanese recipes, and the flavor is a nice, mild dashi.

2 cups kombu dashi (see recipe on p. 330)
1/2 cup bonito flakes

This broth can be made immediately following preparation of kombu dashi, or heat the previously made kombu dashi to boiling. Add bonito flakes, remove from heat, and let stand for 10 minutes or until flakes have settled to the bottom. Place a fine strainer in a bowl and pour in the dashi (a paper towel in a colander works fine if you don't have a strainer).

MISO SOUP BASE

This soup is ubiquitous in Japan, and it is served at breakfast, lunch, and dinner. A great variety of flavorful soups can be created with various additions, including tofu, scallions and other onions, vegetables, and a wide variety of mushrooms. A small amount of vinegar intensifies the flavor, without the high salt content of traditional miso soup.

2 cups dashi or kombu dashi (see recipes on pp. 331 and 330)
2 teaspoons vinegar
1 to 2 tablespoons miso paste (depending on salt content and flavor desired)

Pour dashi or kombu dashi and vinegar in a saucepan and heat on high until about to boil, then reduce heat and simmer on medium-low. Add the miso and stir vigorously until all the miso is dissolved.

OPTIONAL: Try adding tofu; shiitake, shimeji, or enoki mushrooms; and scallions. Also try adding a bit of herring, sardine, or anchovy.

Okinawan Soba Noodle Soup

Okinawan soba noodles are made of white flour. If you can't find them, substitute Japanese udon noodles or trenette, which is a common Ligurian pasta.

Servings: 4

4 cups commercial miso broth or miso soup base (see recipe on p. 332)
1/2 cup dried shiitake mushrooms
7 ounces dry Okinawan soba noodles
3 to 4 bite-size squares firm tofu per serving

In a medium saucepan, add miso broth and shiitake mushrooms. Simmer on low heat for about 15 minutes while you cook the noodles. In a second saucepan, cook the noodles according to the package directions, then drain. Add the noodles and tofu to the broth, and cook on medium heat for 5 minutes.

SARDINE AND SORREL SOUP

There are countless variations of this standard Japanese miso-based soup. Miso paste can now be found in many supermarkets. To make a vegetarian version, simply omit the sardines and use tofu. Tofu is an optional addition to the sardine-based version.

Servings: 4

4 cups low-sodium vegetable broth
1 tablespoon vinegar
2 tablespoons miso paste
1/2 4- to 5-ounce can sardines in water (2 small sardines), or 1/2 cup cubed tofu
1/2 cup fresh brown or shiitake mushrooms (or canned or rehydrated dried shiitake mushrooms)
A few leaves sorrel, sliced into short, thin strips
Black, Szechuan, or sansho pepper to taste

Add broth and vinegar to a saucepan over medium heat. Place miso paste in a small mixing bowl and add about 1/2 cup warmed broth. With a whisk, rapidly mix the miso into the broth. Once the miso is fully dissolved, add the mixture to the pan. Add sardines, if using, to the broth and mash with a fork. Remove the mushroom stems and discard, then thinly slice mushrooms. Add mushroom slices, sorrel strips, and tofu cubes, if using, to the pan. Cook about 10 minutes, then season with black, Szechuan, or sansho pepper.

OPTIONAL: Japanese dashi or another fish broth can substitute for the sardine broth.

SHRIMP AND VEGETABLE SOUP

This is an adaptation of a typical Japanese soup. A vegetarian preparation of this soup substitutes tofu for the shrimp and vegetable broth for chicken broth. All ingredients should be available at most supermarkets, including pickled ginger and shiitake mushrooms. Make a homemade chicken broth or select a commercial brand by the highest available amount of protein (this is a sign of how watery the broth is).

Servings: 4

4 cups low-sodium chicken or vegetable broth
1/2 small onion
1 teaspoon pickled ginger
1 small carrot
4 medium fresh brown or shiitake mushrooms (or canned shiitake mushrooms)
2 ounces snow peas (about 25)
2 teaspoons soy sauce
1 teaspoon vinegar or sake
4 large peeled shrimp, or about 1/2 cup cubed tofu
Black pepper to taste

Add broth to a saucepan over medium heat. Finely chop onion and stir into the broth. While the onion cooks (about 8 to 10 minutes), prepare the other ingredients. First chop the pickled ginger into small pieces and add to the broth. Cut the carrot into very thin slivers up to 2 inches long, then add to the broth. Turn heat up to a slow boil while preparing the remaining ingredients. Remove and discard the mushroom stem ends and cut the mushrooms into thin slices, then add them to the broth. Remove and discard the ends and strings from the snow peas, then slice into slivers similar to the carrots. Add soy sauce and vinegar or sake to the saucepan, then add shrimp or tofu and snow peas, and cook until the shrimp turn pink. Season with pepper. Ladle into bowls and serve immediately.

OPTIONAL: Instead of shrimp, you can substitute fish, scallops, crab, other seafood, or even chicken or meat.

SANDWICHES AND EASY FINGER FOODS

PUMPKIN BREAD GRILLED CHEESE SANDWICH

This sandwich is made with homemade pumpkin semolina bread, using the recipe on p. 419. Cheddar cheese, like most hard cheeses, is low in lactose — and it happens to be the perfect cheese for this sandwich.

Servings: 1

1 slice Cheddar or other hard cheese
2 slices pumpkin semolina bread
Butter
2 teaspoons extra virgin olive oil

For each sandwich, place 1 slice of cheese between 2 slices of bread and butter the top of the sandwich. Add olive oil to a medium frying pan and heat over medium heat. Once the pan is hot, place the sandwich in the pan, butter side up. Brown the bottom slice for about 4 minutes, occasionally lifting to ensure that the bottom isn't burning. Once the bottom is a golden-brown color, flip the sandwich onto the buttered side. Cook another 3 to 4 minutes.

OPTIONAL: Other good cheeses to try

are Gouda, Monterey Jack, Brie, dill Havarti, Swiss, and Emmentaler.

EGG SALAD SANDWICH

Eggs are a flavorful, low-iron source of protein — and they even inhibit absorption of iron from other foods! For these reasons, they are one of the best sources of animal protein. Nevertheless, don't go egg wild since they have high levels of methionine. Make sure you buy organic, to ensure a good omega-3 to omega-6 balance. The mayo is an excellent way to get additional omega-3 into your diet.

Servings: 4

6 large eggs
3 tablespoons canola oil or soybean oil
  mayonnaise
1 tablespoon extra virgin olive oil
1 teaspoon brown or Dijon mustard
1 tablespoon finely chopped scallion
1/4 teaspoon paprika

1. Cover the eggs with about 1 inch of water in a large saucepan. Bring the water to a boil, place the lid on the pan, turn off the heat, and let stand for 10 minutes. Run cool water into the pan to cool. Once they are cool, peel the eggs. In a medium to large mixing bowl, mash the eggs with a fork and then mix with the other ingredients.

2. This sandwich can be made with bread slices or as a wrap with a flour tortilla. Top with tomato slices and lettuce.

OPTIONAL: Try subtracting 1 tablespoon mayonnaise, mashing in an avocado, and adding a small amount of chopped ham, to make delicious "Green Eggs and Ham" salad sandwiches!

AVOCADO HUMMUS DIP OR WRAP

This avocado hummus can be used as a dip or in a wrap sandwich. The high-fiber and MUFA-rich avocado largely replaces the sesame tahini, which is the traditional ingredient of this Middle Eastern dish.

Servings: 4

1 15-ounce can chickpeas (garbanzo
   beans), drained
2 medium Hass avocados, peeled and pitted
1 tablespoon finely chopped red onion
2 garlic cloves, minced
1 to 2 tablespoons sesame tahini
2 tablespoons extra virgin olive oil
1 tablespoon lemon juice
1 tablespoon vinegar
1/2 to 1 teaspoon salt
Black pepper to taste

1. Place chickpeas and avocado flesh in a medium mixing bowl and mash with a large fork or potato masher. Mix in the remaining ingredients.
2. As a dip, serve with small pieces of bread and an array of raw vegetables, including broccoli and cauliflower florets, cherry tomatoes, artichoke hearts, and bite-size sticks

of carrot, zucchini, and celery.

3. This can be made as a wrap with a flour tortilla. Add lettuce, tomato, or slices of sweet pickled red pepper. (For a sandwich, use slices of bread.) Serve with a dill pickle quarter on the side.

OPTIONAL: Add a dash of hot sauce.

SARDINE SANDWICH

Sub this simple sardine sandwich for your usual tuna on rye. It's easy to make and has far more healthful very long chain omega-3s than most canned tuna — plus, it's even more flavorful and contains a lot less mercury.

Servings: 1

1 tablespoon mayonnaise (with olive, canola, or soybean oil)
1 teaspoon finely chopped onion
1/2 teaspoon sweet relish
2 teaspoons chopped celery (optional)
1 teaspoon ketchup (optional)
Black pepper to taste
3 ounces canned sardines

1. Place all ingredients except the sardines in a small mixing bowl and blend together. Add the sardines, chop into coarse chunks with a fork, and mix until well blended, but leave the sardines slightly chunky.
2. This sandwich can be made with slices of bread or as a wrap with a flour tortilla. Top with lettuce and tomato. The optional ketchup gives the dressing a Thousand Is-

land quality. Serve with a dill pickle quarter on the side.

BEAN AND CHEESE BURRITOS

This fiber-filled meal is rich in plant-based protein and healthful carbs. Make sure you stick to a hard cheese, like Cheddar or Monterey Jack, which are low in lactose.

Servings: 4

1 cup water
1 15-ounce can beans (black, pinto, etc.), drained
1 large onion, diced
1/2 teaspoon cumin
1 bay leaf
1 1/2 cups chopped vegetables (zucchini, bell peppers, etc.)
1 tablespoon olive oil
2 cups precooked white rice
1 teaspoon lime juice
4 large tortillas (not iron-enriched)
Cheddar, Monterey Jack, or similar hard cheese
Avocado slices
Chopped cilantro
Salt, cayenne pepper, crushed red pepper flakes, or hot sauce to taste

1. In a small saucepan, cook water, beans, onions, cumin, and bay leaf for 15 minutes over medium heat. Meanwhile, in a medium skillet, sauté vegetables in olive oil. After 15 minutes add rice, cooked beans, and lime juice to the vegetables in the skillet. Remove the bay leaf. Heat burrito filling until rice is hot. Fill each tortilla, top each with cheese, and fold them into burrito shapes.

2. Top with avocado slices, a dollop of sour cream, chopped cilantro, and a squeeze of lime juice.

OPTIONAL: Beans can be mashed and spooned into the tortillas instead of mixed whole with the vegetables.

EAST MEETS WEST

There is not much overlap between Japanese and Western cuisines, but there is one Western cuisine that combines the best of both worlds: the Mediterranean Rivieran cuisine. Some common foods you'll find on both menus: Japanese eggplant, bell peppers, fava and other beans, sardines, eggs, rice and wheat, noodles, bread, many kinds of mushrooms, pumpkin and other squash, carrots, peas, cucumbers, onions, garlic, spinach and other greens, nuts (including favored chestnuts), and various fish and seafood. Unlike many other cuisines, a main ingredient in both is dried fish. Rivierans love dried cod and the Japanese use dashi (a broth flavored with dried, smoked, and fermented skipjack tuna) in many dishes. You won't find much cheese, extra virgin olive oil, or tomatoes in traditional Japanese cuisine, but otherwise they are nutritionally similar and, of course, have both raised their respective populations to the mindspan pinnacle of the world.

VEGETABLES

RIVIERAN EGGPLANT

Japanese eggplant, onion, garlic: Japanese or Mediterranean? Both! Japanese eggplant is even more versatile than the standard variety due to its thin skin. It's got a spongy, fleshy inside, making it easy for it to soak up the other flavors of tomato, garlic, and even honey or maple syrup that permeate this dish.

Servings: 4

6 small to medium Japanese eggplants, sliced 1/2 inch thick or thinner
1 medium onion, sliced
1 large or 2 small tomatoes, sliced, or 4 ounces low-salt tomato paste, or 1 14-ounce can diced or crushed Italian-style tomatoes
2 or 3 garlic cloves, pressed or diced
2 teaspoons basil
1 teaspoon oregano
Dash of salt and black pepper
2 tablespoons olive oil
2 teaspoons honey or maple syrup
4 ounces Parmigiano-Reggiano or mozzarella cheese, grated or thinly sliced
Light sprinkle of grated Parmesan or other hard cheese

1. In a casserole dish, layer half each of the eggplant, onion, and tomato slices. Top with half of the garlic, basil, oregano, and salt and pepper. Drizzle with half the olive oil and honey or maple syrup, then top with half the Parmigiano-Reggiano or mozzarella cheese. Repeat to form a second layer, and sprinkle with grated Parmesan or other cheese. Bake at 375°F for 45 minutes covered; uncover for the final 15 minutes.

2. Let cool. Serve on a plate in rectangular pieces with rice or pasta. Begin meal with a side salad that includes vinegar.

OPTIONAL: May vary with seasonal vegetables, sliced zucchini, or other squash. You may double or triple the recipe; it freezes well and can be reheated.

PIGEON PEAS AND VEGETABLES

Like fava beans and chickpeas, pigeon peas have their own unique and wonderful flavor, and they are high in fiber and protein.

Servings: 4

1 tablespoon extra virgin olive oil
1 green bell pepper, cut into small strips
1 red bell pepper, cut into small strips
1 small sweet onion, cut into small strips
1 cup diced very ripe tomatoes, or 1 15-ounce can crushed or diced tomatoes
1 15-ounce can fava beans or pigeon peas, drained
Kernels cut from 2 ears fresh corn, or 1 cup frozen corn
Salt, black pepper, and cayenne pepper to taste

1. Add olive oil to a medium skillet, and sauté the bell peppers and onions over medium-high heat for 10 minutes. Add the tomatoes and fava beans or pigeon peas. Cook on medium heat for 15 minutes. Add the corn and cook for an additional 2 minutes to heat the corn. Season with salt, black pepper, and cayenne pepper.
2. Serve with rice.

FAVA BEAN AND EGGPLANT STEW

This stew provides many of the delicious staples — fava beans, kalamata olives, colorful vegetables — of a traditional Greek diet. It's also packed with fiber, to help power your microbiome.

Servings: 4

4 medium to large tomatoes, sliced
2 tablespoons extra virgin olive oil
3 Japanese eggplants, cut into 1/2-inch cubes
1 15- to 20-ounce can fava beans
1 small garlic clove, pressed or minced
1 medium zucchini, cut into semicircles
2 teaspoons tomato paste
1 2-ounce tin anchovies in olive oil
10 to 12 kalamata olives, chopped
12 capers, halved
2 chicken thighs (optional)
1/2 teaspoon coriander
1/2 teaspoon marjoram or oregano
Salt and black pepper to taste

1. Place the tomato slices in a single layer in a glass baking dish coated with 1 tablespoon of the olive oil. Roast at 425°F for 30 minutes, turn the slices over, and roast an additional 30 minutes.

2. While the tomatoes are roasting, add the remaining tablespoon olive oil to a large skillet, and sauté the eggplant over medium-high heat for 15 minutes. Add the remaining ingredients to the skillet and cook covered over medium-low heat for 45 minutes. Once the tomatoes are roasted, chop them up and then add them to the skillet and cook covered for an additional 40 minutes, with occasional stirring.

3. Serve over rice.

Pumpkin and Bean Patties

A common complaint about veggie burgers is they crumble apart when you're cooking them. This recipe uses plenty of healthful ingredients such as beans, pumpkin, and egg as sticky binders. You can substitute canned pumpkin if you're pressed for time.

Servings: 6

2 pounds fresh pumpkin, or 2 15-ounce cans cooked pumpkin
1 teaspoon chopped capers
1 15-ounce can chickpeas (garbanzo beans), black beans, or kidney beans
2 tablespoons chopped scallion
1 tablespoon sage
1/2 teaspoon salt
2 teaspoons lemon or lime juice
1 large egg
1/2 cup breadcrumbs
Salt and black pepper to taste
1/2 cup flour
1 tablespoon light olive oil

1. If using fresh pumpkin, seed and chop the pumpkin into 4 to 6 pieces and add to a baking dish containing about 1/2 inch of water. Roast the pumpkin in a 375°F oven

for 45 minutes. Scrape the pumpkin flesh from the skin (try a grapefruit spoon).

2. Place the roasted pumpkin or canned pumpkin, if using, in a food processor with chopped capers, beans, scallion, sage, 1/2 teaspoon salt, and the lemon or lime juice. Pulse until mixed evenly. Add the egg and breadcrumbs and mix until uniform but individual chunks remain visible. Season with salt and pepper.

3. Shape the mixture into patty sizes appropriate for individual servings. Add the flour to a large, shallow bowl or flat work surface, and flour each side of the patties. Add the light olive oil to a large frying pan and heat to medium-high heat. Once the oil is hot, place the patties gently in the pan. Cook about 3 minutes on each side until golden brown.

4. Serve as a main dish without a bun, or on a bun or bread as a burger.

OPTIONAL: Instead of sage, try cilantro or parsley.

ROMANO BEANS

If you like green beans (a.k.a. string beans), then you'll love Romano beans. They are similar to green beans but longer, broader, and flatter. This recipe is incredibly easy, and the flavor is fabulous! This simple recipe also works great for green or wax beans, but the flavor of fresh Romano beans is unequaled.

Servings: 4

1 pound fresh Romano beans, ends removed
1 tablespoon extra virgin olive oil
1 tablespoon butter
1 garlic clove, finely chopped

Add the beans to a large pot of boiling water, return to a boil, and cook for 5 minutes, then drain. Add the olive oil, butter, garlic, and beans to large skillet and sauté the beans until they are slightly tender.

OPTIONAL: Try sautéing with a teaspoon of lemon juice or some chopped chives, or topping with just a bit of your favorite grated hard cheese.

BAKED SQUASH

This squash recipe could hardly be easier, and if you select a good squash the flavor is unbeatable!

Servings: 4

2 medium to large delicata squash

Preheat the oven to 375°F. Select a baking dish that will hold all four halves of the squash and add about 3/4 inch of water. Cut the squash in half lengthwise and place cut side down in the water. Bake for 45 minutes, remove from the oven, turn the squash cut side up, and bake for an additional 20 minutes or until all the flesh is soft.

OPTIONAL: Try other squash like acorn or spaghetti, but I think you'll discover that delicata is unsurpassed for flavor.

GREEK LEMON ROASTED POTATOES

This potato dish is ubiquitous throughout Greece. It makes a fabulous side dish for most entrées, especially Mediterranean dishes. Although cutting up the potatoes can be time-consuming, it's essential because the potato chunks absorb more of the seasonings and broth. Many kinds of potatoes work well for this dish, so experiment or use what you have on hand.

Servings: 6

3 pounds potatoes, cut into 1- to 1 1/2-inch chunks
1/3 cup extra virgin olive oil
Juice of 2 medium lemons, or 2 tablespoons lemon juice
4 garlic cloves, chopped
2 teaspoons dried marjoram, or 1 1/2 teaspoons dried oregano
2 tablespoons white wine vinegar
1 teaspoon salt
A few grinds of black pepper
2 cups vegetable broth or water
Chopped fresh marjoram, oregano, or parsley

1. Preheat the oven to 400°F. In a large

baking dish, add all the ingredients except the broth or water and fresh herbs. Stir the potatoes in the dish to coat completely with oil. Add the broth or water and cook for 45 minutes. Turn the potatoes, and cook for an additional 20 to 30 minutes, or until a fork passes easily through.

2. Serve topped with a bit of fresh marjoram, oregano, or parsley.

STEWED CHICKPEAS

This is a standard dish of Genoese cuisine. It has a terrific, mildly nutty flavor that goes with pretty much anything: serve it as a side dish with rice, or with rustic bread as an appetizer.

Servings: 6

2 15-ounce cans chickpeas (garbanzo beans), drained
2 to 3 tablespoons extra virgin olive oil
1 medium onion, chopped
6 medium to large leaves Swiss chard, finely chopped
1 celery stalk, finely chopped
1 garlic clove, chopped or pressed
1 tablespoon finely chopped fresh parsley
1 teaspoon lemon juice
1 cup diced fresh tomatoes, or 3/4 cup diced or crushed canned tomatoes
Grated Parmigiana-Reggiano, fontina, or Parmesan cheese

1. Cover the chickpeas with 1 inch of water in a large stockpot, cover loosely, and simmer for 1 hour. Sauté the onions, Swiss chard, celery, garlic, and parsley in the olive oil in a frying pan on medium heat for about

30 minutes. Drain the chickpeas and add the lemon juice, tomatoes, and sautéed mixture to the chickpeas. Cook the mixture on low heat for an additional hour.

2. Top with the cheese.

ZUKE CHANPURU
(OKINAWAN STIR-FRY)

This recipe is made traditionally with goya, a.k.a. bitter melon, which is an acquired taste. People vary in their tolerance/preference for bitter flavors, and goya is *very* bitter. The primary recipe here substitutes zucchini, but I also provide instructions for how to make the traditional version. Look for the lighter, yellower goya for a less bitter flavor. If you can't find goya or if you simply don't like its strong, bitter flavor, go with the zucchini. The goya recipe is more traditional with pork, but feel free to leave it out, since the egg and tofu provide plenty of flavor and protein.

Servings: 4 to 6

4 medium zucchini, or 2 medium goya
1 teaspoon salt, if using goya
1/4 cup water, if using goya
1 14- to 16-ounce package extra firm tofu
2 tablespoons light olive or canola oil
4 ounces pork belly, sliced 1/8 to 1/4 inch
    thick, or 2 ounces bacon
1 medium onion, diced
2 teaspoons miso paste

1 tablespoon sake (optional)
3 eggs, lightly beaten
1 tablespoon soy sauce
Salt and black pepper to taste

1. For zucchini, slice the zucchini lengthwise down the center, then cut into 1/4-inch-thick half-moon slices.
2. For goya, cut the goya lengthwise and scoop out and discard the white fleshy center. Cut into crescent-moon slices about 1/4 inch thick. Mix in a large bowl with 1 teaspoon salt and water, stir occasionally for 20 minutes, then blanch the melon slices in a large pot of boiling water for 3 minutes (this reduces the bitter flavor). Remove the goya slices to a colander and dry with paper towels.
3. Remove the tofu from the package, discard the liquid, cut into 1/2-inch cubes, and set aside. Place the oil and pork in a wok or large skillet, and cook until it is lightly browned. Add the zucchini or goya, onions, and miso paste, and stir-fry on medium heat until the onions are translucent and golden. Add the tofu, stir-fry an additional minute, then add the sake, if desired, and eggs on top and let cook without stirring until the eggs are mostly set. Add the soy sauce and salt and pepper, and stir gently to mix.

4. This stir-fry goes great on a bed of rice, or on the side.

MUSHROOMS, CARROTS, AND SEA VEGETABLES ON NOODLES

This Japanese staple is a great way to squeeze in sea vegetables, which offer a wide array of minerals (and you can even pick up sheets of nori seaweed in mainstream supermarkets or megastores like Walmart). Soba noodles make a great base, absorbing the flavor of the soy and seaweed. You can also serve this with rice.

Servings: 4

10 ounces fresh shiitake or oyster
  mushrooms, or 2 ounces dried shiitake
  mushrooms, rehydrated
2 teaspoons canola oil
1 1/2 cups julienned carrots
1/4 cup dashi (see recipe on p. 331) or
  water
1 tablespoon vinegar
2 sheets nori seaweed
2 teaspoons soy sauce
7 ounces soba noodles
Sesame seeds (optional)

1. Slice the mushrooms. Add the canola oil and carrots to a large skillet or wok over medium heat. Stir the carrots in the oil and then add the dashi or water and vinegar. Chop or slice the nori into bite-size bits or strips. It helps to wet it slightly, but don't get it too wet or it will disintegrate. Cook the carrots until the liquid has evaporated, then add the mushrooms and nori. Cook another 3 minutes, stirring occasionally. Stir in the soy sauce.

2. Cook the soba noodles according to the package instructions. Serve the stir-fry over noodles. Sprinkle with sesame seeds, if desired.

GINGER CARROTS

This fiber-rich, sweet, and tangy side dish gets a major flavor and health boost with the addition of X factors vinegar and mirin.

Servings: 4

1/3 cup vinegar, preferably rice vinegar
1/2 pound carrots, peeled and julienned
1/2 teaspoon grated gingerroot
1 teaspoon mirin

Pour the vinegar in a small saucepan. Add the carrots, ginger, and mirin. Bring to a boil, then reduce heat and cover with a lid. Cook on medium-low heat for 12 minutes, or until the carrots are tender.

PASTA, RICE, AND BARLEY

Once again, always select grains that are not enriched with iron.

Keep rice and pasta at the ready. I always have precooked rice and pasta stored in the refrigerator. I typically make enough for three to four days. Not only is it convenient when you're busy, but cycles of heating and cooling promote the formation of digestion-resistant starch. Cook pasta according to the manufacturer's directions, and cook only until al dente (firm). Instructions on cooking rice can be found in the recipes. I also precook barley, but not as much of it as rice or pasta; it also refrigerates well, but I eat less of it.

Pasta. Dry pasta should be boiled in water containing a few shakes of salt and a teaspoon of olive oil. According to the nearly universal preference in Mindspan

Elite Mediterranean areas, pasta must be cooked al dente. Always test the pasta as it nears readiness and drain into a colander once it reaches al dente.

Rice and barley. In general, rice should be steamed with twice the volume of high-quality water. For example, 1 cup rice requires 2 cups water. Rice should always be washed a few times with clean water prior to cooking. Since it is difficult to measure the appropriate amount of water once rice is wet, buy a container (glass, polypropylene, or other non-leaching plastic) that is graduated in thirds. For plain rice, fill the container with rice to one-third, wash the rice thoroughly, and then fill the other two-thirds of the container with water. Cook the rice on the stove or in a microwave for 20 minutes, stir to mix, and leave covered for an additional 5 minutes. Use a similar washing procedure when using an automatic rice maker. All of the same preparation steps and measurements should be used to cook pearled barley, but the cooking time for the quick-cook variety is only 10 to 12 minutes. Any dish that calls for rice can be served with barley, but I recommend and usually eat rice.

HOW MUCH PASTA?

One common refrain we hear about Mediterranean eating is that pasta is only a small side dish. Of course, Italy is the epicenter of pasta production and consumption, but its neighbors of the French Riviera love pasta too. The most authoritative and oft-referenced work on traditional cuisine of the French Riviera was published in 1972 by the mayor of Nice, Jacques Médecin, and he provides a clear answer to the question of how much pasta to serve.

Médecin says he knows "pasta freaks who would not balk at a 1 pound/500 gram helping," but he concluded after consulting with restaurant owners that a "reasonable" serving size is 7 ounces (200 grams) of cooked pasta per person (about 80 grams of dry pasta). At almost half a pound without sauce, this is no side dish. Of course, less should be served to children and smaller people, and more to larger ones. And by all means, eat less to lose weight, but that applies to any food.

TOMATO SAUCE NIÇOISE

This tomato sauce has elements of both the French and Italian Rivieras. It can be served with any noodle. I like all pastas but prefer bite-size ones like rotini and farfalle, since they're less likely to flip and have crevices that hold sauce. This is a traditional-style recipe from Nice for what we might think of as spaghetti and tomato sauce, although it has less tomato. This sauce is enough for about 1 pound of dry pasta.

Servings: 6

2 tablespoons extra virgin olive oil
3 medium garlic cloves, pressed or finely chopped
1 teaspoon marjoram
1 small sprig thyme (optional)
1 1/2 cups chopped onions
3 cups diced very ripe tomatoes, or 1 28-ounce can crushed or diced tomatoes
Salt and black pepper to taste
Grated Parmigiano-Reggiano or Parmesan cheese

1. In a medium frying pan heat the olive oil, garlic, marjoram, and thyme, if desired, until the garlic bubbles for about 1 minute. Add

the chopped onions and cook until translucent and beginning to brown. Add the tomatoes and cook for 12 to 15 minutes, or until thickened. Season with salt and pepper.

2. Place drained noodles on a plate, top with a layer of sauce, and sprinkle with cheese.

OPTIONAL: This dish can also be topped with fresh basil leaves coarsely chopped or torn (about 1 leaf per serving).

PESTO SAUCE

In most parts of Italy, tomato-based sauces reign supreme, but in Liguria, pesto is king. It is also very popular in Nice and Provence (where it is called pistou). The heart, soul, and essence of this sauce is fresh basil, preferably Genoese basil. According to tradition in the region, there is only one truly superior way to prepare the basil for pesto: by crushing it to a paste in a mortar and pestle. They say this releases all the basil flavor, but there also might be good health-based reasons for the complete breakdown of the basil leaves. I have burned out blenders making pesto, so if you want an alternative to the mortar and pestle, try a food processor. If using the mortar method, you'll need a large one, or reduce the recipe size.

Servings: 6

2 cups fresh basil leaves
4 tablespoons fresh pine nuts
1 garlic clove, peeled
Salt to taste
1/2 cup grated Parmigiano-Reggiano, or a
    mix of Parmigiano-Reggiano and pecorino
    sardo

1/3 cup extra virgin olive oil

1. Wash and dry the basil leaves. This can be done quickly in a lettuce dryer or spinner. Place the pine nuts, garlic, and salt in the mortar and crush to a paste. Add the basil leaves a small bunch at a time, crushing the entire mixture to a paste. Repeat this process with the cheese. Add olive oil in a few parts and continue crushing to a smooth consistency.

2. If using a food processsor, add the washed and dried basil, pine nuts, garlic, salt, and one-third of the oil, and pulse until a coarse paste. Use a spatula to move leaves down from the sides of the processor as needed. Continue this process with another third of the oil. Add the final third of the oil and the cheese, and pulse until the mixture is uniform. Cut basil and pesto oxidize quickly, so cover with plastic wrap if you aren't going to use immediately.

3. Immediately before use, mix the pesto to desired consistency with warm water (you can use water from the boiling pasta). An ideal consistency is thinner than the stock paste, but not so thin as to be runny. Try about a 4 or 5 to 1 ratio of pesto stock to water. Almost any noodle goes well with this sauce.

OPTIONAL: Walnuts can be used instead of pine nuts. The French version, pistou, can be made with the addition of 2 ounces of butter.

Roasted Tomato and Pesto Sauce

This sauce provides a taste of several different Italian regions — but the pine nuts and basil give it a strong northwest Italian accent. The amount of sauce is enough for 10 ounces of dry pasta, for 4 people. Roasting the tomatoes complements the pesto and gives the sauce a rich, deep flavor.

Servings: 4

6 large fresh tomatoes
4 tablespoons extra virgin olive oil
1 medium onion, chopped
4 garlic cloves, minced or pressed
1 teaspoon oregano
1/6 6-ounce can tomato paste
1 15-ounce can diced or crushed tomatoes
1/2 cup dry red wine (Cabernet Sauvignon, Merlot, etc.)
1 cup water
1 cup fresh basil leaves
2 tablespoons fresh pine nuts
1/2 cup grated Parmigiano-Reggiano, or a mix of Parmigiano-Reggiano and pecorino sardo
Salt and black pepper to taste

1. Slice the fresh tomatoes into 4 pieces

(slices, not wedges) and place in a single layer in a glass baking dish coated with 2 tablespoons of the olive oil. Roast at 425°F for 30 minutes, turn slices over, and roast an additional 30 minutes.

2. While the tomatoes are roasting, in a large skillet, add onions, garlic, oregano, and remaining 2 tablespoons olive oil, and cook on medium heat about 10 minutes, or until slightly golden. Stir in the tomato paste, canned tomatoes, wine, and water. Finely chop or crush in a mortar the basil and pine nuts, and add to the sauce. Add the cheese. Once the tomatoes are roasted, add them and any remaining juice to the sauce and cook for an additional 5 minutes, stirring occasionally. Season with salt and pepper.

3. Place drained noodles on a plate and top with a layer of sauce.

LES GNOCCHI VERTS
(RIVIERA GREEN GNOCCHI)

Gnocchi and Swiss chard are staple foods in the Riviera regions. This recipe from Nice combines them into a single delicious dish.

Servings: 6

3 pounds soft, older medium potatoes
1 pound leaves Swiss chard, finely chopped
1 tablespoon extra virgin olive oil
1 teaspoon salt
3 cups white, non-enriched, unbleached flour
2 large eggs
Grated Parmigiano-Reggiano or Parmesan cheese

1. Peel the potatoes, halve them, and boil in salted water in a large pot for 20 to 25 minutes. While the potatoes cook, in a second pot, blanch the chopped chard leaves in salted boiling water for 5 minutes. Drain the pot and remove residual moisture by stirring the chard on low heat for a couple of minutes, then remove the pan from the heat. While the potatoes are still hot, place them in a large mixing bowl and stir in the olive oil and then the chard, 1 teaspoon salt, and flour. Beat and then add the eggs. At this point, the dough should be firm enough to work with your hands. Fold and knead the dough to ensure uniformity. Roll the dough into rods slightly larger than 5/8 inch in diameter, and cut into pieces about an inch long. Cook for 4 to 8 minutes in a large pot of boiling water with a pinch of salt and a small amount of oil. When they float, they are done. Drain the gnocchi well in a colander.

2. Place the drained gnocchi on a plate, top with a layer of sauce (tomato sauce is the Mediterranean preference), and then sprinkle with Parmigiano-Reggiano or Parmesan cheese.

OPTIONAL: Try substituting semolina flour for up to a third of the white flour. This makes the gnocchi more pasta-like. You can also substitute chestnut flour, which is a common variation in Liguria.

CREAMY ANCHOVY BASIL SAUCE

This amount of sauce is enough for a pound of dry pasta, for 6 people. It's a Rivieran staple, and the anchovies are a great way to squeeze in an extra serving of omega-3s. It's versatile enough to go with virtually any noodle.

Servings: 6

1/2 cup extra virgin olive oil
4 garlic cloves, pressed or very finely
　chopped
6 to 8 fresh basil leaves, or 1 tablespoon
　dried basil
1/2 medium onion, finely chopped
2 tablespoons butter
1 2-ounce tin anchovies, mashed with a fork
3 tablespoons heavy cream
Salt and black pepper to taste
Grated pecorino, Parmigiano-Reggiano,
　or Parmesan cheese

1. In a large frying pan, heat the olive oil, garlic, basil, and onions and cook until the onions become translucent and begin to brown. Stir in the butter, mashed anchovies, and cream. Continue to stir over medium

heat for 5 minutes. Season with salt and pepper.

2. Almost any noodle goes well with this
sauce. Top with cheese.

Eggplant Tomato Sauce

This simple but delicious recipe is a great way to sneak in a couple of extra servings of vegetables for picky eaters (and they won't even notice the eggplant!). This amount of sauce is enough for 10 ounces of dry pasta.

Servings: 4

2 tablespoons extra virgin olive oil
1 medium onion, chopped
3 garlic cloves, pressed or minced
4 Japanese eggplants, cut into ½-inch cubes or strips
1/2 teaspoon marjoram or oregano
1/4 cup water, or more if needed
3 cups diced very ripe tomatoes, or one 28-ounce can crushed or diced tomatoes
1/4 cup fresh basil leaves, chopped immediately before use
Salt and black pepper to taste
Grated Parmigiano-Reggiano or Parmesan cheese

1. In a large frying pan, heat olive oil, onions, and garlic, and cook until the onions are translucent and beginning to brown. Add the eggplant, marjoram or oregano, and water, and cook on medium heat for about

20 minutes, with occasional stirring, especially near the end. Add the tomatoes and cook another 15 minutes, or until the sauce reaches the desired consistency. Add the basil and cook for an additional 2 minutes while stirring to distribute the basil flavor. Season with salt and pepper.

2. Almost any noodle goes well with this sauce. Top with cheese.

GREENS AND BEANS PASTA

Greens are a staple in Mediterranean Riviera regions. If you're feeling adventurous, try swapping out some of the spinach for more traditional greens such as borage, purslane, nettles, dandelion leaves, arugula/rocket, burdock, salsify, and kale. (Try small amounts at first, since some of these are fairly bitter.) This amount of sauce is enough for 1 pound of dry pasta.

Servings: 6

1 pound dry pasta
2/3 cup plus 2 tablespoons extra virgin olive oil
5 garlic cloves, pressed or very finely chopped
5 plum tomatoes, diced
1/2 cup chicken or vegetable broth
1 15-ounce can cannellini or northern beans
6 cups spinach or 6 leaves Swiss chard, chopped
1 cup shredded mozzarella cheese
1 cup grated Parmigiano-Reggiano or Parmesan cheese
Salt and black pepper to taste

1. In a large pot, cook the pasta according to the manufacturer's directions until al dente. Drain the pasta in a colander, place in a large serving container, coat with ⅔ cup olive oil, and let cool. In a large frying pan, heat 2 tablespoons olive oil, the garlic, and tomatoes, and stir occasionally for 4 minutes. Stir in the broth, beans, and spinach or chard, and cook for 5 minutes. Add the cooked pasta to the pan and mix. Stir in the mozzarella cheese and Parmigiano-Reggiano or Parmesan cheese. Season with salt and pepper.

2. Serve with crusty bread and extra virgin olive oil.

PASTA SALAD

This is a Mediterranean classic cold pasta dish. A wide variety of noodles work very well, but select a noodle that has crevices to hold the sauce and flavor. First choices are rotini, farfalle, and fusilli.

Servings: 6 to 8

1 pound dry pasta
2/3 cup extra virgin olive oil
8 large sun-dried tomatoes
1/2 green pepper, thinly sliced
1/2 red pepper, thinly sliced
2 garlic cloves, finely chopped or pressed
1 large ripe tomato, diced
3/4 cup kalamata or black olives, sliced
1/4 cup red wine vinegar (plus additional
    for rehydrating tomatoes)
1 teaspoon marjoram or oregano
1 cup grated Parmigiano-Reggiano or
    Parmesan cheese (optional)
1/2 teaspoon salt
Black pepper to taste

1. In a large pot, cook the pasta according to the manufacturer's directions until al dente. Drain the pasta in a colander, place in a large serving container, coat with the olive oil, and let cool. In a small bowl, rehydrate the sun-dried tomatoes with about 2 volumes of an equal mixture of water and red wine vinegar, and let stand for 6 to 8 minutes. Once the tomatoes are soft, chop into 1/4-inch pieces. Mix the chopped tomatoes and all the remaining ingredients together with the pasta.

2. Spoon onto a plate with a side garnish of parsley. On a hot summer day, serve with a mint iced tea.

OPTIONAL: Without cheese, this dish is vegan. Try it with feta cheese, in addition to or instead of the Parmigiano-Reggiano. For more veggies, add a couple of sautéed zucchini. Also try chopped capers, which add another layer of complexity to this amazing dish!

READY RICE

This should be prepared in medium to large batches and stored in the refrigerator. I prefer a mix of about 1/2 to 2/3 Japonica rice and 1/2 to 1/3 long-grain rice (generally parboiled). This mix is still slightly sticky, but it doesn't clump like Japonica alone, especially when stored in the refrigerator.

Servings: Variable

3 cups uncooked rice (2 cups Japonica,
   1 cup long-grain parboiled)

1. This rice can be prepared in a rice cooker, in the microwave, or on the stovetop. For microwave preparation, add the rice to a suitable lidded container, wash the rice several times, and then add water to the fill line equal to three volumes of the rice (for example, if you use 1 cup of rice, then add water to the 3-cup fill line). Slightly less water makes for a drier rice. Microwave the container on maximum power until the water begins to boil (record the amount of time for future preparation). Let stand for about 10 minutes, stir the rice up from the bottom of the container, then heat the container another 1 to 2 minutes in the microwave.

2. For stovetop preparation, add the rice and rinse several times with water. Drain as much of the rinse water as possible, add 1 to 1.5 volumes of fresh water (more water makes for softer and stickier rice), and bring to a boil. Turn down heat to low, cover, and simmer for 20 to 25 minutes (depending on the type of rice). Stir the rice, replace the lid, and let cool for at least 15 minutes.

3. This rice can be eaten alone, or paired with many side dishes and entrées.

HERBED RICE

This rice can be used as an alternative to plain rice and eaten with sauces and vegetable dishes.

Servings: 4

3 tablespoons extra virgin olive oil
2 bay leaves
2 teaspoons thyme, fresh rosemary, or marjoram
1/4 cup water
3 cups precooked rice

1. In a large frying pan, heat the olive oil to medium heat, place the bay leaves on the oil, and add the thyme, rosemary, or marjoram and water. Add the rice, stir well, and cover. After 10 minutes, stir and remove from the heat. The bay leaves can be left in the rice, but do not serve.
2. This rice can be eaten alone, or paired with many side dishes and entrées.

RICE WITH FAVA BEANS

This classic rice dish from Nice is an outstanding side dish, or even a main course for a delicious and filling lunch. The recipe contains a small amount of petit salé or bacon for flavor, but it can be made vegetarian by simply omitting the meat. The fava beans are so deliciously rich you'll hardly notice its absence.

Servings: 4

2 tablespoons extra virgin olive oil
1 medium onion, chopped
1 garlic clove, finely chopped
2 ounces petit salé or bacon, diced
1 cup vegetable or chicken broth
1 20-ounce can fava beans, drained
4 leaves Swiss chard, chopped (optional)
3 cups precooked rice
1 tablespoon butter
Salt and black pepper to taste

In a large skillet heat the olive oil to medium heat, add the onions, garlic, and diced petit salé or bacon, and cook until golden brown. Add the broth, beans, and chard, if desired, and cook with occasional stirring over medium-low heat for 15 minutes, or until most of the moisture has been cooked off. Add the rice and butter, mix well, and cook until the rice is hot. Season with salt and pepper.

RICE SALAD NIÇOISE

This classic rice dish from Nice is an outstanding side dish, or even a main course for a quick lunch.

Servings: 4

7 tablespoons extra virgin olive oil
1 1/2 cups rice
3/4 cup water
5 large tomatoes, or 1 28-ounce can diced or crushed tomatoes
1 cup frozen small green peas
1 green pepper, thinly sliced
1 tablespoon vinegar
1/2 teaspoon marjoram or oregano
1/2 teaspoon salt
Black pepper to taste
2 ounces pitted olives
4 spring onions
1 tablespoon homemade ketchup (optional; see recipe on p. 430)
1 sprig mint

1. In a medium saucepan, heat 4 tablespoons of the olive oil to medium heat. Add the rice and stir well to coat the rice completely with oil. After the rice turns milky white, add the water, stir, cover, and cook on low heat for 20 minutes. Stir the rice, cover, and let sit an additional 5 minutes. In another saucepan, place the tomatoes over low heat and simmer until reduced by about half, then add the peas and green pepper and simmer, stirring, for an additional 5 minutes. In a small mixing bowl, mix the remaining 3 tablespoons olive oil, vinegar, marjoram or oregano, salt, black pepper, and ketchup, if desired. Slice the olives and onions, and mix them in a large salad bowl with the cooled tomato, the rice, and the dressing.

2. Top with mint sprig.

FISH, MEAT, AND TOFU

I can't stress enough that minimizing red meat in your diet is a key to maximizing mindspan, especially in the second half of life. Whenever possible, replace red meat with tofu or moderate servings of fish.

MEDITERRANEAN ROLLED FISH

Fish is an exceptional source of low-iron protein and very long chain omega-3 fatty acids, which is why I recommend featuring it on the menu at least two to three times a week. This recipe is a particular favorite of mine because it's simple and easy to whip together even after a long day at work. Just be careful to check where your fish is from and whether it is endangered.

Servings: 2

1 tablespoon olive oil
Four 2- to 3-ounce fish fillets (tilapia or flounder are good choices)
2 scallions, minced or diced
4 ounces spinach, fresh or frozen (defrosted and drained)
2 garlic cloves, pressed or diced
2 teaspoons basil, marjoram, and/or thyme
1 teaspoon Worcestershire sauce
Dash of salt and black pepper
2 ounces feta cheese, grated
2 ripe lemons
Paprika

1. Moderately heat the olive oil in a small pan. Rinse the fish fillets under warm water and place in pan. In a small mixing bowl, mix the scallions, spinach, garlic, herbs, Worcestershire sauce, salt, and pepper and add feta cheese. Spread the mixture over the fillets and roll lengthwise. Squeeze 1 lemon over the rolled fillets and sprinkle with paprika. Bake at 400°F for 40 minutes covered. **2.** Let cool a bit. Cut the remaining lemon into wedges. Serve two fish rolls on a plate with a lemon wedge on the side. You can place the fish over 2 to 3 heaping tablespoons of prepared rice. A simple side green vegetable goes nicely. Try steamed asparagus spears topped with lemon juice.

OPTIONAL: Add a side salad: lettuce and sliced fresh tomatoes, topped with a sprinkle of grated cheese (fresh asiago or fontina) and a fresh basil leaf, and dressed with a garlic vinaigrette.

GRILLED SALMON

This is a flavorful East meets West salmon dish. Salmon is fairly low in iron and rich in EPA and DHA very long chain fatty acids.

Servings: 4

3 tablespoons light olive oil
1 scallion, chopped
2 tablespoons soy sauce
1 teaspoon vinegar
1 tablespoon brown sugar
Dash of crushed red pepper flakes
One 14-ounce fresh salmon fillet

1. In a small bowl, mix 2 tablespoons of the light olive oil, scallions, soy sauce, vinegar, brown sugar, and red pepper flakes until the brown sugar has dissolved. Pour the marinade into a sealable plastic bag. Wash the salmon, place in the bag, and marinate for 2 to 4 hours. Take out of the refrigerator about 30 minutes prior to cooking, to allow the salmon to come to room temperature. Heat the remaining 1 tablespoon light olive oil in a large skillet until it begins to bubble or smoke faintly, then place the salmon in the pan. Cook for 5 to 6 minutes, spoon over the fillet about 1 teaspoon of the marinade, then turn with a spatula and cook for another 4 minutes, or until the thinner parts of the fillet begin to flake. Allow to rest in the pan 1 to 2 minutes.

2. Serve with a couple of generous sides of vegetables (steamed asparagus or broccoli go very well) and rice or pasta.

OPTIONAL: This recipe is spectacular on the grill. Be careful as the salmon nears the finish line, as it can flake at the edges and fall into the grill. To avoid this problem, you can place a piece of foil on the grill and move the salmon onto it for the final 2 to 3 minutes of cooking.

SAGE ROASTED CHICKEN

Historically, meat is not eaten in large portions by the Mediterranean Mindspan Elite, but various kinds of meat stuffed or rubbed with sage are favorites. Fresh sage has a special flavor that fades as it dries, so always try to use fresh sage whenever possible.

Servings: 4 to 6

One 2 1/2- to 3-pound chicken, cut into
 pieces (breasts, thighs, drumsticks, wings)
10 to 12 leaves fresh sage, washed and dried
1 tablespoon light olive oil
1 teaspoon thyme

1. You can either buy a cut chicken or have your butcher cut the chicken into pieces. Lift the skin away from the meat without tearing or removing it and insert enough sage leaves to cover about half to two-thirds of the meat. Pull the skin back into place to seal in the sage. Preheat the oven to 375°F. Add olive oil to a glass baking dish large enough to hold all the chicken pieces. Roll the chicken pieces in the dish to coat with oil, and place the pieces skin side down in the dish. Sprinkle with about half the thyme. Bake for 45 minutes. Turn the pieces over, sprinkle with the remaining thyme, and bake for an additional 20 minutes. The top should be golden and crispy, and the juices should run clear.

2. Serve with rice or potatoes.

OPTIONAL: Pork loin or chops can be used instead of chicken. Buy thicker cuts, cut a slit deep into the side, and roast or panfry. This dish goes very well with applesauce and green beans.

EAST OF EASY CURRY

Curry is common in Okinawa.

Servings: 4

3/4 pound chicken breasts, boneless and skinless, cut into 1/2-inch cubes or 1/4-inch strips
2 teaspoons soy sauce
3 1/2 teaspoons curry powder
3 tablespoons canola oil
1 medium onion, chopped
1 medium red bell pepper, cut into thin slices
1 cup fresh peapods or frozen peas
1 medium apple, chopped
4 garlic cloves, finely chopped
1 tablespoon very finely chopped or grated gingerroot
1 1/2 cups low-sodium vegetable or chicken broth
1 tablespoon cornstarch
1/4 cup low-fat sour cream

1. In a medium bowl, coat the chicken with soy sauce, then add 1 1/2 teaspoons of the curry powder and coat all pieces. In a wok or large skillet on medium heat, add 1 tablespoon of the canola oil, and when the oil begins to smoke, add the chicken and stir-fry for 3 minutes; then remove from pan and set aside. Add the remaining 2 tablespoons oil, onions, red pepper, and peapods or frozen peas to the pan, and stir-fry for 6 minutes, or until the onions are golden and translucent. Add the apple, garlic, ginger, and remaining 2 teaspoons curry powder to the pan, and stir-fry for 2 minutes. Reduce heat. In a small mixing bowl, with a fork or whisk, mix the broth and cornstarch until there are no clumps. Add the mixture to the pan, stir to mix all ingredients, increase heat to a boil, and then reduce to medium heat and stir and cook for 5 minutes. Stir in the chicken and sour cream and cook for 5 minutes on medium-low heat.

2. Serve over a bed of rice, or with rice on the side.

OPTIONAL: Tofu can be used for a vegetarian option, or pork loin strips can be used instead of chicken.

OKINAWAN KIMCHI PORK

This recipe is made with kimchi, a favorite fermented food in many Asian countries, including Japan. It's a typical Okinawan chanpuru (stir-fry), and it is a great dish even without the pork. I suggest you purchase kimchi, rather than make it yourself, but watch the salt, and make sure it is fermented rather than just salted. Some brands, like Mother-in-Law's, say on the jar that they are fermented. Be careful, this stuff is spicy! If it is too hot for your palate, cook some napa, or Chinese, cabbage and mix it with the kimchi before adding to the recipe. See the recipe options for how to do this.

Servings: 4

1 tablespoon canola oil
1 medium onion, chopped
6 ounces pork, cut into strips 1/4 inch thick and 1 1/2 inches long
8 ounces firm tofu, diced or shredded into 3/4-inch pieces
1 1/2 cups kimchi (or mix with napa cabbage)
1 tablespoon soy sauce
6 eggs, lightly beaten

1. Add canola oil to a wok or large skillet on medium-high heat. Once the pan is hot, add onions and stir-fry for 2 minutes. Add pork and stir-fry until it is browned through. Add tofu and stir-fry another 2 minutes, then add kimchi and soy sauce and mix well. Pour eggs over the top and allow to cook until mostly set. Stir gently to finish cooking the eggs and then serve hot.

2. This dish goes perfectly with a bit of rice. Serve with about 1/2 to 3/4 cup cooked rice per person.

OPTIONAL: If the kimchi is too spicy, mix it with steamed or boiled napa, or Chinese, cabbage. To do this, simply wash, chop, and steam or boil the cabbage for 5 minutes prior to use.

NON-MEAT OPTION: Try this dish without the pork. In this variation the kimchi and egg flavor shine through.

DESSERTS

Desserts aren't traditionally a major dietary feature among the Mindspan Elite, who are more likely to opt for flavorful coffee, tea, and/or fresh fruit. But if you still want to soothe your sweet tooth, try one of these options.

SARDINIAN SEMOLINA PUDDING

This is a classic Sardinian dish. Semolina is made from durum wheat, which gives foods a low glycemic index. The cream and optional egg further lower the glycemic index.

Servings: 4

1 1/2 cups water
1 cup heavy cream
2 tablespoons sugar
1 teaspoon salt
3/4 cup coarsely ground semolina

Pour water and cream into a medium saucepan, place over medium heat, and add sugar and salt. When the liquid boils, gradually stir or whisk in all of the semolina. Cook while stirring until the mixture thickens, which should take 8 to 10 minutes. Let the pudding cool to room temperature, or refrigerate to enhance formation of resistant starch. Rewarm to eat, but if you cook until hot, let it return to a warm temperature before eating.

NONVEGETARIAN OPTION: One egg can be stirred into the cooled pudding. Stir the egg in completely, and re-heat until very hot. Let cool until warm before eating.

IDEAL OPTION: Top with a bit of fruit or berry sauce or preserves. Here is one recipe for a delicious berry sauce.

Berry Sauce

1/4 cup unsweetened orange juice
1 pint blueberries, blackberries, or
   raspberries
Up to 2 tablespoons sugar (optional)

To prepare the sauce, mix the orange juice, berries, and sugar, if desired, in a small saucepan. Bring to a light boil while stirring over medium heat. Reduce heat and simmer, stirring occasionally for 15 to 20 minutes, or until the berries have disintegrated. Allow to cool until warm, and then spoon over the pudding.

DARKBERRY DIPS

This recipe is an excellent way to get a dose of dark chocolate, one of my — and the entire world's — favorite saturated fats.

Servings: 4

Dash vanilla, mint, or almond extract
12 to 14 medium-large strawberries, or about 40 raspberries

Dipping Chocolate

About 4 ounces 70% to 85% dark chocolate
2 teaspoons heavy cream
or
3 squares (3 ounces) unsweetened baking chocolate
2 teaspoons heavy cream
1 level tablespoon sugar

1. In a small coffee cup combine ingredients for the dipping chocolate and heat in microwave on medium power for about 40 seconds, or until the chocolate melts. Add the flavor extract and stir until cooler and thicker but still liquid. If using strawberries, hold each berry by the stem. Dip in chocolate until almost covered, remove excess, and then place on a plate covered with plastic wrap or waxed paper. If using raspberries, drizzle chocolate over berries placed on plastic wrap or waxed paper. Put in freezer for about 10 minutes until the chocolate hardens.

2. Serve on the chilled plate with a few mint leaves.

SNACKS

Most Mindspan Elite don't snack much or at all, but if you are running low on fuel, here are some simple, healthful snacks.

Pickled Herring or Sardines on a Cracker
Pickled herring is a fantastic snack, as are canned sardines (in water or olive oil). Eat up to 4 pieces of herring or 2 medium sardines for a snack. As always, select a cracker free of added iron.

Veggies and Vinaigrette or Nut Butter
Slice some carrots and celery and dip them in vinaigrette dressing, or coat them with almond or peanut butter.

A Handful of Nuts
Nuts are an excellent and healthful snack. Macadamia nuts, pecans, walnuts, and almonds are all top choices.

Roasted soybeans and peanuts aren't actually nuts, but are also good snacks.

Sourdough Bread with Cheese and Apples
Pair 3 or 4 small pieces of sourdough bread with an ounce of goat cheese, fontina, asiago, or Brie. (All are excellent choices, but feel free to try others.) Add half a sliced apple. The fat and protein in the cheese blunt the tartness of the apple and contribute to a heavenly combination.

BREADS AND FOCACCIA

Many breads presented in this section are made most easily with a bread machine, although they usually are not as authentic or quite as nicely textured as oven-baked breads. To make a chewier bread, use starter rather than yeast, add gluten, and/or replace some of the flour with semolina flour starter. Adding gluten can also give a higher rise. Try adding 1 teaspoon gluten flour and 1 teaspoon water to any bread recipe to improve the texture. Adding vegetables like pumpkin or zucchini can also increase firmness. The dough of the focaccia can be made in a bread machine, but it is baked in an oven. Focaccia and tarts (torte) are common in Ligurian cuisine, and can be found with many kinds of stuffing or toppings.

When working with dough on a countertop, prevent sticking by first sprinkling flour onto the surface. To shape a loaf prior to placing it on a cooking sheet, first wet the work surface with a bit of water or a damp sponge, then place a large piece of plastic wrap on the surface. Then flour the surface of the plastic wrap prior to placing the dough on it. This allows you to transfer a formed loaf to a baking pan. This technique works very well with the rustic loaf or rustic sourdough recipe.

FERMENTATION THROUGHOUT THE AGES

Breads and alcohols have been made and consumed for millennia. Written histories of ancient Egypt and Mesopotamia describe breadmaking essentials. The first time breads and alcohols were produced was almost certainly accidental, but inevitable, since yeasts — the microscopic fungi that produce ethanol and the carbon dioxide bubbles in bread — are ubiquitous and even float through the air. Around 1500 B.C. chance became less of a factor through the use of fermentation "starters." But it wasn't until the mid-nineteenth century that Louis Pasteur discovered that microbes were responsible for food and alcohol fermentation. By the late nineteenth century, yeasts had been isolated and pure yeast strains began to be used in the production of various alcohols and breads.

It took until the middle of the twentieth century for industrial breadmaking to largely supplant traditional breads throughout most parts of developed nations. But some Mediterranean backwaters were more resistant to the change. Traditional breads are made with non-sour starter cultures or preferments (poolish, biga, levain, etc.) that promote the growth of bacteria during prefermentation. Most bacteria grow much faster than yeast, and so even a small starting amount of bacteria can expand very rapidly and contribute to the overall quality of the dough. The range of tartness of traditional starter-based breads — from unnoticeable to noticeably tart — is due to lactic acid produced by lactobacillus bacteria, which are symbiotic to the yeasts that produce carbon dioxide and cause dough to rise. Even in the absence of tart lactic acid, the many rich and varied flavors of traditional breads come partly from the products of both bacterial and yeast fermentation.

BASIC SOURDOUGH SEMOLINA BREAD

Yield: 2-pound loaf

1 cup water
2 teaspoons sugar
About 1 cup sourdough starter (see p. 428)
2 1/4 cups white, non-enriched flour
1 cup ground semolina flour (not iron-
  enriched)
1 teaspoon salt
1 tablespoon butter or oil

Put water in a microwave-safe container and heat for 30 seconds at high power in a microwave oven (until warm but not hot to the touch). Transfer to the bread machine pan. Add other ingredients in the order presented (make sure starter does not contact salt or butter or oil). Bake using the standard bread machine program for a 2-pound loaf.

OPTIONAL: Other flours can be added instead of the semolina.

PUMPKIN SEMOLINA BREAD

Yield: 2-pound loaf

1 15-ounce can pumpkin, or 1½ cups roasted fresh pumpkin
1/2 cup water
2 teaspoons sugar
1 teaspoon salt
1 tablespoon butter or oil
3 cups white, non-enriched flour
1 cup ground semolina flour (not iron-enriched)
2 teaspoons yeast, or 1/2 cup starter (see p. 428)

Mix pumpkin and water in a small microwave-safe container and heat for 60 seconds at high power in a microwave oven (until warm but not hot to the touch). Transfer to the bread machine pan. Add other ingredients in the order presented. (Make sure the yeast doesn't contact the salt or butter or oil.) Bake using the standard bread machine program for a 2-pound loaf.

OPTIONAL: Add 1 cup rehydrated dried and sweetened cranberries. To prepare the cranberries, put 3/4 cup cranberries and 1 teaspoon water in a microwave-safe container and microwave on high or medium heat for 90 seconds, or until hot. Let stand for 5 minutes and then add to bread machine pan.

You can use a higher proportion of semolina flour (up to three-fourths).

BASIC FOCACCIA

Focaccia is *the* classic Italian bread. In Liguria and across most of Italy, it is a staple, snack, and fast food.

Yield: 1 loaf

3 cups white, non-enriched flour
2 teaspoons salt
1 cup water
1 teaspoon yeast
2 tablespoons olive oil

1. Mix the flour and salt together in a medium mixing bowl. Heat the water until warm (about 90°F). Add the yeast to the water and let stand a few minutes to rehydrate the yeast. Add the yeast water to the flour and salt mixture and mix, then add the olive oil and continue to mix well with a sturdy spatula or spoon. If the mixture appears dry, add a small amount of water. Continue mixing until uniform.
2. Coat the palms of your hands with flour prior to handling the dough. Knead the dough on a floured flat work surface until the dough is firm and pliable. Put the dough ball into a medium or large bowl lightly coated with olive oil and cover with a kitchen

towel. Let the dough rise in the bowl for 2 hours, or place in a refrigerator and let it rise overnight.

3. Shape the dough into an oblong shape slightly smaller than the size of a rectangular loaf pan and flatten with a rolling pin. Lightly oil the pan and then place the dough in the pan. Cover with a towel and let rest for 45 minutes. At the end of 45 minutes, preheat oven to 450°F. When the oven is at temperature, brush the top of the loaf lightly with olive oil and sprinkle with a pinch of salt. Carefully place the loaf in the oven and bake it for 20 to 25 minutes. Let cool on a wire rack.

OPTIONAL: Add chopped olives to the dough, or caramelized onions to the top of the loaf.

Rustic Loaf or Rustic Sourdough

Yield: 2-pound loaf

2 1/2 cups white, non-enriched, unbleached flour
1/2 teaspoon yeast (for sourdough, replace the yeast and 1/2 cup flour with 1 cup starter, p. 428)
1 1/2 cups semolina flour (not iron-enriched)
2 cups water
1 tablespoon olive oil
1 1/2 teaspoons salt
Coarse semolina or cornmeal

1. Place the flour and yeast (or sourdough starter) in a large mixing bowl and mix together well. Add the semolina, water, olive oil, and salt and mix with a heavy spatula or spoon until all the ingredients are uniformly mixed. Cover the bowl with aluminum foil, place in a cool location (away from heaters or sunny windows), and let rise for 12 hours.
2. Shape the dough into a loaf about 12 inches long, and place on a baking sheet lightly greased with light olive oil (if you are using a nonstick baking sheet, the olive oil can be omitted), and lightly coated with coarse semolina or cornmeal. Sprinkle sem-

olina or white flour over the top and lightly rub over the surface of the dough, drape a kitchen towel over the loaf, and let rise for 1 1/2 to 2 hours. Bake for 30 to 40 minutes until the loaf is golden and gives a resonant thump when tapped firmly.

OPTIONAL: For an onion herb loaf, add 3/4 cup cooked onions, 1 teaspoon oregano, 1 teaspoon thyme, and 1 teaspoon rosemary to the dry ingredients prior to mixing.

HOMEMADE STAPLES

Some of *The Mindspan Diet* recipes require select ingredients that are important for maximizing mindspan. There are no substitutes. I make my own breads and I suggest you do the same. Bread machines make the process almost automatic. Certain vegetables enhance both the flavor and texture of breads, and the only way to have bread exactly as you want it is to make it yourself. I also make my own pickles. Both are so good I prefer them to any commercial alternative.

I include milk and buttermilk substitutes for lactose digesters (made from sour cream or cream). If you're able to digest lactose, you unfortunately absorb additional carb calories in the form of the highly reactive sugar galactose. If you cannot digest lactose, count yourself lucky and consume milk or buttermilk and lactose-containing dairy in moderation. Do not use lactose-reduced milk (such as Lactaid), since this predigests lactose, releases the harmful galactose, and deprives you of the benefits of the increased feeding of your microbiome. People who have high LDL cholesterol (above 130 mg/dL) should use reduced-fat sour cream or skip this staple altogether and opt for soy milk or another option with low saturated animal fat.

For those able to digest lactose, sour cream has at least three benefits relative to milk or buttermilk: low lactose, less methionine, and the X factor lactic acid. Use full-fat sour cream. Do not use nonfat sour cream (this concoction has nothing to do with cream). If you use reduced-fat sour cream, make sure it has low carbohydrate and protein amounts, proportional to full-fat varieties (check the nutrition labels).

Sour cream milk substitute is very easy to make. For a lighter blend similar to skim milk, just add 2 tablespoons of sour cream per cup of water in a mixing bowl or container with a screw-on lid, and either mix or shake until the sour cream is completely dispersed. For a creamier blend, more similar to whole milk or buttermilk, use 4 tablespoons of sour cream per cup of water. You can also add 1/2 teaspoon of sugar per cup to counter the tartness of the lactic acid. If you want to replicate the full X factor effects of milk, you can even add inulin, lactulose, or fructooligosaccharides, up to about 10 grams per cup.

This milk substitute works great for granola and other breakfast cereals. It isn't as good for coffee or tea, but you can use cream instead of sour cream for these. It also doesn't work in recipes that require protein from milk. For such recipes, add one large egg per cup of sour cream milk substitute.

HOMEMADE SOURDOUGH STARTER

You can make sourdough starter at home with nothing but flour, water, and time. Add about 2 ounces unbleached or whole wheat flour to 2 ounces of clean, low-chlorine water. Stir well until there is no dry flour remaining. Place in a location where the temperature will remain 68° to 90°F. Split starter, and renew every day with an equal amount of flour and water. After five days, your starter is ready to use! Try adding about 1 cup of starter per recipe. If you are using a bread machine, it might require a slow rise or customizable cycle, but give your machine a try! The worst that can happen is that you'll get a low-rise but still flavorful loaf. If the conditions in your area aren't producing suitable results, consider a commercial sourdough starter, many of which can be found online.

HOMEMADE PICKLING BRINE

This recipe works with cucumbers and most other vegetables. You should use about an equal amount of brine and vegetables.

2 cups water
1 3/4 cups white vinegar
1 cup chopped fresh or frozen dill
1/2 cup sugar
1 1/2 tablespoons salt
1 1/2 tablespoons brown mustard
1 tablespoon commercial pickling spice
8 garlic cloves, chopped
1/2 teaspoon crushed red pepper flakes

Mix all of the ingredients in a large mixing bowl or a pickling container that will hold at least 10 cups. If you plan to fill multiple smaller containers (glass jar, sealable plastic, etc.), after preparing the brine, fill the containers about halfway, then add the vegetables. Refrigerate for at least 1 week, and preferably longer. After 2 months in the brine, some softer vegetables, like cucumbers, lose their crispness.

HOMEMADE KETCHUP

Yield: Just under 1 1/2 cups

1 6-ounce can tomato paste
1/4 cup sugar
1/2 cup white vinegar or flavored vinegar
  of your choice
1/4 cup water
1/4 teaspoon onion powder
1/4 teaspoon or less garlic powder

1. Combine all ingredients in a medium saucepan over medium heat. Whisk until smooth. When the mixture comes to a boil, reduce heat to low and simmer for 15 minutes, stirring often.
2. Remove pan from heat and cover until cool. Chill and store in a covered container.

OPTIONAL: Using brown sugar rather than white will result in a flavor more like barbecue sauce. Other flavors you can add for variations on barbecue sauce: pineapple juice, smoke flavor, molasses, garlic, and tamarind.

ACKNOWLEDGMENTS

I have many people to thank for bringing my life and this project to fruition. I'll begin in the present and move in roughly reverse chronological order. This lengthy project might not have happened without the love and support of my wife, Martha. She and my friend Ed Maxwell, an outstanding chef, taught me much of what I know about cooking. This book was improved greatly by the efforts of my agent, Mitchell Waters, as well as those of Steven Salpeter, Tim Knowlton, Jonathan Lyons, Sarah Perillo, and the rest of the team at my agency, Curtis Brown, Ltd. My original manuscript was transformed into its present readable form by Hallie Levine and the rest of the talented crew led by my editor, Marnie Cochran, including proofreader Barb Jatkola, and many others behind the scenes at Ballantine Books and Random House.

I can't thank enough Madeleine Ball, Mike

Chou, Sasha Wait Zaranek, Ward Vandewege, Tom Clegg (and the rest of the Curoverse team), Jason Bobe, and everyone on the Personal Genome Project staff. Thank you for all your hard and smart work over many years and for having me as part of the team building a visionary project — and for understanding my scarcity as I researched and wrote this book. I owe similar apologies and gratitude to everyone at my other organizations. Thank you, Ron Kessler, Martine Rothblatt, Alex Hoekstra, and Ranjan Ahuja at the Mind First Foundation. This book is but one contribution to our goal of maximizing mindspan. I'm also grateful to Mirza Cifric, Jonathan Zhao, Dominic Paratore, and my talented colleagues at Veritas Genetics and Samplify Bio. A special thanks to my sister Shelly Estep, who holds everything together.

Many people have helped me to think like a scientist, and to bring the benefits of real science into people's everyday lives. The wisest choices I made in my life led on a long and winding road to an eventual meeting with my mentor, George Church. George has exerted a profound influence on me as a scientist, and an even greater influence on me personally. Most scientists can't even imagine the box that George thinks outside of. Peter Medawar and George C. Williams also have been major influences. Unfortunately, just as I was getting to know him by email, George told me he recently had been diagnosed with Alzheimer's disease. Matt Kaeberlein has been an important contributor to my own understanding of aging and longevity, and Eugene Weinberg made me realize the extent of the dangers of iron. Both are model scientists, pursuing evidence wherever it might lead. Going way back, thank you, Thomas Podleski; Carl Sagan; my ninth-grade math teacher, Robert Fieberg; and thinkers and researchers in all disciplines who don't care who is right, only what is right.

My four grandparents navigated the difficult times of world wars and the Great Depression, and then the two who lived the longest, Mimi Estep and Scott Player, were taken from me by dementia. They and my parents, Sallie and Tony, brought me into existence, and helped me get on the path toward who I am today. My efforts to make the most of every mind are a living embodiment of their lives and their legacies.

APPENDIX A.
ALZHEIMER'S DISEASE AND DEMENTIA RESOURCES

- Alzheimer's Disease Fact Sheet at the National Institute on Aging: nia.nih.gov/alzheimers/publication/alzheimers-disease-fact-sheet
- Alzheimer's Association: alz.org/research/funding/advisory_council_alzheimers_association.asp
- The 10/66 Dementia Research Group: alz.co.uk/1066

APPENDIX B.
RECOMMENDED GENETIC
AND BIOMARKER TESTING

Before you embark on the Mindspan Diet or as soon as possible after you begin, I recommend testing a small number of key biomarkers so that you know rather than guess where you stand and where you are headed. Many important biomarker tests are provided in routine physical exams, but some of the following important biomarkers typically are not.

- Fasting glucose
- Fasting insulin
- Serum iron
- Serum ferritin
- Hemoglobin
- Total iron-binding capacity (TIBC) or unsaturated iron-binding capacity (UIBC)
- Telomere length

Unsaturated iron-binding capacity (UIBC) typically is superior to total iron-binding capacity (TIBC), but facilities that test for this can be more difficult to locate.

I also recommend some key genetic tests. Minimally, you should know your genetics for the ability to digest lactose (the relevant gene is LCT) and your status for the main iron overload gene (HFE). Recommended genes, methods, and suppliers are subject to rapid change, so for additional and updated information on genetic testing and biomarker measurement, visit mindspandiet.com.

APPENDIX C.
IRON-RICH AND IRON-POOR
MEATS AND FISH

Many meats have a high content of absorbable heme iron. However, other meats and some fish have low heme iron content. The table below shows the total iron and heme iron per 3-ounce serving (cooked) and the percentage of iron that is heme iron.

Type of Meat/ fish		Iron (mg)	Heme Iron (mg)	Percent Heme
Fish	Cod	0.4	0.1	20
	Mackerel	1.4	0.3	28
	Salmon	0.6	0.1	17*
	Catfish	1.5	0.4	28
	Red snapper	1.2	0.2	15
	Sardines and herring	2.2	0.4	18*
	Anchovies	1.9	0.6	28*
Seafood	Mussels	4.6	2.1	48

Type of Meat/ fish		Iron (mg)	Heme Iron (mg)	Percent Heme
	Lobster	1.6	0.6	40
	Giant prawn	0.6	0.1	11
	Shrimp	2.0	0.6	30
Chicken	Breast	0.3	0.1	23
	Leg	1.2	0.3	22
Venison		4.5	2.2	51
Lamb		3.1	1.6	55
Beef	Sirloin	2.5	1.2	52
	Round steak	3.2	1.5	50
	Top round	2.5	1.1	48
	Ground	2.5	0.9	40
Pork	Tenderloin	0.8	0.3	31
	Loin	2.4	1.1	45
	Blood	12.2	15.3	80
Liver pâté		5.0	0.8	16

* Canned salmon (with bones), whole sardines, and anchovies contain substantial amounts of calcium, which inhibits iron absorption if a minimum of about 300 mg calcium is consumed.

Data from various sources, including irondisorders.org.

APPENDIX D.
OMEGA FATS OF GRAINS
AND COMMON OILS

OMEGA FATS OF GRAINS

Linoleic acid (LA, omega-6), alpha-linolenic acid (α-LA, omega-3) content, and their ratio (milligrams per 100 grams of grain)

Grain	LA	α-LA	LA/α-LA ratio
Barley	505	55	9.2
Brown rice	1850	81	22.8
Buckwheat	961	78	12.3
Corn	2100	65	32.3
Millet	2010	115	17.5
Oats	2420	110	21.8
Rye	958	157	6.1
Whole wheat	740	40	18.5

OMEGA FATS OF COMMON OILS

Linoleic acid (LA, omega-6), alpha-linolenic acid (α-LA, omega-3) content, and their ratio (in grams/ tablespoon)

Oil	LA	α-LA	LA/α-LA ratio
Canola	2.8	1.3	2.2
Coconut	0.24	none	>100
Corn	7.2	0.16	45
Cottonseed	7.0	0.03	>100
Flaxseed (linseed)	2.2	8.0	0.28
Olive	1.1	0.1	11
Palm kernel	0.2	none	>100
Peanut	4.3	none	>100
Safflower, high LA	10.0	none	>100
Safflower, high MUFA	0.5 to 1.9	none	>100
Sesame	5.6	0.04	>100
Soybean	6.8	0.9	7.8
Sunflower, low LA	5.4	0.03	>100

NOTES

Introduction

The first draft of the human genome J. C. Venter et al., "The Sequence of the Human Genome," *Science* 291, no. 5507 (2001): 1304–51; E. S. Lander et al., "Initial Sequencing and Analysis of the Human Genome," *Nature* 409, no. 6822 (2001): 860–921.

One public example John Lauerman, "My DNA Results Spur Alzheimer's Anxiety at $12,000 Cost," Bloomberg.com, accessed November 5, 2015, bloomberg.com/news/articles/2012 -11-06/my-dna-results-spur-alzheimer-s -anxiety-at-12-000-cost; Ira Flatow, "Genetic Test Reveals Unexpected Data," NPR.org, accessed November 5, 2015, npr.org/2012/02/24/147356658/ genetic-test-reveals-unexpected-data.

Recent research suggests that Parkinson's C. C. Johnson et al., "Adult Nutrient Intake as a Risk Factor for

Parkinson's Disease," *International Journal of Epidemiology* 28, no. 6 (December 1, 1999): 1102–9, doi:10.1093/ije/28.6.1102; K. M. Powers et al., "Parkinson's Disease Risks Associated with Dietary Iron, Manganese, and Other Nutrient Intakes," *Neurology* 60, no. 11 (June 10, 2003): 1761–66, doi:10.1212/01.WNL.0000068021.13945.7F.

hemochromatosis, which is fairly common Wint Nandar and James R. Connor, "HFE Gene Variants Affect Iron in the Brain," *The Journal of Nutrition* 141, no. 4 (April 1, 2011): 729S–739S, doi:10.3945/jn.110.130351.

1. Mindspans on the Move

According to recent polls Reuters News Service, "Americans Rank Alzheimer's as Most Feared Disease, According to New Marist Poll for Home Instead Senior Care | Reuters," accessed November 5, 2015, reuters.com/article/2012/11/13/idUS129170+13-Nov-2012+BW20121113.

Genetic evidence shows R. L. McGeachin and J. R. Akin, "Amylase Levels in the Tissues and Body Fluids of Several Primate Species," *Comparative Biochemistry and Physiology. A, Comparative Phys-*

iology 72, no. 1 (1982): 267–69.

The changes with the largest effect George H. Perry et al., "Diet and the Evolution of Human Amylase Gene Copy Number Variation," *Nature Genetics* 39, no. 10 (October 2007): 1256–60, doi:10.1038/ng2123.

In fact, mummies Randall C. Thompson et al., "Atherosclerosis Across 4000 Years of Human History: The Horus Study of Four Ancient Populations," *Lancet* 381, no. 9873 (April 6, 2013): 1211–22, doi:10.1016/S0140-6736(13)60598-X.

In fact, the age-adjusted rates B. Guyer et al., "Annual Summary of Vital Statistics: Trends in the Health of Americans During the 20th Century," *Pediatrics* 106, no. 6 (December 2000): 1307–17; Centers for Disease Control and Prevention (CDC), "Decline in Deaths from Heart Disease and Stroke — United States, 1900–1999," *Morbidity and Mortality Weekly Report* (*MMWR*) 48, no. 30 (August 6, 1999): 649–56.

When they were children Elizabeth Arias, *National Vital Statistics Reports* 64, no. 11 (September 22, 2015), accessed November 5, 2015, cdc.gov/nchs/data/nvsr/nvsr64/nvsr64_11.pdf.

Between 2000 and 2010 Jean-Marie Robine and Graziella Caselli, "An Unprecedented Increase in the Number of Centenarians," *Genus* 61, no. 1 (January 1, 2005): 57–82; Jean-Marie Robine, Yasuhiko Saito, and Carol Jagger, "The Emergence of Extremely Old People: The Case of Japan," *Experimental Gerontology, Proceedings of the 2nd Symposium on Organisms with Slow Aging (SOSA-2),* 38, no. 7 (July 2003): 735–39, doi:10.1016/S0531-5565(03)00100-1; Kaare Christensen et al., "Ageing Populations: The Challenges Ahead," *Lancet* 374, no. 9696 (October 3, 2009): 1196–1208, doi:10.1016/S0140-6736(09)61460-4.

As with life expectancy Mercedes D. Dickinson and Merrill Hiscock, "The Flynn Effect in Neuropsychological Assessment," *Applied Neuropsychology* 18, no. 2 (April 2011): 136–42, doi:10.1080/09084282.2010.547785; Jakob Pietschnig and Martin Voracek, "One Century of Global IQ Gains: A Formal Meta-Analysis of the Flynn Effect (1909–2013)," *Perspectives on Psychological Science: A Journal of the Association for Psychological Science* 10, no. 3 (May 2015): 282–306, doi:10.1177/1745691615577701.

Some of these reports suggest Archana

Singh-Manoux et al., "Timing of Onset of Cognitive Decline: Results from Whitehall II Prospective Cohort Study," *BMJ (Clinical Research Ed.)* 344 (2012): d7622.

According to a recent study Rafael Lozano et al., "Global and Regional Mortality from 235 Causes of Death for 20 Age Groups in 1990 and 2010: A Systematic Analysis for the Global Burden of Disease Study 2010," *Lancet* 380, no. 9859 (December 15, 2012): 2095–2128, doi:10.1016/S0140-6736(12)61728-0.

Alzheimer's disease is responsible Alzheimer's Association, "ff_infographic _2015.pdf," accessed November 1, 2015, alz.org/facts/downloads/ff_infographic _2015.pdf.

The Lyon, France, heart study M. De Lorgeril et al., "Effect of a Mediterranean Type of Diet on the Rate of Cardiovascular Complications in Patients with Coronary Artery Disease: Insights into the Cardioprotective Effect of Certain Nutriments," *Journal of the American College of Cardiology* 28, no. 5 (November 1, 1996): 1103–8, doi:10.1016/S0735 -1097(96)00280-X.

2. Genes and Environment, Fuel and Fire

Currently, most experts agree that genes Jacob vB Hjelmborg et al., "Genetic Influence on Human Lifespan and Longevity," *Human Genetics* 119, no. 3 (April 2006): 312–21, doi:10.1007/s00439-006-0144-y; A. M. Herskind et al., "The Heritability of Human Longevity: A Population-Based Study of 2872 Danish Twin Pairs Born 1870–1900," *Human Genetics* 97, no. 3 (March 1996): 319–23.

Consider one extraordinary example Michel Allard et al., *Jeanne Calment: From Van Gogh's Time to Ours, 122 Extraordinary Years* (Thorndike, Maine: Thorndike Press, 1999).

Identical twins . . . score nearly identically Herskind et al., "The Heritability of Human Longevity"; K. Christensen et al., "Perceived Age as Clinically Useful Biomarker of Ageing: Cohort Study," *BMJ (Clinical Research Ed.)* 339 (2009): b5262; David Andrew Gunn et al., "Mortality Is Written on the Face," *The Journals of Gerontology Series A: Biological Sciences and Medical Sciences,* August 11, 2015, doi:10.1093/gerona/glv090.

In fact, even the average low-fiber Western diet P. Brøbech Mortensen and

M. Rye Clausen, "Short-Chain Fatty Acids in the Human Colon: Relation to Gastrointestinal Health and Disease," *Scandinavian Journal of Gastroenterology* 31, no. s216 (January 1996): 132–48, doi:10.3109/00365529609094568; I. Nordgaard and P. B. Mortensen, "Digestive Processes in the Human Colon," *Nutrition* (Burbank, Calif.) 11, no. 1 (February 1995): 37–45.

3. Key Similarities of Mindspan Elite Cuisines

Regardless of method World Health Organization, *World Health Statistics 2008* (Geneva, Switzerland: World Health Organization, 2008), site.ebrary.com/id/10233806.

Finland, Iceland, the United States World Health Organization, "WHO | Causes of Death in 2008," WHO, accessed November 8, 2015, who.int/gho/mortality_burden_disease/causes_death_2008/en/.

The best of the best is Japan It's important to keep in mind that history is replete with countless tales of extraordinary longevity — many of which are literally unbelievable. For example, in 2010, demographers in Japan discovered that estimates of Japanese elderly were inflated by over 230,000 people. Most had died and many deaths went unreported by relatives who continued to collect their pensions. Since then, researchers have done a thorough housecleaning of past survey methods, and we can now have full confidence in current Japanese longevity data, including the fact that Japan has the highest proportion of validated centenarians and both current and past supercentenarians. L. Fratiglioni et al., "Incidence of Dementia and Major Subtypes in Europe: A Collaborative Study of Population-Based Cohorts. Neurologic Diseases in the Elderly Research Group," *Neurology* 54, no. 11 suppl. 5 (2000): S10–15; Blossom Stephan and Carol Brayne, "Prevalence and Projections of Dementia," accessed November 6, 2015, mheducation.co.uk/openup/chapters/9780335223756.pdf.

Japanese women are the real stars At least part of the difference is explained by the smoking gap. Over the past decades only about 10 percent of women smoked cigarettes, versus over 80 percent of men in the mid-1960s, which has declined gradually to below 30 percent today. It is quite astounding that the Japanese have long led worldwide life expectancy despite being among the world's heaviest smokers. They must be doing everything else just about right.

The highest longevity concentration Pedro Reques Velasco, "Longevidad y territorio: Un análisis geodemográfico de la población centenaria en España," *Revista Española de Geriatría y Gerontología* 43, no. 2 (March 2008): 96–105, doi:10.1016/S0211-139X(08)71162-4.

In the United States, vegetarian and pescatarian M. J. Orlich et al., "Vegetarian Dietary Patterns and Mortality in Adventist Health Study 2," *JAMA Internal Medicine* 173, no. 13 (July 8, 2013): 1230–38, doi:10.1001/jamainternmed .2013.6473.

These countries and regions have the unfortunate distinction Fratiglioni et al., "Incidence of Dementia and Major Subtypes in Europe"; Johan P. Mackenbach, Marina Karanikolos, and Caspar W. N. Looman, "The Rise of Mortality from Mental and Neurological Diseases in Europe, 1979–2009: Observational Study," *BMC Public Health* 14 (August 13, 2014), doi:10.1186/1471-2458-14 -840.

The Longest-Lived People in the World My analysis of data on validated centenarians and supercentenarians from the Gerontology Research Group shows that Liguria has the highest proportion of centenarian residents and the highest supercentenarian rate among all twenty regions of Italy. The only other region with a comparable proportion of supercentenarian residents is Aosta Valley, which had only one supercentenarian lifetime resident, compared to twelve who have lived in Liguria. Aside from Aosta Valley, the supercentenarian resident rate in Liguria is more than twice that of all other Italian regions, including third-place Sardinia. Dan Buettner, *The Blue Zones Solution: Eating and Living Like the World's Healthiest People* (Washington, D.C.: National Geographic, 2015); Dan Buettner, *The Blue Zones: Lessons for Living Longer from the People Who've Lived the Longest* (Washington, D.C.; Enfield: National Geographic Society; Publishers Group UK [distributor], 2010); A. Herm, K. S. L. Cheung, and M. Poulain, "Emergence of Oldest Old and Centenarians: Demographic Analysis," 2012, hub.hku.hk/handle/10722/198087; "Emma Morano," *Wikipedia,* *the Free Encyclopedia,* November 3, 2015, en.wikipedia.org/w/index.php ?title=Emma_Morano; Robine, Saito, and Jagger, "The Emergence of Extremely Old People"; Jean-Marie Robine and Yasuhiko Saito, "The Number of Centenarians in Europe," *European Papers on the New Welfare,* October 10, 2009, eng.newwelfare.org/2009/10/10/ the-number-of-centenarians-in-europe/; Allard et al., *Jeanne Calment.*

There's no doubt that diet K. Hatada et al., "Further Evidence of Westernization of Dementia Prevalence in Nagasaki, Japan, and Family Recognition," *International Psychogeriatrics/IPA* 11, no. 2 (June 1999): 123–38; L. White et al., "Prevalence of Dementia in Older Japanese-American Men in Hawaii: The Honolulu-Asia Aging Study," *JAMA* 276, no. 12 (September 25, 1996): 955–60.

Contrary to popular belief Food and Agriculture Organization of the United Nations (FAOSTAT), accessed November 8, 2015, faostat3.fao.org/home/E.

France is last and Japan second to last World Health Organization, "WHO | Causes of Death in 2008."

Some Core Commonalities of the Mindspan Elite Food and Agriculture Organization of the United Nations (FAOSTAT); Colman Andrews, *Flavors of the Riviera: Discovering Real Mediterranean Cooking* (New York: Bantam Books, 1996); Jacques Médecin and Peter John Graham, *Cuisine Niçoise: Recipes from a Mediterranean Kitchen* (London: Grub Street, 2002); S. Miyagi et al., "Longevity and Diet in Okinawa, Japan: The Past, Present and Future," *Asia-Pacific Journal of Public Health* 15, no. 1 suppl. (March 1, 2003): S3–9, doi:10.1177/10105 3950301500S03; D. Craig Willcox et al., "The Okinawan Diet: Health Implications of a Low-Calorie, Nutrient-Dense, Antioxidant-Rich Dietary Pattern Low in Glycemic Load," *Journal of the American College of Nutrition* 28, suppl. (August 1, 2009): 500S–516S, doi:10.1080/073157 24.2009.10718117; Bradley J. Willcox, D. Craig Willcox, and Makoto Suzuki, *The Okinawa Program: How the World's Longest-Lived People Achieve Everlasting Health — and How You Can Too* (New York: Three Rivers Press, 2002); Buettner, *The Blue Zones*; Buettner, *The Blue Zones Solution*; G. M. Pes et al., "Lifestyle and Nutrition Related to Male Longevity in Sardinia: An Ecological Study," *Nutrition, Metabolism, and Cardio-*

vascular Diseases: NMCD 23, no. 3 (March 2013): 212–19, doi:10.1016/j. numecd.2011.05.004.

In the Italian Riviera regions A. Turrini et al., "Food Consumption Patterns in Italy: The INN-CA Study 1994–1996," *European Journal of Clinical Nutrition* 55, no. 7 (July 2001): 571–88, doi:10.1038/ sj.ejcn.1601185.

These aren't just side dishes Médecin and Graham, *Cuisine Niçoise.*

In his classic book *Flavors of the Riviera* Andrews, *Flavors of the Riviera.*

Just as with their Mediterranean neighbors LiveWell for LIFE, "Food Patterns and Dietary Recommendations in Spain, France, and Sweden," accessed November 5, 2015, livewellforlife.eu/wp -content/uploads/2012/05/LiveWell_A4 -Food-Patterns-Report_web.pdf.

In 1961, about 45 percent of food energy Food and Agriculture Organization of the United Nations (FAOSTAT).

In Japan, about half of calories Ibid.

But Okinawans haven't consumed Hidemi Todoriki, D. Craig Willcox, and Bradley Willcox, "The Effects of Post-War Dietary Change on Longevity and Health in Okinawa," in *Okinawan Journal of American Studies,* 1 (2004), 52–61.

Gallo pinto Buettner, *The Blue Zones.*

In other words, at the same age Raj N. Kalaria et al., "Alzheimer's Disease and Vascular Dementia in Developing Countries: Prevalence, Management, and Risk Factors," *Lancet Neurology* 7, no. 9 (September 2008): 812–26, doi:10.1016/S14 74-4422(08)70169-8; Cleusa P. Ferri et al., "Global Prevalence of Dementia: A Delphi Consensus Study," *Lancet* 366, no. 9503 (December 17, 2005): 2112–17, doi:10.1016/S0140-6736(05) 67889-0.

4. Changing Bodies, Changing Needs

This double-edged sword effect G. C. Williams, "Pleiotropy, Natural Selection, and the Evolution of Senescence," *Evolution* 11 (1957): 398–411; R. M. Nesse and G. C. Williams, *Why We Get Sick: The New Science of Darwinian Medicine* (New York: Random House, 1996).

I call this one *synchrony of senescence* P. W. Estep, "The Promise of Human Life Span Extension," in *Biopsychosocial Approaches to Longevity*, ed. L. W. Poon and T. T. Perls (New York: Springer, 2007), 29–61.

The same is true with very low or high blood sugar Kyle M. Walsh et al.,

"Telomere Maintenance and the Etiology of Adult Glioma," *Neuro-Oncology* 17, no. 11 (November 2015): 1445–52, doi:10.1093/neuonc/nov082; R. A. Marciniak, F. B. Johnson, and L. Guarente, "Dyskeratosis Congenita, Telomeres and Human Ageing," *Trends in Genetics* 16, no. 5 (2000): 193–95; Veryan Codd et al., "Identification of Seven Loci Affecting Mean Telomere Length and Their Association with Disease," *Nature Genetics* 45, no. 4 (April 2013): 422–27, 427e1–2, doi:10.1038/ng.2528.

That means environment is responsible Herskind et al., "The Heritability of Human Longevity"; vB Hjelmborg et al., "Genetic Influence on Human Lifespan and Longevity"; M. McGue et al., "Longevity Is Moderately Heritable in a Sample of Danish Twins Born 1870–1880," *Journal of Gerontology* 48, no. 6 (November 1993): B237–44.

When Japanese move to other countries White et al., "Prevalence of Dementia in Older Japanese-American Men in Hawaii."

Many studies have shown that people who adopt Theodora Psaltopoulou et al., "Mediterranean Diet, Stroke, Cognitive Impairment, and Depression: A

Meta-Analysis," *Annals of Neurology* 74, no. 4 (October 2013): 580–91, doi:10 .1002/ana.23944.

And the difference can be measured Daniel W. Belsky et al., "Quantification of Biological Aging in Young Adults," *Proceedings of the National Academy of Sciences of the United States of America* 112, no. 30 (July 28, 2015): E4104–10, doi:10.1073/pnas.1506264 112.

Longevity and mindspan are at much greater risk Paik-Seong Lim et al., "Enhanced Oxidative Stress in Haemodialysis Patients Receiving Intravenous Iron Therapy," *Nephrology Dialysis Transplantation* 14, no. 11 (November 1, 1999): 2680–87, doi:10.1093/ndt/14.11 .2680; Corinna Brandsch, Robert Ringseis, and Klaus Eder, "High Dietary Iron Concentrations Enhance the Formation of Cholesterol Oxidation Products in the Liver of Adult Rats Fed Salmon Oil with Minimal Effects on Antioxidant Status," *The Journal of Nutrition* 132, no. 8 (August 1, 2002): 2263–69; Sharlene M. Day et al., "Chronic Iron Administration Increases Vascular Oxidative Stress and Accelerates Arterial Thrombosis," *Circulation* 107, no. 20 (May 27, 2003):

2601–6, doi:10.1161/01.CIR.00000669
10.02844.D0; Wei-Yi Ong and Barry
Halliwell, "Iron, Atherosclerosis, and
Neurodegeneration: A Key Role for Cholesterol in Promoting Iron-Dependent
Oxidative Damage?," *Annals of the New
York Academy of Sciences* 1012, no. 1
(March 1, 2004): 51–64, doi:10.1196/
annals.1306.005; Tzong-Shyuan Lee et
al., "Iron-Deficient Diet Reduces Ath-
erosclerotic Lesions in ApoE-Deficient
Mice," *Circulation* 99, no. 9 (March 9,
1999): 1222–29, doi:10.1161/01.CIR
.99.9.1222.

Some variants of the gene PCSK9 Jonathan C. Cohen et al., "Sequence Variations in PCSK9, Low LDL, and
Protection Against Coronary Heart Disease," *The New England Journal of Medicine* 354, no. 12 (March 23, 2006):
1264–72, doi:10.1056/NEJMoa054013;
Ilaria Guella et al., "Effects of PCSK9
Genetic Variants on Plasma LDL Cholesterol Levels and Risk of Premature
Myocardial Infarction in the Italian Population," *Journal of Lipid Research* 51,
no. 11 (November 2010): 3342–49,
doi:10.1194/jlr.M010009.

**But clinical trials of HDL-boosting
drugs** Bronwyn A. Kingwell et al.,

"HDL-Targeted Therapies: Progress, Failures and Future," *Nature Reviews Drug Discovery* 13, no. 6 (June 2014): 445–64, doi:10.1038/nrd4279.

Similarly, increases in HDL by gene variants Benjamin F. Voight et al., "Plasma HDL Cholesterol and Risk of Myocardial Infarction: A Mendelian Randomisation Study," *Lancet* 380, no. 9841 (August 11, 2012): 572–80, doi:10.1016/S0140-6736(12)60312-2.

And while HDL level N. Barzilai et al., "Unique Lipoprotein Phenotype and Genotype Associated with Exceptional Longevity," *JAMA* 290, no. 15 (2003): 2030–40.

The authors of this study G. S. Roth et al., "Biomarkers of Caloric Restriction May Predict Longevity in Humans," *Science* 297, no. 5582 (2002): 811.

In fact, it seems that the opposite is true T. Laukkanen et al., "Association Between Sauna Bathing and Fatal Cardiovascular and All-Cause Mortality Events," *JAMA Internal Medicine* 175, no. 4 (April 1, 2015): 542–48, doi:10.1001/jamainternmed.2014.8187.

Metformin also boosts insulin sensitivity V. N. Anisimov, A. V. Semenchenko, and A. I. Yashin, "Insulin and Longevity: Antidiabetic Biguanides as Geroprotectors," *Biogerontology* 4, no. 5 (2003): 297–307; V. N. Anisimov et al., "Effect of Metformin on Life Span and on the Development of Spontaneous Mammary Tumors in HER-2/neu Transgenic Mice," *Experimental Gerontology* 40, no. 8–9 (2005): 685–93; Daniel L. Smith et al., "Metformin Supplementation and Life Span in Fischer-344 Rats," *The Journals of Gerontology Series A: Biological Sciences and Medical Sciences* 65A, no. 5 (May 1, 2010): 468–74, doi:10.1093/gerona/glq033.

Over many years of life, the telomeres Yiqiang Zhan et al., "Telomere Length Shortening and Alzheimer Disease — A Mendelian Randomization Study," *JAMA Neurology* 72, no. 10 (October 1, 2015): 1202–3, doi:10.1001/jamaneurol.2015.1513; Mary Armanios and Elizabeth H Blackburn, "The Telomere Syndromes," *Nature Reviews Genetics* 13, no. 10 (October 2012): 693–704, doi:10.1038/nrg3246.

Most long-lived people in their eighties and nineties Kyle Lapham et al., "Automated Assay of Telomere Length Measurement and Informatics for 100,000 Subjects in the Genetic Epidemiology

Research on Adult Health and Aging (GERA) Cohort," *Genetics* 200, no. 4 (August 2015): 1061–72, doi:10.1534/genetics.115.178624.

But the largest and most impressive study Nawab Qizilbash et al., "BMI and Risk of Dementia in Two Million People over Two Decades: A Retrospective Cohort Study," *Lancet Diabetes & Endocrinology* 3, no. 6 (June 2015): 431–36, doi:10.1016/S2213-8587(15) 00033-9.

One 2009 *Lancet* review that looked at around 900,000 Europeans Prospective Studies Collaboration et al., "Body-Mass Index and Cause-Specific Mortality in 900,000 Adults: Collaborative Analyses of 57 Prospective Studies," *Lancet* 373, no. 9669 (March 28, 2009): 1083–96, doi:10.1016/S0140-6736(09)60318-4.

For middle-aged and older men Kenneth F. Adams et al., "Overweight, Obesity, and Mortality in a Large Prospective Cohort of Persons 50 to 71 Years Old," *The New England Journal of Medicine* 355, no. 8 (August 24, 2006): 763–78, doi:10.1056/NEJMoa055643; Leon Flicker et al., "Body Mass Index and Survival in Men and Women Aged 70 to

75," *Journal of the American Geriatrics Society* 58, no. 2 (February 2010): 234–41, doi:10.1111/j.1532-5415.2009 .02677.x.

Calorie restriction (CR) came into vogue "Calorie Restriction," *Wikipedia, the Free Encyclopedia,* October 17, 2015, en.wikipedia.org/w/index.php?title =Calorie_restriction.

However, some recent and careful studies J. M. Harper, C. W. Leathers, and S. N. Austad, "Does Caloric Restriction Extend Life in Wild Mice?," *Aging Cell* 5, no. 6 (2006): 441–49.

DHEA-S Bradley J. Willcox et al., "Caloric Restriction, the Traditional Okinawan Diet, and Healthy Aging: The Diet of the World's Longest-Lived People and Its Potential Impact on Morbidity and Life Span," *Annals of the New York Academy of Sciences* 1114 (October 2007): 434–55, doi:10.1196/annals .1396.037.

One publication from this study showed that Joyce M. J. de Vos-Houben et al., "Telomere Length, Oxidative Stress, and Antioxidant Status in Elderly Men in Zutphen and Crete," *Mechanisms of Ageing and Development* 133, no. 6 (June 2012): 373–77, doi:10.1016/j.mad.2012

.04.003; Brian Buijsse et al., "Oxidative Stress, and Iron and Antioxidant Status in Elderly Men: Differences Between the Mediterranean South (Crete) and Northern Europe (Zutphen)," *European Journal of Cardiovascular Prevention and Rehabilitation* 14, no. 4 (August 2007): 495–500, doi:10.1097/HJR.0b013e3280 111e41.

According to Japan's 2006 National Health and Nutrition Survey Ministry of Health, Labour, and Welfare, Japan, "The National Health and Nutrition Survey in Japan, 2006," 2009.

In a publication from 1996 M. Akisaka et al., "Energy and Nutrient Intakes of Okinawan Centenarians," *Journal of Nutritional Science and Vitaminology* 42, no. 3 (June 1996): 241–48.

Key Biomarker Summary (table) Biomarker comparisons can be challenging, in part because of differing genetics. Also, historical biomarkers often are not available. An ideal way to compare dynamic and easily changed biomarkers is an intervention trial in which people adopt different diets. The comparisons presented here on cholesterol (total, LDL, HDL), triglycerides, C-reactive protein, glucose, and insulin are from this kind of study, based on a Mediterranean-style diet.

Cholesterol (table) A. Ferro-Luzzi et al., "Changing the Mediterranean Diet: Effects on Blood Lipids," *The American Journal of Clinical Nutrition* 40, no. 5 (November 1984): 1027–37; M. de Lorgeril et al., "Mediterranean Diet, Traditional Risk Factors, and the Rate of Cardiovascular Complications After Myocardial Infarction: Final Report of the Lyon Diet Heart Study," *Circulation* 99, no. 6 (February 16, 1999): 779–85.

C-reactive protein (table) K. Esposito et al., "Effect of a Mediterranean-Style Diet on Endothelial Dysfunction and Markers of Vascular Inflammation in the Metabolic Syndrome: A Randomized Trial," *JAMA* 292, no. 12 (September 22, 2004): 1440–46, doi:10.1001/jama.292.12.1440.

As blood pressure values rise P. C. van den Hoogen et al., "The Relation Between Blood Pressure and Mortality Due to Coronary Heart Disease Among Men in Different Parts of the World. Seven Countries Study Research Group," *The New England Journal of Medicine* 342, no. 1 (January 6, 2000): 1–8, doi:10.1056/NEJM200001063420101.

5. Iron, the Sharpest Sword

Its rust comes in the form A. Terman, "Garbage Catastrophe Theory of Aging: Imperfect Removal of Oxidative Damage?," *Redox Report* 6, no. 1 (2001): 15–26; D. A. Gray and J. Woulfe, "Lipofuscin and Aging: A Matter of Toxic Waste," *Science of Aging Knowledge Environment* no. 5 (February 2, 2005): re1.

Rust also comes in the form Kay Keyer and James A. Imlay, "Superoxide Accelerates DNA Damage by Elevating Free-Iron Levels," *Proceedings of the National Academy of Sciences of the United States of America* 93, no. 24 (November 26, 1996): 13635–40; B. Halliwell and J. M. Gutteridge, "Oxygen Toxicity, Oxygen Radicals, Transition Metals and Disease," *The Biochemical Journal* 219, no. 1 (April 1, 1984): 1–14.

Still, free iron occasionally escapes Eugene D. Weinberg and Cheryl D. Garrison, *Exposing the Hidden Dangers of Iron: What Every Medical Professional Should Know About the Impact of Iron on the Disease Process* (Nashville, Tenn.: Cumberland House, 2004).

However, after menopause L. R. Zacharski et al., "Association of Age, Sex, and Race with Body Iron Stores in Adults:

Analysis of NHANES III Data," *American Heart Journal* 140, no. 1 (July 2000): 98–104, doi:10.1067/mhj.2000.106646; Nandar and Connor, "HFE Gene Variants Affect Iron in the Brain."

In youth, iron is a critical nutrient Neda Jahanshad et al., "Brain Structure in Healthy Adults Is Related to Serum Transferrin and the H63D Polymorphism in the HFE Gene," *Proceedings of the National Academy of Sciences* 109, no. 14 (April 3, 2012): E851–59, doi:10.1073/pnas.1105543109; Amina Sow et al., "Oligodendrocyte Differentiation Is Increased in Transferrin Transgenic Mice," *Journal of Neuroscience Research* 83, no. 3 (February 15, 2006): 403–14, doi:10.1002/jnr.20741.

However, high body iron stores George Bartzokis et al., "Brain Ferritin Iron May Influence Age- and Gender-Related Risks of Neurodegeneration," *Neurobiology of Aging* 28, no. 3 (March 2007): 414–23, doi:10.1016/j.neurobiolaging.2006.02.005.

The brain typically has a higher concentration of iron M. Gerlach et al., "Altered Brain Metabolism of Iron as a Cause of Neurodegenerative Diseases?," *Journal of Neurochemistry* 63, no. 3 (September 1994): 793–807.

After menopause, they gradually lose this protection Zacharski et al., "Association of Age, Sex, and Race with Body Iron Stores in Adults."

However, women who have undergone a premenopausal hysterectomy Todd A. Tishler et al., "Premenopausal Hysterectomy Is Associated with Increased Brain Ferritin Iron," *Neurobiology of Aging* 33, no. 9 (September 2012): 1950–58, doi:10.1016/j.neurobiolaging.2011.08.002; W. A. Rocca et al., "Increased Risk of Cognitive Impairment or Dementia in Women Who Underwent Oophorectomy Before Menopause," *Neurology* 69, no. 11 (September 11, 2007): 1074–83, doi:10.1212/01.wnl.0000276984.19542.e6.

Studies on lab animals and people Luigi Zecca et al., "Iron, Brain Ageing and Neurodegenerative Disorders," *Nature Reviews Neuroscience* 5, no. 11 (November 2004): 863–73, doi:10.1038/nrn1537.

In the late 1950s it was noted that people with hemorrhages B. Hallgren and P. Sourander, "The Effect of Age on the Non-Haemin Iron in the Human Brain," *Journal of Neurochemistry* 3, no. 1 (October 1958): 41–51.

In late 2015, a study of people who ate a Mediterranean-style Yian Gu et al., "Mediterranean Diet and Brain Structure in a Multiethnic Elderly Cohort," *Neurology*, October 21, 2015, doi:10.1212/WNL.0000000000002121.

The difference between the two groups In this study by Gu and colleagues, low meat consumption was the most significant association with larger brain structures and overall brain size. The next most significant was higher fish consumption. Moderate alcohol consumption also showed positive effects. However, contrary to typical nutritional guidelines, higher fruit intake was also associated with smaller sizes of certain brain structures. This doesn't surprise me greatly, since fruit is a primary source of vitamin C, which promotes absorption of iron.

In 1991 the iron chelator drug deferoxamine D. R. Crapper McLachlan et al., "Intramuscular Desferrioxamine in Patients with Alzheimer's Disease," *Lancet* 337, no. 8753 (June 1, 1991): 1304–8.

More recent studies show that this drug Chuang Guo et al., "Intranasal

Deferoxamine Reverses Iron-Induced Memory Deficits and Inhibits Amyloidogenic APP Processing in a Transgenic Mouse Model of Alzheimer's Disease," *Neurobiology of Aging* 34, no. 2 (February 2013): 562–75, doi:10.1016/j.neuro biolaging.2012.05.009; Maria Noêmia Martins de Lima et al., "Reversion of Age-Related Recognition Memory Impairment by Iron Chelation in Rats," *Neurobiology of Aging* 29, no. 7 (July 2008): 1052–59, doi:10.1016/j.neuro biolaging.2007.02.006.

Those genes are called APOE and APP Only one other gene has shown a reproducible association with human longevity: FOXO3. The effect of the beneficial variant is small relative to those of APOE and APP.

This gene — which has repeatedly been proven Almut Nebel et al., "A Genome-Wide Association Study Confirms APOE as the Major Gene Influencing Survival in Long-Lived Individuals," *Mechanisms of Ageing and Development* 132, no. 6–7 (June 2011): 324–30, doi:10.1016/j.mad.2011.06.008.

The e3 variant is most common D. T. Eisenberg, C. W. Kuzawa, and M. G. Hayes, "Worldwide Allele Frequencies of the Human Apolipoprotein E Gene: Climate, Local Adaptations, and Evolutionary History," *American Journal of Physical Anthropology* 143, no. 1 (2010): 100–111.

Even though Africans have the highest proportion M. X. Tang et al., "The APOE-epsilon4 Allele and the Risk of Alzheimer Disease Among African Americans, Whites, and Hispanics," *JAMA* 279, no. 10 (March 11, 1998): 751–55.

An international consortium of several Alzheimer's disease studies Scott Ayton et al., "Ferritin Levels in the Cerebrospinal Fluid Predict Alzheimer's Disease Outcomes and Are Regulated by APOE," *Nature Communications* 6 (2015): 6760, doi:10.1038/ncomms7760.

Research suggests that the job of APP in the brain Christa J. Maynard et al., "Overexpression of Alzheimer's Disease Amyloid-ß Opposes the Age-Dependent Elevations of Brain Copper and Iron," *Journal of Biological Chemistry* 277, no. 47 (November 22, 2002): 44670–76, doi:10.1074/jbc.M204379200.

Three copies of the APP gene R. E. Tanzi et al., "Amyloid Beta Protein Gene: cDNA, mRNA Distribution, and

Genetic Linkage Near the Alzheimer Locus," *Science* 235, no. 4791 (February 20, 1987): 880–84; Anne Rovelet-Lecrux et al., "APP Locus Duplication Causes Autosomal Dominant Early-Onset Alzheimer Disease with Cerebral Amyloid Angiopathy," *Nature Genetics* 38, no. 1 (January 2006): 24–26, doi:10.1038/ng1718. Other mechanisms can lead to greater than normal copy numbers of APP. One is called copy number variation (CNV), which produces a duplication of the APP gene during fetal development. Similar to Down syndrome, this kind of duplication probably contributes to earlier onset of Alzheimer's disease.

In other words, this system is very rare Jack Rogers et al., "Iron and the Translation of the Amyloid Precursor Protein (APP) and Ferritin," *Biochemical Society Transactions* 36, no. Pt 6 (December 2008): 1282–87, doi:10.1042/BST0361282.

In 2012, Icelandic scientists discovered Thorlakur Jonsson et al., "A Mutation in APP Protects Against Alzheimer's Disease and Age-Related Cognitive Decline," *Nature Advance* online publication (2012), doi.org/10.1038/nature

11283; nature.com/nature/journal/vaop/ ncurrent/abs/nature11283.html #supplementary-information.

This doesn't seem ideal C. A. Szekely et al., "No Advantage of A Beta 42-Lowering NSAIDs for Prevention of Alzheimer Dementia in Six Pooled Cohort Studies," *Neurology* 70, no. 24 (June 10, 2008): 2291–98, doi:10.1212/01.wnl .0000313933.17796.f6; C. A. Szekely et al., "NSAID Use and Dementia Risk in the Cardiovascular Health Study: Role of APOE and NSAID Type," *Neurology* 70, no. 1 (January 1, 2008): 17–24, doi:10 .1212/01.wnl.0000284596.95156.48.

Here is a brief overview of just some Weinberg and Garrison, *Exposing the Hidden Dangers of Iron*. Many of the studies in this overview are covered in detail in this excellent collection.

This is the same mechanism L. B. Yanoff et al., "Inflammation and Iron Deficiency in the Hypoferremia of Obesity," *International Journal of Obesity* 31, no. 9 (April 17, 2007): 1412–19, doi:10.1038/ sj.ijo.0803625.

This helps explain why GI infections increase Tanja Jaeggi et al., "Iron Fortification Adversely Affects the Gut Microbiome, Increases Pathogen Abundance and Induces Intestinal Inflammation in Kenyan Infants," *Gut* 64, no. 5 (May 1, 2015): 731–42, doi:10.1136/gutjnl-2014-307720.

In an alarming study of over 300,000 people Chi Pang Wen et al., "High Serum Iron Is Associated with Increased Cancer Risk," *Cancer Research* 74, no. 22 (November 15, 2014): 6589–97, doi:10.1158/0008-5472.CAN-14-0360.

Another study found that across a wide range Qun Xu et al., "Multivitamin Use and Telomere Length in Women," *The American Journal of Clinical Nutrition* 89, no. 6 (June 2009): 1857–63, doi:10.3945/ajcn.2008.26986.

Increased dietary iron has been associated J. I. Wurzelmann et al., "Iron Intake and the Risk of Colorectal Cancer," *Cancer Epidemiology Biomarkers & Prevention* 5, no. 7 (July 1, 1996): 503–7; R. L. Nelson, "Iron and Colorectal Cancer Risk: Human Studies," *Nutrition Reviews* 59, no. 5 (May 2001): 140–48.

Atherosclerosis (plaque buildup in arteries) Stefan Kiechl et al., "Body Iron Stores and the Risk of Carotid Atherosclerosis: Prospective Results from the Bruneck Study," *Circulation* 96, no. 10 (November 18, 1997): 3300–3307, doi:10.1161/01.CIR.96.10.3300.

Plaques have high iron levels Douglas B. Kell, "Towards a Unifying, Systems Biology Understanding of Large-Scale Cellular Death and Destruction Caused by Poorly Liganded Iron: Parkinson's, Huntington's, Alzheimer's, Prions, Bactericides, Chemical Toxicology and Others as Examples," *Archives of Toxicology* 84, no. 11 (November 2010): 825–89, doi:10.1007/s00204-010-0577-x.

High-frequency blood donors José Manuel Fernández-Real, Abel López-Bermejo, and Wifredo Ricart, "Iron Stores, Blood Donation, and Insulin Sensitivity and Secretion," *Clinical Chemistry* 51, no. 7 (July 1, 2005): 1201–5, doi:10.1373/clinchem.2004.046847.

The Bioavailability Puzzle Leif Hallberg and Lena Hulthén, "Prediction of Dietary Iron Absorption: An Algorithm for Calculating Absorption and Bioavailability of Dietary Iron," *The American Journal of Clinical Nutrition* 71, no. 5 (May 1, 2000): 1147–60.

In the Framingham Heart Study Diana J. Fleming et al., "Dietary Factors Associated with the Risk of High Iron Stores in the Elderly Framingham Heart

Study Cohort," *The American Journal of Clinical Nutrition* 76, no. 6 (December 1, 2002): 1375–84.

Multiple studies have shown that these factors R. M. Wright, J. L. McManaman, and J. E. Repine, "Alcohol-Induced Breast Cancer: A Proposed Mechanism," *Free Radical Biology & Medicine* 26, no. 3–4 (February 1999): 348–54; Wen et al., "High Serum Iron Is Associated with Increased Cancer Risk"; Weinberg and Garrison, *Exposing the Hidden Dangers of Iron.*

A more likely explanation is that there's another compound H. R. Massie, V. R. Aiello, and T. R. Williams, "Inhibition of Iron Absorption Prolongs the Life Span of Drosophila" *Mechanisms of Ageing and Development* 67, no. 3 (April 1993): 227–37; Richard F. Hurrell, Manju Reddy, and James D. Cook, "Inhibition of Non-Haem Iron Absorption in Man by Polyphenolic-Containing Beverages," *British Journal of Nutrition* 81, no. 4 (April 1999): 289–95, doi:10.1017/S0007114599000537.

The ranges of normal serum ferritin Weinberg and Garrison, *Exposing the Hidden Dangers of Iron;* Yutaka Kohgo et al., "Body Iron Metabolism and Pathophysiology of Iron Overload," *International Journal of Hematology* 88, no. 1 (July 2008): 7–15, doi:10.1007/s12185-008-0120-5.

Normal Range of Ferritin in Japan Kohgo et al., "Body Iron Metabolism and Pathophysiology of Iron Overload."

Ideal Range of Ferritin T. Tsukahara et al., "No Significant Effect of Iron Deficiency on Cadmium Body Burden or Kidney Dysfunction Among Women in the General Population in Japan," *International Archives of Occupational and Environmental Health* 76, no. 4 (May 2003): 275–81, doi:10.1007/s00420-003-0432-y.

6. Cracking the Mindspan Code

More important, the primary fuel Luc Pellerin and Pierre J. Magistretti, "Food for Thought: Challenging the Dogmas," *Journal of Cerebral Blood Flow and Metabolism: Official Journal of the International Society of Cerebral Blood Flow and Metabolism* 23, no. 11 (November 2003): 1282–86, doi:10.1097/01.WCB.00000 96064.12129.3D.

The standard way of measuring L.S.A. Augustin et al., "Glycemic Index, Glycemic Load and Glycemic Response: An International Scientific Consensus Summit from the International Carbohydrate Quality Consortium (ICQC)," *Nutrition, Metabolism & Cardiovascular Diseases: NMCD* 25, no. 9 (September 2015): 795–815, doi:10.1016/j.numecd.2015.05.005.

Surprisingly, people of European ancestry M. Kataoka et al., "Glycaemic Responses to Glucose and Rice in People of Chinese and European Ethnicity," *Diabetic Medicine: A Journal of the British Diabetic Association* 30, no. 3 (March 2013): e101–7, doi:10.1111/dme.12080; B. S. Venn, S. M. Williams, and J. I. Mann, "Comparison of Postprandial Glycaemia in Asians and Caucasians," *Diabetic Medicine: A Journal of the British Diabetic Association* 27, no. 10 (October 2010): 1205–8.

Lost is the over-eighty-year-old knowledge Harold Himsworth, "Diet and the Incidence of Diabetes Mellitus," *Clinical Science* 2 (1935): 117–48.

These sugary glues are called advanced glycation end products Estep, "The Promise of Human Life Span Extension."

In the U.S. today NIH, Office of Dietary

Supplements, "Dietary Supplement Fact Sheet: Iron — Health Professional Fact Sheet," accessed November 10, 2015, ods.od.nih.gov/factsheets/Iron-Health Professional/.

Iron fortification of flour Institute of Medicine (US) Committee on Use of Dietary Reference Intakes in Nutrition, National Academy of Sciences, "Overview of Food Fortification in the United States and Canada," 2003, ncbi.nlm.nih.gov/books/NBK208880/.

Most people think carbs cause diabetes R. Jiang et al., "Body Iron Stores in Relation to Risk of Type 2 Diabetes in Apparently Healthy Women," *JAMA* 291, no. 6 (February 11, 2004): 711–17, doi:10.1001/jama.291.6.711; Jukka T. Salonen et al., "Relation Between Iron Stores and Non–Insulin Dependent Diabetes in Men: Case-Control Study," *BMJ* 317, no. 7160 (September 12, 1998): 727–30; Fernández-Real, López-Bermejo, and Ricart, "Iron Stores, Blood Donation, and Insulin Sensitivity and Secretion."

Insulin response (per gram of food) for red meat S. H. Holt, J. C. Miller, and P. Petocz, "An Insulin Index of Foods: The Insulin Demand Generated by 1000-

kJ Portions of Common Foods," *The American Journal of Clinical Nutrition* 66, no. 5 (November 1997): 1264–76.

The actual prevalence of celiac disease A. Fasano et al., "Prevalence of Celiac Disease in At-Risk and Not-at-Risk Groups in the United States: A Large Multicenter Study," *Archives of Internal Medicine* 163, no. 3 (February 10, 2003): 286–92; doi:10.1001/archinte.163.3.286.

Gluten-free pastas made of rice C. Berti et al., "In Vitro Starch Digestibility and in Vivo Glucose Response of Gluten-Free Foods and Their Gluten Counterparts," *European Journal of Nutrition* 43, no. 4 (January 6, 2004): 198–204, doi:10.1007/s00394-004-0459-1.

Some of the GI values I have seen are over 100 J. B. Miller, E. Pang, and L. Bramall, "Rice: A High or Low Glycemic Index Food?," *The American Journal of Clinical Nutrition* 56, no. 6 (December 1992): 1034–36; Holt, Miller, and Petocz, "An Insulin Index of Foods."

Because, based on abundant iron in modern diets K. S. Olsson et al., "The Effect of Withdrawal of Food Iron Fortification in Sweden as Studied with Phlebotomy in Subjects with Genetic

Hemochromatosis," *European Journal of Clinical Nutrition* 51, no. 11 (November 1997): 782–86.

Here is the status of iron fortification Food Fortification Initiative, "Global Progress — Food Fortification Initiative," accessed November 10, 2015, ffinetwork.org/global_progress/.

And Okinawans traded their sweet potato staple Willcox et al., "Caloric Restriction, the Traditional Okinawan Diet, and Healthy Aging."

Nevertheless, I agree with leading Paleo food researcher Loren Cordain, "Cereal Grains: Humanity's Double-Edged Sword," in *Evolutionary Aspects of Nutrition and Health: Diet, Exercise, Genetics and Chronic Disease. World Review of Nutrition and Dietetics,* vol. 84 (Basel: Karger, 1999), 19–73.

Scientists who study animals that eat F. D. Provenza et al., "Linking Herbivore Experience, Varied Diets, and Plant Biochemical Diversity," *Small Ruminant Research* 49, no. 3 (September 1, 2003): 257–74, doi:10.1016/S0921-4488(03)00143-3.

The Japanese began a countrywide effort S. Kono, M. Ikeda, and M. Ogata, "Salt and Geographical Mortality of Gastric Cancer and Stroke in Japan," *Journal of Epidemiology and Community Health* 37, no. 1 (March 1983): 43–46.

Japanese and other scientists T. Iwaoka et al., "The Effect of Low and High NaCl Diets on Oral Glucose Tolerance," *Klinische Wochenschrift* 66, no. 16 (August 1988): 724–28, doi:10.1007/BF01 726415; Taisuke Iwaoka et al., "Dietary NaCl Restriction Deteriorates Oral Glucose Tolerance in Hypertensive Patients with Impairment of Glucose Tolerance," *American Journal of Hypertension* 7, no. 5 (May 1, 1994): 460–63, doi:10.1093/ ajh/7.5.460.

Sweat loss of salt and other minerals like iron M. Brune et al., "Iron Losses in Sweat," *The American Journal of Clinical Nutrition* 43, no. 3 (March 1986): 438–43; T. Laukkanen et al., "Association Between Sauna Bathing and Fatal Cardiovascular and All-Cause Mortality Events," *JAMA Internal Medicine* 175, no. 4 (April 1, 2015): 542–48, doi:10.1001/ jamainternmed.2014.8187; M. F. Waller and E. M. Haymes, "The Effects of Heat and Exercise on Sweat Iron Loss," *Medicine and Science in Sports and Exercise* 28, no. 2 (February 1996): 197–203.

There were two major and related

changes Todoriki, Willcox, and Willcox, "The Effects of Post-War Dietary Change on Longevity and Health in Okinawa"; Colin Joyce, "Japanese Get a Taste for Western Food and Fall Victim to Obesity and Early Death," *Telegraph*, accessed November 5, 2015, telegraph.co .uk/news/health/news/3342882/Japanese -get-a-taste-for-Western-food-and-fall -victim-to-obesity-and-early-death.html.

7. Fat Friends and Foes

Research shows more probably doesn't help Penny M. Kris-Etherton, Jessica A. Grieger, and Terry D. Etherton, "Dietary Reference Intakes for DHA and EPA," *Prostaglandins, Leukotrienes and Essential Fatty Acids,* Workshop on DHA as a Required Nutrient, 81, no. 2–3 (August 2009): 99–104, doi:10.1016/j. plefa.2009.05.011.

So even though omega-3 intakes in Mediterranean countries Artemis P. Simopoulos, "The Importance of the Omega-6/Omega-3 Fatty Acid Ratio in Cardiovascular Disease and Other Chronic Diseases," *Experimental Biology and Medicine* 233, no. 6 (June 1, 2008): 674–88, doi:10.3181/0711-MR-311.

Fat intake of traditional diet of Sardin-

ian shepherds Pes et al., "Lifestyle and Nutrition Related to Male Longevity in Sardinia."

What was problematic about the Okinawan fat increase Todoriki, Willcox, and Willcox, "The Effects of Post-War Dietary Change on Longevity and Health in Okinawa."

As you consider the healthful properties of olive oil Turrini et al., "Food Consumption Patterns in Italy."

So did those women who replaced other fats Dariush Mozaffarian, Eric B. Rimm, and David M. Herrington, "Dietary Fats, Carbohydrate, and Progression of Coronary Atherosclerosis in Postmenopausal Women," *The American Journal of Clinical Nutrition* 80, no. 5 (November 1, 2004): 1175–84.

A year earlier, a group of Australian scientists D. M. Colquhoun et al., "Cheese Added to a Low Fat Diet Does Not Affect Serum Lipids," *Asia Pacific Journal of Clinical Nutrition* 12 (2003): S65.

People who had already suffered one heart attack De Lorgeril et al., "Effect of a Mediterranean Type of Diet on the Rate of Cardiovascular Complications in Patients with Coronary Artery Disease:

Insights into the Cardioprotective Effect of Certain Nutriments."

8. Solving the Protein Part of the Puzzle

In the early 1990s, scientists discovered that the key Norman Orentreich, Jonathan R. Matias, Anthony DeFelice, and Jay R. Zimmerman, "Low Methionine Ingestion by Rats Extends Life Span," *Journal of Nutrition* 123, no. 2 (February 1994): 269–74.

Animals on methionine-restricted diets Liou Sun et al., "Life-Span Extension in Mice by Preweaning Food Restriction and by Methionine Restriction in Middle Age," *The Journals of Gerontology Series A: Biological Sciences and Medical Sciences,* January 1, 2009, glp051, doi:10.1093/gerona/glp051.

Later in life, the methionine-restricted animals Richard A. Miller et al., "Methionine-Deficient Diet Extends Mouse Lifespan, Slows Immune and Lens Aging, Alters Glucose, T4, IGF-I and Insulin Levels, and Increases Hepatocyte MIF Levels and Stress Resistance," *Aging Cell* 4, no. 3 (June 1, 2005): 119–25, doi:10.1111/j.1474-9726.2005 .00152.x.

Yet even with such diets, low methio-

nine Pilar Caro et al., "Forty Percent and Eighty Percent Methionine Restriction Decrease Mitochondrial ROS Generation and Oxidative Stress in Rat Liver," *Biogerontology* 9, no. 3 (February 19, 2008): 183–96, doi:10.1007/s10522-008-9130-1; Inés Sanchez-Roman et al., "Effects of Aging and Methionine Restriction Applied at Old Age on ROS Generation and Oxidative Damage in Rat Liver Mitochondria," *Biogerontology* 13, no. 4 (May 13, 2012): 399–411, doi:10.1007/s10522-012-9384-5; Virginia L. Malloy et al., "Methionine Restriction Decreases Visceral Fat Mass and Preserves Insulin Action in Aging Male Fischer 344 Rats Independent of Energy Restriction," *Aging Cell* 5, no. 4 (August 1, 2006): 305–14, doi:10.1111/j.1474-9726.2006.00220.x.

Simply adding methionine undermines these benefits Daniela Omodei and Luigi Fontana, "Calorie Restriction and Prevention of Age-Associated Chronic Disease," *FEBS Letters* 585, no. 11 (June 6, 2011): 1537–42, doi:10.1016/j.febslet.2011.03.015.

The China Study, a well-known study done in the 1980s T. Colin Campbell and Thomas M. Campbell, *The China*

Study: The Most Comprehensive Study of Nutrition Ever Conducted and the Startling Implications for Diet, Weight Loss and Long-Term Health, 1st paperback ed. (Dallas: Benbella Books, 2006).

A 2006 Finnish study followed middle-aged men for fourteen years Jyrki K. Virtanen et al., "High Dietary Methionine Intake Increases the Risk of Acute Coronary Events in Middle-Aged Men," *Nutrition, Metabolism and Cardiovascular Diseases* 16, no. 2 (March 2006): 113–20, doi:10.1016/j.numecd.2005.05.005.

Research from the mid-1960s Kelly M. West and John M. Kalbfleisch, "Glucose Tolerance, Nutrition, and Diabetes in Uruguay, Venezuela, Malaya, and East Pakistan," *Diabetes* 15, no. 1 (January 1, 1966): 9–18, doi:10.2337/diab.15.1.9.

But there is no reason to be confused Kevin D. Hall et al., "Calorie for Calorie, Dietary Fat Restriction Results in More Body Fat Loss Than Carbohydrate Restriction in People with Obesity," *Cell Metabolism* 22, no. 3 (September 1, 2015): 427–36, doi:10.1016/j.cmet.2015.07.021.

Even in these hot spots of crummy carbs Jiang et al., "Body Iron Stores in Relation to Risk of Type 2 Diabetes in

Apparently Healthy Women"; Salonen et al., "Relation Between Iron Stores and Non–Insulin Dependent Diabetes in Men"; Fernández-Real, López-Bermejo, and Ricart, "Iron Stores, Blood Donation, and Insulin Sensitivity and Secretion."

Seventh-day Adventists typically don't smoke or drink alcohol Orlich et al., "Vegetarian Dietary Patterns and Mortality in Adventist Health Study 2."

Most people I've told this to are shocked Andrews, *Flavors of the Riviera*; Fred Plotkin, *Recipes from Paradise: Life and Food on the Italian Riviera,* 1st ed. (Boston: Little, Brown, 1997).

Seventh-day Adventist pescatarians Orlich et al., "Vegetarian Dietary Patterns and Mortality in Adventist Health Study 2."

Only 6 percent of Japanese eat fish twice or more per day Yasuyuki Nakamura et al., "Association Between Fish Consumption and All-Cause and Cause-Specific Mortality in Japan: NIPPON DATA80, 1980–99," *The American Journal of Medicine* 118, no. 3 (March 2005): 239–45, doi:10.1016/j.amjmed.2004.12.016.

Nicoyans of Costa Rica also eat only

moderate amounts Buettner, *The Blue Zones Solution.*

9. X Factors — The Last Piece of the Puzzle

These compounds provide Nordgaard and Mortensen, "Digestive Processes in the Human Colon"; G. Livesey, "Metabolizable Energy of Macronutrients," *The American Journal of Clinical Nutrition* 62, no. 5 suppl. (November 1995): 1135S–1142S.

These animals all eat the same amount Vanessa K. Ridaura et al., "Gut Microbiota from Twins Discordant for Obesity Modulate Metabolism in Mice," *Science* 341, no. 6150 (September 6, 2013): 1241214, doi:10.1126/science.1241214.

Excess food iron increases disease-causing Weinberg and Garrison, *Exposing the Hidden Dangers of Iron.*

This property is called the second-meal effect T. M. Wolever et al., "Second-Meal Effect: Low-Glycemic-Index Foods Eaten at Dinner Improve Subsequent Breakfast Glycemic Response," *The American Journal of Clinical Nutrition* 48, no. 4 (1988): 1041–47; Furio Brighenti et al., "Colonic Fermentation of Indigestible Carbohydrates Contributes to the Second-Meal Effect," *The American Journal of Clinical Nutrition* 83, no. 4 (April 1, 2006): 817–22.

Unlike Mindspan Risk populations According to a 1999 study by the Foreign Agricultural Service of the U.S. Department of Agriculture (USDA), the highest per capita consumers of cheese were Greece, France, and Italy, in descending order. The Greeks ate about 52 pounds of cheese annually — about two-fifths more than in the United States, and more than twice that of the U.K.

However, there's a crucial difference Yuval Itan et al., "A Worldwide Correlation of Lactase Persistence Phenotype and Genotypes," *BMC Evolutionary Biology* 10, no. 1 (February 9, 2010): 36, doi:10.1186/1471-2148-10-36; "Lactase Persistence," *Wikipedia, the Free Encyclopedia,* November 4, 2015, en.wikipedia.org/w/index.php?title=Lactase_persistence&oldid=688944614.

A study of Japanese and Okinawan elderly H. Shibata et al., "Nutrition for the Japanese Elderly," *Nutrition and Health* 8, no. 2–3 (1992): 165–75.

Naturally, nutritionists have long puzzled M. Kuratsune et al., "Dietary

Fibre in the Japanese Diet," *Princess Takamatsu Symposia* 16 (1985): 247–53.

10. The Mindspan Diet in Action

Japanese eat a fair amount of fish Nakamura et al., "Association Between Fish Consumption and All-Cause and Cause-Specific Mortality in Japan."

The foods and recipes that form the core Recipes were inspired by and based on traditional recipes from various sources, including the following: Médecin and Graham, *Cuisine Niçoise;* Plotkin, *Recipes from Paradise;* Andrews, *Flavors of the Riviera;* Mireille Johnston, *The Cuisine of the Sun: Classic Recipes from Nice and Provence,* 1st ed. (New York: Random House, 1976); Willcox, Willcox, and Suzuki, *The Okinawa Program.*

11. Stocking Up

Two of the most important for your health M. Ramesh, "What Is the True Amylose Content of Rice Starch?," accessed November 5, 2015, nottingham.ac.uk/ncmh/harding_pdfs/Paper234.PDF.

THE MINDSPAN DIET
CHEAT SHEET

❏ **LIMIT IRON.** The Percent Daily Value of iron listed on nutrition labels is calibrated for male teens and menstruating women. If you don't fall into either of these classes you need to divide the Percent Daily Value by 4. You should watch your iron and ferritin levels, and try to keep them at the low end of normal (have them tested at least annually; see appendix B for more information). If you drink tap water and have older metal supply pipes, let the water run until clean and cold, and then fill clean bottles for immediate use and storage.

❏ **LIMIT RED MEAT.** The best nutrition for mental longevity is a mostly vegetarian diet, with little or no red meat. Preferred primary protein sources are, in descending order, grains and vegetables > fish > poultry > red meat.

❑ **SLOW DOWN.** Japanese and Mediter-ranean foods and eating styles ease the body into digestion. Start a meal with X factors and a low glycemic index soup and salad. Place healthful carbs in the second half of the meal.

❑ **EAT GOOD CARBS AND GOOD FATS.** Mindspan champs of the world eat lots of healthful carbs. Eat more vegetables, LIGIR (low iron and glycemic index refined) carbs, pasta, white rice (preferably parboiled or converted), barley, and sourdough bread. Be very wary of iron-enriched grain prod-ucts.

❑ **DITCH THE MILK (IF YOU CAN DIGEST LACTOSE).** Do not consume milk and minimize ice cream, yogurt, cot-tage cheese, and other milk products that contain substantial amounts of the lactose (milk sugar). Cheese, cream, sour cream, butter, and other dairy products without lac-tose are fine in moderation for most people. It might sound counterintuitive, but only consume lactose if you cannot digest it, which allows it to be metabolized by mi-crobes in the gut.

❑ **FEED YOUR BRAIN.** Mindspan leaders of the world eat more fish and seafood than most others, but most don't overdo it. Eat a few small to moderate servings of fish a week, perhaps a bite-size piece of pickled herring once or twice a day, and a dish with sardines or anchovies at least once a week. If you are vegetarian or vegan, I suggest you consider supplemental DHA plus EPA.

❑ **DRINK COFFEE, TEA, OR RED WINE *WITH MEALS*.** These beverages inhibit the absorption of iron (and other minerals, so don't overdo it). Relative to tea, coffee, cocoa, and other common inhibitors, red wine is a weak inhibitor of iron absorption. But other forms of alcohol actually promote iron absorption, so red wine is a better choice overall.

❑ **DRINK ALCOHOL IN MODERATION.** If you drink alcohol, limit yourself to two drinks a day and spread out your drinking. Red wine is best; drink it slowly with meals. If you don't drink, don't start.

❑ **LIMIT SUGAR.** Cut back on table sugar, and when choosing between a sweet fruit and a non-sweet one (squash, tomato, cucumber, bell pepper, etc.), choose the latter. The problem isn't the carbs; it is fructose, a primary ingredient in table sugar and fruits.

❑ **TAKE B AND D VITAMINS.** Take a B vitamin supplement (containing at least folic acid or folate, B6, B12, and niacin) and a vitamin D supplement, at least occasionally. Take vitamin D more often if you spend most of your days indoors. Look for a high-quality supplement that provides 100 percent of the Percent Daily Value. No need for more.

WHAT TO EAT
CHEAT SHEET

Foods to Consume at Most Meals
- Good carbs: pasta or high-amylose white rice (preferably parboiled or converted) boiled or steamed, stored in your fridge, and then reheated for immediate use
- Vegetables, including leafy greens such as leaf lettuce, kale, borage, seaweed or kelp, and spinach
- Legumes
- Vinegar
- Coffee or tea (caffeinated or herbal, but not decaf tea) *with meals*
- Moderate amounts of olive oil and smaller amounts of butter

Foods to Consume in Moderation
- Fish and other seafood. Try to get at least 2 percent of your calories from fish and seafood. Emphasize smaller, fattier fish, low in mercury. Examples

are herring, sardines, and anchovies.
- Rustic breads, like Italian ciabatta or sourdough bread
- Fruits, especially non-sweet ones such as tomatoes
- Cheese and other non-lactose-containing dairy
- Eggs

Foods to Avoid
- Red meat. Reduce dramatically or eliminate altogether. One standout commonality of all Mindspan Elite is that meat plays a small role in their traditional cuisines.
- Most other sources of animal protein, including poultry, liquid milk, and other dairy foods that contain liquid milk
- High glycemic index carbs (most commercial white and whole wheat breads) absent synergistic X factors
- Added sugar, sugary beverages, and other sources of large and concentrated quantities of sugar and milk sugar (lactose, sweetened condensed milk)
- Deep-fried foods, especially those fried in an unknown oil when eating out

Foods for Men and Nonmenstruating Women *Never* to Consume

- Iron-enriched foods, especially super-enriched breakfast cereals (both hot and cold). Avoid enriched white flour, crackers, commercial white breads, white rice, most grits and farina, pizza, pasta, tortillas, muffins, cookies, cakes and cake mixes — the list goes on and on. Look for the words "enriched," "iron," "ferrous," and "ferric." The most confusing of all is "reduced iron." This does not indicate less iron, but is a form of iron that is added to food.

INDEX

alpha-linolenic acid (α-LA), 187, 202, 205, 441–42
ALS (Lou Gehrig's disease), 120
Alzheimer's disease, 32–33, 66, 69, 85, 117, 119, 250–51
  gender differences in risk of, 121
  genes and, 36, 123–32
  iron and risk of, 120–23
  NSAIDs and, 132
  obesity and, 104
amino acids, 56–57
  essential, limiting, 208–10
amyloid plaques, 126, 127, 132
amyloid precursor protein (APP) gene, 126–32
amylose content (AC), 175, 178, 269
anchovy(ies), 204, 255, 276–77
  Basil Sauce, Creamy, 382–83
  heme iron content of, 440
Andrews, Colman, 79, 195
anemia, 107, 110, 118, 122, 226
animal protein, 253, 260
  fatty acids in, 187
  Mindspan Elite's low intake of, 213–14
  see also fish and seafood; red meat
animal studies, problems with applying results to humans, 209
antagonistic pleitropy (AP rule), 88–89, 93, 99
antioxidants, 141

504

blood sugar, 53, 91
  finely grinding grains and, 169
  glycemic index (GI) and, 154–56
  salt intake and, 181, 233
  second-meal effect and, 231–32
  slowing down carbs and, 178–79
body fat, 104, 159
  bad fats stored as, 203–4
  daily food intake and, 152–53
  humans' need for, 207–8
body mass index (BMI), 95, 104–7, 111,
    113
body temperature, 133
  longevity and, 101
body weight:
  cause of gain in, 222
  gut microbes and, 225
  see also obesity
brain, human, 151, 187–88, 207
  iron accumulation in, 120–22
  Mediterranean diet and, 160
bran, of grains, 76, 81, 169, 172, 173, 175,
    271
bread machines, 273, 415, 425
breads, 248–49
  enriched with iron, 160–61, 164
  fermentation and, 416–17
  Focaccia, Basic, 421–22
  home-baked, 249, 272–73, 415–24, 425
  Rustic Loaf or Rustic Sourdough, 423–24

buckwheat noodle(s) (soba), 172
  Mushrooms, Carrots, and Sea Vegetables
    on, 367–68
  Soup, Okinawan, 333
Buettner, Dan, 287
bulgur wheat, in Greek Tabbouleh Salad,
    315–16
burritos:
  Bean and Cheese, 347–48
  Breakfast, South of the Border, 296
butter, 58, 205, 223, 239, 240, 248, 255,
    264, 275
  French paradox and, 197
buttermilk, 58, 223, 238, 240, 425, 426
butyric acid, 58, 223
B vitamins, 93, 208, 257, 496

calcium, 139, 173, 181, 216, 440n
calcium supplements, 241
Calment, Jeanne, 41, 43, 69
calorie restriction (CR), 100, 107–8, 207–8
calories, 152–53, 222
cancer, 27, 28, 109, 134–36, 158, 189,
    193, 210, 239
  breast, 142
  colon or colorectal, 136, 226, 237
  iron levels and, 119, 134–35
  telomere length and, 103, 134–36
cannellini:
  Greens and Beans Pasta, 386–87

China Study, 210
Chinese cuisines, 182, 184, 262, 263
chocolate, dark, 248
  Darkberry Dips, 411–12
cholesterol, 29, 61, 91, 110, 209, 210, 248
  see also HDL cholesterol; LDL
    cholesterol
citric acid, 59
cocoa, 256
coffee, 74–75, 256, 259, 263, 495
  iron absorption and, 143
colon and colorectal cancers, 136, 226, 237
complex carbohydrates:
  defined, 53
  see also grains; starches
Congee, Egg (Rice Porridge), 292–93
constipation, 172, 175
copper, 127n, 139, 266
Cordain, Loren, 171
corn:
  omega fats of, 441, 442
  Pigeon Peas and Vegetables, 353
Cornaro, Luigi, 107
corn products, iron fortification of, 166
coronary heart disease (CHD), 111, 136
Costa Rican diet (Nicoyans), 63–64, 65,
    68–69, 83, 166, 218, 229, 262
Costa Rican Gallo Pinto, 287–88
cottage cheese, 255
Couscous Salad, Provençal, 313–14

garbanzo beans, *see* chickpea(s)
garlic, 227, 241
  and Onion Soup, 323–24
  Vinaigrette, 300
gender differences, 121
  longevity and, 70, 136
genes, 40–50
  APOE, 124–25, 129–30, 198
  APP, 126–32
  AP rule and, 88–89, 93, 99
  dementia or Alzheimer's disease and, 36,
    123–32
  DNA chains in, 43–45
  heart disease and, 98–99
  interaction of environment and, 40–50,
    92
  senescence and, 87–92
genetic testing, 438
genomics, 19–21
ginger:
  Carrots, 369
  Dressing, Japanese, 302
glucose, 52, 102, 134, 151, 157, 165
  fasting (biomarker), 111, 113
  glycemic index (GI) and, 154–56
glucose disorders, 213
gluten, 161–63, 274
glycemic index (GI), 53, 154–56, 268–69
  gluten-free pastas and, 163
  salt intake and, 180

mercury, in fish and seafood, 255, 260, 277
metabolic dysfunction, 134
metabolic syndrome, 101, 152, 154–55,
    212, 225, 254
metformin, 102
methionine, 208–10, 214, 217, 219, 253,
    341, 426
microbiome, *see* gut microbiome
milk, 73, 234–35, 236, 238–41, 249, 255,
    260, 264, 275, 494
  lactose-reduced, 426
  substitute for, 426–27
millet:
  omega fats of, 441
mindspan:
  optimal health and, 29–30
  trends in, 30–35
  use of term, 13
Mindspan Elite, 14–15, 63–85
  biomarker relevance and, 96, 109–12
  BMI of, 104–7
  diverse cuisines, similar diets of, 71–73
  fat preferences of, 190–92
  fermentable carbs in diet of, 62
  key similarities of cuisines of, 63–85
  longevity of, 65–66
  protein preferences of, 213, 214–21
  refined grains in diet of, 76–84
  see also specific people and countries

nonsteroidal anti-inflammatory drugs
(NSAIDs), 132, 141–42, 259
noodle(s):
  Mushrooms, Carrots, and Sea Vegetables
    on, 367–68
  Soba, Soup, Okinawan, 333
  see also pasta
northern beans, in Greens and Beans
    Pasta, 386–87
nutrient needs, aging and, 93–95
nuts, 201–2, 205, 260, 276, 413–14
  as snacks, 202, 413–14

oat(meal)(s), 61, 172, 174, 229, 272
  omega fats of, 441
  X Factor Rice and, 290–91
obesity, 48, 65, 152–53, 233, 242
  factors contributing to, 74, 197, 222
  Mindspan Elite's low rates of, 67, 72,
    107
  risks associated with, 104–7, 158
oils, 201–2, 275–76
  common, omega fats of, 441–42
  partially hydrogenated, 200
  see also canola oil; olive oil
Okinawan recipes:
  East of Easy Curry, 404–5
  Kimchi Pork, 406–7
  Soba Noodle Soup, 333
  Stir-Fry (Zuke Chanpuru), 364–66

ABOUT THE AUTHOR

Preston Estep III, Ph.D., received his doctorate in genetics from Harvard Medical School. He is the director of gerontology at the Harvard Personal Genome Project, and he manages the project's genome sequencing pipeline. A co-founder and adviser to multiple biomedical start-ups and nonprofit organizations, Dr. Estep is a founder and the chief scientific officer of Veritas Genetics, and the chairman of the Mind First Foundation, a mental health nonprofit that he established with professors at Harvard Medical School. Dr. Estep lives with his wife in the Boston area. This is his first book.

The employees of Thorndike Press hope you have enjoyed this Large Print book. All our Thorndike, Wheeler, and Kennebec Large Print titles are designed for easy reading, and all our books are made to last. Other Thorndike Press Large Print books are available at your library, through selected bookstores, or directly from us.

For information about titles, please call:
  (800) 223-1244

or visit our Web site at:
  http://gale.cengage.com/thorndike

To share your comments, please write:
  Publisher
  Thorndike Press
  10 Water St., Suite 310
  Waterville, ME 04901